Legal Naturalism

Legal Naturalism

A MARXIST THEORY OF LAW

Olúfẹ́mi Táíwò

CORNELL UNIVERSITY PRESS

Ithaca and London

PUBLICATION OF THIS BOOK WAS MADE POSSIBLE, IN PART,
BY A GRANT FROM LOYOLA UNIVERSITY OF CHICAGO.

First published 1996 by Cornell University Press
First printing, Cornell Paperbacks, 2015

Library of Congress Cataloging-in-Publication Data

Taiwo, Olufemi.
Legal naturalism : A Marxist theory of law / Olufemi Taiwo.
p. cm.
Includes bibliographical references and index.
ISBN 978-0-8014-2851-7 (cloth : alk. paper)
ISBN 978-0-8014-5659-6 (pbk. : alk. paper)
1. Natural law.   2. Law and socialism.   3. Marx, Karl, 1818–1833.   I. Title.
K460.T35   1995
340'.112—dc20   95-9334

Cornell University Press strives to use environmentally responsible
suppliers and materials to the fullest extent possible in the publishing of
its books. Such materials include vegetable-based, low-VOC inks and
acid-free papers that are recycled, totally chlorine-free, or partly
composed of nonwood fibers. For further information, visit our
website at www.cornellpress.cornell.edu.

Paperback printing   10 9 8 7 6 5 4 3 2 1

For my mother
Christianah Iyìolá
and
in memory of my father
Samuel Okùnolá Táíwò (S.O.T.)
died 06.12.92

the dog never forgets its benefactor

Contents

Acknowledgments

This book has been many years in the making. In the nomadic existence that I led in those years, I have benefited so often from the generosity and kindness of so many that the gratitude expressed here can only be regarded as partial recompense. Help has come from friends, colleagues, and family in Nigeria, Canada, and the United States. Professor David Lyons of Cornell University deserves my profound gratitude for his friendship and continuing interest in my work. I am grateful to Professor Allen Wood of the same university for not only agreeing to read the manuscript on which this book is based, but for the special efforts he made to discuss his reactions with me. Professor William McBride of Purdue University continues to be a valued friend and a source of professional inspiration. I also thank Professors Frank Cunningham, Daniel Goldstick, André Gombay, and Ernest Weinrib, all of the University of Toronto, who enthusiastically directed the original project on which this book is based, and Charles Mills, Sandra Bartky, Paul Gomberg, David Schweickart, Holly Graff, and David Ingram for helpful and spirited responses to the penultimate drafts of Chapters 2, 3, and 6.

An earlier version of Chapter 1 was presented to the Colloquium, Department of Philosophy, Dalhousie University, Halifax, Nova Scotia. I acknowledge with gratitude the contributions of those who attended and the generosity of the Department in hosting me.

Roger Haydon, my editor at Cornell University Press, has shepherded this manuscript with diligence and enthusiasm. I cannot thank him enough for the energy he has expended to see this project come to fruition. The anonymous reviewers for the press were very helpful and have made this a better book than it would otherwise have been. I also thank Charles Purrenhage for very sensitive but no less efficient copyediting.

In the years that I have worked on this book, friends and family have been forgiving of my delinquencies and unstinting in their support. No one has been more blessed than I. For this I thank Ibrahim Abdullah, Deolu Ademoyo, Femi Akindele, Adeyinka Alade, Victor Alumona, Bisi Anyadike, Chima Anyadike, Kofi Anyidoho, Susan Babbitt, Keren Brathwaite, Anthony Dawahare, Mike Faborode, Dipo Fashina, David Gandolfo, Julius Ihonvbere, Tunde Lawuyi, Dele Layiwola, Toyin Mejiuni, Ann Miller, Hugh Miller, Charles Mills, Nkiru Nzegwu, Bola Odeleye, Kayode Odeleye, Moji Olaniyan, Teju Olaniyan, Tola Pearce, Kemi Rotimi, Remi Sonaiya, Bernard Walker, Sheila Walker, and Julie Ward. I also thank Leslie Brissette and Jeanne Huchthausen for humanizing the workplace at Loyola University Chicago. Wendy Chiaramonte of LUCID helped with the Law Tree diagram. Bernard Walker helped prepare the index.

I would like to express my profound appreciation for the support and encouragement of my wife, Faith Adams, Rita Adams, Denise Phillips, and my brothers, Kayode Taiwo and Gbadebo Taiwo. I hope this is some proof that my exile has not been in vain. This book is dedicated to my parents, my first and still two of my best teachers.

I gratefully acknowledge the following publishers for permission to reprint copyrighted materials: International Publishers, New York, for Marx and Engels, *Collected Works*; and Monthly Review Press, New York, for Thiago de Mello's poem excerpt from Robert Marquez, ed., *Latin American Revolutionary Poetry*.

O. T.

Legal Naturalism

Introduction

This book reinterprets the Marxist general theory of law. I argue that a plausible, coherent, and adequate theory of law must carve a niche for itself in the wide ambit of the natural law tradition. Hence I have called the theory "Legal naturalism." Legal naturalism shares some of the formal elements of theories within the natural law tradition. First, it posits a duality of legal existence: natural law and positive law. Second, it holds that positive law is an emanation from the precepts of natural law and that natural law is superior to positive law. Natural law provides criteria of identity, justification, and evaluation for positive law. Finally, it establishes a link between the natural law that ought to be and the positive law that is, such that positive law strives to realize *in concreto* natural law. All natural law theories share these three attributes. But legal naturalism (i.e., the Marxist theory of natural law) differs from other theories within the tradition. Unlike the others, it locates natural law in the *social formation* or *mode of production*, broadly conceived.

On this view, the positive law of any particular society is reflective of deeper structures. These deeper structures are not solely, or even significantly, economic. They are legal, but *naturally* legal. They are constituted by those legal relations which are essential and necessary to the social formation in which they occur, such that if that social formation were to lack them it would be not what it is but something else. They are the legal relations the lack of which will make us conclude that a given social formation lacks a constituent element. In this sense, law, a given natural law, is constitutive of and at the same time reflects a given structure of rights, privileges, entitlements, immunities, and so on, presupposed by the relevant social formation. The social formation or mode of production refers to the forces and relations of production as well as to how production is organized (i.e., the social organization of production). In some epochs, the mode of social organization includes law, and that legal regime which is essential to the relevant mode of social organization is its natural law. When we say that the positive law of a specific society is the juridical expression of deeper structures, we mean or ought to mean that it is an expression of the constitutive natural law of the mode of production concerned. By the same token, there are and will be forms of state etc. that are constitutive of some mode of production such that it would be inconceivable for the mode of production to exist and thrive if the form of state or law natural to it were to be nonexistent.

I have called this theory "legal naturalism" because the law that is expressed in the positive legal system of a society is a constitutive part of the *nature* of the mode of production. It is similar to other natural law theories to the extent that it appropriates law from the nature of something. Thomists derive law from divine nature and from human nature as it participates in this divine nature. For social contract and natural rights theorists, the law is appropriated from human nature. Legal naturalists, however, derive law from the nature of the mode of production or social formation. Of the other forms of deriving natural law, only the divinely inspired one is incompatible with this interpretation. For legal naturalism human nature is an integral element of social formation so that when we say law derives from the nature of the social formation, "social formation" is a rich concept that encompasses the raw materials and instruments of production as well as human nature as it has developed up to the moment of which we are speaking. In a sense, then, the locus of law posited by legal naturalism is wider than that supplied by other theories within the natural law tradition.

This reinterpretation of the Marxist theory of law is warranted for several reasons. Marxism, excepting one or two interpretations, has remained for too long a spectator in the area of legal philosophy generally. It is no exaggeration to say that, with few exceptions, Marxists have shared an ambivalent attitude toward law and its empirical analogues. On the one hand, they are hostile, and the reason for hostility is not far below the surface. Marxist theories of law are dominated by a positivist orientation that sees law as the will of the ruling class in its efforts to make the subaltern classes cooperate with or accede to its dominance. As such, law is regarded as a component of *state* activity and, hence, a branch of politics. As an element of politics, law becomes a weapon in the class struggle, and the subordinate classes are called upon to overthrow the ruling class, *its* state and, by extension, *its* law. Consequently, representing an essentially hostile presence in the social formation, Marxists and their allies should struggle against law and seek its abolition. But there is a problem.

It is true that the ruling classes under capitalism make law to further their class interests and do so in light of their class-inspired understanding of what their societies and their social formation require. It is equally true that many people in society outside the ruling circles obey these laws, accept them, or at least acquiesce in them. We know, too, that many people whose interests are frequently subverted by the operations of the legal system are seldom stinting in their praise of the law. They regard the law as rightful. Their conception of justice is permeated by the content of the law. We may not dismiss these attitudes as the result of false consciousness on the part of the people concerned. Very few Marxists resort to this explanation nowadays. In the major Marxist responses to this reality we see the second aspect of the ambivalence alluded to above.

Confronted with the undeniable allegiance to law of members of the subordinate classes, and the realization that law is defined not strictly by its policing functions but also by its regulative and coordinating functions, Marxists have adopted an *instrumentalist* approach. Marxists and their allies seek to maximize whatever advantages law has to offer under conditions of class rule. Without any abiding faith or confidence in the justice or rightness of the prevailing law, they mine it for what it has to offer; but they never cease to undermine it in order thereby to effectuate its overthrow. This instrumentalism engenders a dilemma that has attracted comments from supporters as well as opponents of Marxism.

As long as Marxists remain hostile to law and its empirical analogues they cannot urge their followers and sympathizers to go to the law to seek redress for any injustice they suffer. This situation, however, is bound to breed some quietism, if not defeatism, on the part of the ruled that will prevent them from securing the justice enjoined by the social formation in which they operate. Simultaneously, it will leave the ruling classes unchallenged in their operation of the social system. Worse still, it will not permit the subordinate classes to hold their rulers to playing by the latter's own rules or by the rules mandated by the structures of the social formation. Yet, if hostility is muted and the instrumentalist moment prevails, then—the ultimate horror—the ruled may actually succeed in holding the rulers to their own rules and secure such justice for themselves as is possible within their social formation. If they succeed often enough, they may even begin to trust in the capacity of law to ameliorate their sometimes desperate situation. This problem is acute enough for the Marxist practitioner who has to work alongside workers in the class struggle. It is more acutely posed for the Marxist legal practitioner whose advocacy, especially of the winning variety, on behalf of the masses in collective bargaining, tort, and constitutional cases, may have the unintended consequence of kindling the hope of his or her clients for melioration within the system. Here is the kernel of the problem Tom Gerety discusses in his "Iron Law: Why Good Lawyers Make Bad Marxists." To be a good lawyer is to maintain some faith in the meliorative possibilities within the system, a faith that drives all good advocacy; whereas to be a good Marxist is insistently to point out the incapacity of law to promote real change or offer genuine resolutions. This ambivalence explains in part why Marxists have not been central or important players in the area of legal theory.

Legal naturalism does not share this ambivalence toward law. It remains critical of law without being hostile to it. Nor does it operate with an instrumentalist conception. It takes seriously law's complexity and the presence of real conflicts over the law and its manifestations. Positive law seeks to embody in specific enactments the natural law presuppositions of the social formation. Within the sphere of positivization, possibilities exist for divergent perceptions among members of the ruling classes, and between the rulers and the subordinate classes, and these perceptions might be responsible for struggles over the law and the direction of its evolution. Furthermore, given that the social formation of which the relevant natural law is a constitutive element is capable of evolution, we might speak of the positive law as more or less approximating its natural legal foundations. If this is true, then one can embrace the natural law presuppositions of, say, capitalism, even concede that capitalism is a comparatively superior social formation, while insisting that the laws of a municipal legal system are so much in violation of capitalist natural law that they merit disobedience. Similarly, one may grant that capitalism is a better mode of social ordering than feudalism without necessarily embracing the view that capitalism is the best of all possible social formations. As I will demonstrate, this mode of proceeding can claim fidelity to Karl Marx's own method and produces fecund insights into the nature of law and legal phenomena. By restoring the complexity of legal phenomena and reinserting law into the framework of the social formation, we dissolve the dilemma identified above. By turning law into the product of struggles between and within classes, we restore genuine conflict to the notion of class struggle within the law and over its evolution. We thereby create room for Marxism to become a genuine general theory of law equipped to illumine our understanding of concrete, historically specific legal phenomena.

Finally, this book poses anew the question of the future of law. It restates and offers a fresh defense of the withering-away-of-law thesis against the current tenor of thinking in Marxist legal theory. Rather than present the problem in terms of what will happen to law, understood purely in terms of impersonal structures totally impervious to human tinkering, I ask what *should* happen to law. I submit that the withering-away thesis is a programmatic pronouncement of Marxism, a call to change the world and install a mode of social ordering within which law and its analogues are superfluous. This call is best understood in terms of two basic features of Marxism as social theory. The first is its *critical dimension*, which calls for the criticism of all existing social conditions and their supersession by different modes of social living in which the diremptions of social life dominant within capitalism become a thing of the past. The second is its *utopian dimension*, which holds forth the alluring picture of future social orderings without law and all the other forms of mediation that stand between humans and their nature, their fellows, their lives, and their social relations. On this latter view, which Marxism incidentally shares with other theories in the utopian tradition, the necessity for law in social relations hitherto in history bespeaks a radical insufficiency in *la condition humaine*. Marxism contends that the removal, or at least the amelioration, of this insufficiency is conceivable and eminently desirable. I argue that this commitment is an integral part of the Marxist theory of law, and I provide the philosophical foundations for the withering away of law.

This conclusion goes against the grain of current wisdom in Marxist theory, and one may ask why this concept of withering away remains relevant, more so now than in the past. I acknowledge that these are exciting times for law and its empirical analogues. The collapse of Eastern Europe and its misbegotten "socialist revolutions" has sparked a renewed enthusiasm for law and its most potent ideological representation at the present time, the rule of law, not only in Eastern Europe but in other parts of the world where the pretense of socialism had similarly taken root in the recent past. Coupled with this renewed enthusiasm for the rule of law is the revivified commitment—genuine, not so genuine, and downright bogus—to the form of governance typified by liberal democracy with its emphasis on multipartyism and periodic elections. Other related phenomena are resurgent: the emplacement of the market as the preferred vehicle for allocating resources in society; and free trade. These are practices against which Marxism has pledged itself for more than a century. Thus it would appear that this is a most inopportune time to re-state the Marxist suspicion of law as a preferred mode of social ordering.

The widespread enthusiasm for law at the present time must not blind us to the real limits inherent in law as a principle of social ordering. We often go to great lengths to exclude law from our most cherished relation-ships. Rarely do we invoke law or resort to it until we have exhausted the possibilities for mutual understanding and good-neighborliness. It is one of the abiding strengths of Marxism as social theory that it abjures any un-qualified embrace of law and its appurtenances. Hence, a time when the enthusiasm for law is ascendant provides an opportunity to reconsider some of the grounds for the Marxist preference for a postpolitical and postlegal society. That is what I do in the concluding part of this book.

1

The Foundation:
Marx on Law and Laws

I

This chapter provides a historical foundation for the theory of law presented in this book. For a theory that claims a Marxist pedigree, such a foundation is to be found in Marx's early writings on law and laws. These texts have been a favorite quarry for psychologists, political theorists, and philosophical humanists who seek an appropriate philosophical anthropology for their explanation of *la condition humaine* under late capitalism. Others have mined the same texts for elements of a Marxist ethics or the foundations of a moral theory. But Marxist theories of law have in the main ignored these writings or regarded them as being of little significance to the further development of Marx's views on law, or indeed on anything else.[1] Such an attitude tends to make light of the implications of these texts for a correct and adequate Marxist theory of law. I argue that Marx's early texts contain elements for a more adequate theory. Additionally, an analysis of these works holds promise for a better understanding of Marx's general methodological orientation and an unraveling of statements and viewpoints in Marx's work that have baffled commentators. It will also

1. The following list is representative of such theories: E. B. Pashukanis, *Law and Marxism: A General Theory*, ed. and intro. Chris Arthur (London: Ink Links, 1978; reprint London: Pluto Press, 1983); Karl Renner, *The Institutions of Private Law and Their Social Functions* (London: Routledge & Kegan Paul, 1949); Paul Hirst, *On Law and Ideology* (Atlantic Highlands, N.J.: Humanities Press, 1979); Bernard Edelman, *Ownership of the Image* (London: Routledge & Kegan Paul, 1979); Leon S. Jawitsch, *The General Theory of Law* (Moscow: Progress Publishers, 1981).

place us in a better position to chart the trajectory of his development: knowing what he began with, we can put the later views in perspective.

Marx was no stranger to law early in his career. He was at different times a student of law, a legal practitioner and, quite often, a victim of law. It should be no surprise that law and its attributes engaged his attention. And his was not a mere academic fascination. As Maureen Cain and Alan Hunt aptly observe, "circumstances forced Marx to take the law seriously into account in his early years. Until the time of his exile, engaging with the law was for him far more than a theoretical pastime."[2] As a political journalist running an opposition journal, Marx directly experienced the full force of censorship and other assaults on press freedom. As his announcement of March 17, 1843, attests, his editorship of the journal *Rheinische Zeitung* eventually fell prey to the irritations of the censorship.[3] Marx's writings on law at this period of his development hold more than an antiquarian interest. Should we find that in his later years Marx altered his views on law, the reasons for such an outcome would be enlightening. We would be even better served if it turns out that he repudiated his earlier views. What we may not do is behave as if the early writings were merely the confused, exuberant outpourings of a youthful spirit which in the soberness of age were found embarrassing and therefore jettisoned. The basic idea motivating this chapter is that the writings examined here are pivotal to an adequate understanding of the genesis and evolution of the Marxist theory of law. The differences we may find between these writings and the later ones are, I suggest, more of emphasis than of substance, of degree than of kind.

At the commencement of his career, Marx accepted Hegel's legal rationalism.[4] Legal rationalism is the view that law is an embodiment of Reason striving for freedom. Law here means a system of rights. Right is the content of free will acting in the world. Freedom in turn is the essence of

2. Maureen Cain and Alan Hunt, *Marx and Engels on Law* (London: Academic Press, 1979), p. 12.

3. "The undersigned declares that, owing to the *present conditions of censorship*, he has retired as from today from the editorial board of the *Rheinische Zeitung*. Dr. Marx." Karl Marx and Frederick Engels, *Collected Works*, published to date: vols. 1–34; 38–47 (New York: International Publishers, 1975–1995), 1:376. Hereafter cited as MECW.

4. In his writings, Marx acknowledged debts he owed to several authors before him, including Montesquieu, Rousseau, and his teachers Eduard Gans and Karl von Savigny. But it is Hegel that Marx chose to engage in those manuscripts in which he wrote extensively on law. I interpret this choice as an index of the importance Marx placed on Hegel's philosophy of law. For a contrary opinion, see Philip J. Kain, *Marx and Ethics* (Oxford: Clarendon Press, 1988), who argues that Marx is closer to Kant than to Hegel in his ethics.

right and the goal that Reason strives to reach in the world. Reason is human reason, intelligence, which, being the essence of humans, is that element which separates us from the lower animals: it is the element in which is contained the essence of our humanity. For legal rationalism, then, Reason is the constitutive element of law and, simultaneously, its ultimate criterion of identity and evaluation. What we have identified here as legal rationalism is the equivalent in law of a more general position of Hegel's which Z. A. Pelczynski has called "political rationalism."[5] What are the principal features of this legal rationalism? For an answer we turn to the *Philosophy of Right*.

In the Introduction to the *Philosophy of Right*, Hegel distinguishes between two kinds of law: *rational (natural) law* and *positive law*. Natural law is law according to its concept, the concept of Right. Positive law is law posited, law that has become realized *in concreto* in particular countries, peoples, or nations. This is the first feature of Hegel's legal rationalism. "The subject-matter of the philosophical science of right is the Idea of right, i.e. the concept of right together with the actualization of that concept."[6] The philosophical study of the concept of right has the task of developing "the Idea out of the concept, or, what is the same thing, [looking] on at the proper immanent development of the thing itself."[7] The object of this philosophical study is, for Hegel, "natural law." This is distinguished from positive law. "Right is positive in general (a) when it has the *form* of being valid in a particular state, and this legal authority is the guiding principle for the knowledge of right in this positive form, i.e. for the science of positive law. (b) Right in this positive form acquires a positive element in its *content* (through the life, stage of historical development, and culture of a people, particular statutes and other legislations, and the mode of adjudication)."[8] Positive law is the law of a particular country or people—say, Nigeria or Germany. It is the concrete, specific form in which individuals encounter law, are oriented by it, and are constrained in their behavior. Thanks to positive law, what is abstractly represented in natural law is brought to life for individuals through the various modes of positivization mentioned by Hegel.

5. Z. A. Pelczynski, "Introduction," *Hegel's Political Writings*, trans. T. M. Knox (Oxford: Clarendon Press, 1964), p. 29.

6. G. W. F. Hegel, *Philosophy of Right*, trans. T. M. Knox (Oxford: Clarendon Press, 1952), §1.

7. Ibid., §2.

8. Ibid., §3. The latter part in parentheses is a paraphrase of Hegel's three modes in which right acquires a positive element in its content.

Although natural law and positive law are distinct from each other, Hegel cautions that we should not pervert their difference into an opposition and a contradiction. The two kinds of law combine to form, and are moments of, a single whole. In this whole, however, the natural law is the more ultimate of the two, and it is the touchstone by which we determine whether an instance of positive law is ultimately valid regardless of its positivity. Conformity with reason, which natural law embodies, is therefore the criterion by which positive laws are to be evaluated. As Pelczynski puts it, "The belief in rational law as the only legitimate and tenable criterion of laws, institutions, and constitutions is the first basic article of Hegel's political faith."[9] This distinction between natural law and positive law is of cardinal importance to Hegel's, and Marx's, legal philosophy.

The works on law and laws written between 1837 and 1843 bear the stamp of legal rationalism. The abandonment of legal rationalism had its genesis in 1843–44 when Marx retreated first to Kreuznach and then to Paris—the period that gave us the *Contribution to the Critique of Hegel's Philosophy of Law*, *On the Jewish Question*, and the *Economic and Philosophical Manuscripts*. These were works of transition marked by internalist criticisms of the hitherto accepted Hegelian legacy.

The first postlegal-rationalist works were *The Holy Family* and *The German Ideology*, jointly authored with Frederick Engels in 1845. By the time these were completed a transition had been effected, first from idealism to materialism, and then from legal rationalism to what I call *sociolegal naturalism*. Legal naturalism, a theory built on the foundation described in this chapter, will form the subject matter of the rest of this book. The rest of this chapter will be devoted to a discussion of Marx's legal rationalism.

II

Marx's legal rationalism, indeed Marxist legal theory as a whole, rests on a general methodology that informs Marx's explanation of social phenomena. It is this methodology which, in the area of the general theory of law, permits us to locate Marx and the Marxist theory of law in the natural law tradition. To this methodology Scott Meikle has given the name *essentialism*.[10]

Essentialism is an ontological point of view that posits real natures, necessities, and essences and seeks to distinguish these from the alternative

---

9. Pelczynski, "Introduction," p. 29.
10. Scott Meikle, *Essentialism in the Thought of Karl Marx* (La Salle, Ill.: Open Court, 1985).

point of view, which sees in reality a mass of discrete atomistic bits that have no necessary or organic connection. The latter view is generally called atomism. According to Meikle,

> The theoretical core of the opposition between essentialism and atomism (or accidentalism) is absolute. It begins with ancient Greek thought in the struggle between the atomists and Aristotle, carefully reviewed by Marx in his *Doctoral Dissertation* (so he knew all about it). On the one hand there were Democritus and Epicurus who thought of reality as atomistic small-bits that combine and repel in the void, and who had a hard job accounting for the persisting natures of things, species and genera on that basis. On the other hand there was Aristotle, who realized that no account of such things could be possible without admitting a category of form (or essence), because what a thing is, and what things of its kind are, cannot possibly be explained in terms of their constituent matter (atoms), since that changes while the entity retains its nature and identity over time.[11]

The difference between the two points of view turns on their respective ontologies. For essentialism, the world is full of organic wholes which have real natures and necessities. On this view, the constituents of the world are things that persist in time. They are made up of units that are organically related in accordance with their underlying natures or essences.

Opposed to the essentialist view is one that denies that things in the world are made up of organically related elements and asserts instead that there is only a mechanical ordering among them. On the latter view, there is no real nature or underlying essence aside from the contingent unity of the parts that make up what we call a whole.[12] Between the two views is one that suspends judgment on either claim and refrains from making any claim about what there is in the world. The conflict Meikle is talking about is one of opposing ontologies: "The major conflict between essentialism and reductive materialism is between their respective ontologies. Reductive materialism believes in an ontology of simples, of basic building-blocks lacking complexity, and further believes everything else is reducible to them. Essentialism, on the other hand, admits into its ontology what I have referred to up to now as 'organic wholes' or 'entities', and does not consider them to be reducible but rather irreducible."[13] Meikle's general

---

11. Ibid., pp. 8–9.
12. David Hume's account of causation is a good example of such a view.
13. Meikle, *Essentialism*, p. 154.

thesis is that "the work of Marx is thoroughly essentialist in every respect, and that this is the source of its explanatory strength."[14]

Meikle's discussion centers on the character of Marx's ontology. But we are less interested in the ontological thesis than in the methodological thesis. There is no necessary connection between ontological commitments and methodological choices. One should be careful about deriving explanatory models from ontological presuppositions. Sometimes there is a disjuncture between an ontological position and the explanatory thesis held by one and the same person. For instance, one could be an essentialist of a sort that argues that the world is made up of organic wholes (ontological thesis) and still argue that the behavior of those wholes is best explained mechanically. With this caution in mind, I am persuaded that in his explanations, Marx's methodology is unmistakably and thoroughly essentialist. By essentialism here I mean the methodological thesis that a correct, plausible, and adequate explanation of a thing or process must ultimately be couched in terms of the thing's nature: that in virtue of which a thing is what it is and the lack of which will make it not what it is but something else. It will presently be made clear how Marx deployed this thesis. In what follows I attempt to sketch Marx's general methodological postulates. A brief discussion of Marx's essentialism in legal theory follows. This sets the stage for an examination of Marx's legal rationalism in the writings from 1835 to 1843. Finally, I analyze and consider the reasons for Marx's transition to legal naturalism from 1843 to 1845.

III

Marx generally favored and employed essentialist explanations. At several places in his writings he distinguished between explanation by accidents and explanation by essence. Explanations by essence or by nature presuppose that things are not coterminous with what they appear to be: that there is a distinction between things and the phenomenal form in which they are presented to our perception, between appearances that events present to us and what may be their underlying causes. We may say that if things *are* as they appear, efforts at deep explanation will be pointless.

It is fairly easy to secure agreement that things (physical objects) are not necessarily what they appear to be. People readily agree that some qualities of a thing pertain to its being what it is and that some of its attributes are

14. Ibid., p. 4.

mere accidents. It is less easy to do the same with the description and explanation of social phenomena. Social phenomena are not things, and it is not obvious that they persist over time or that they have underlying natures. The general trend of Marx's methodological postulates, however, indicates that we should treat social phenomena in analogous ways. We must go beyond the phenomenal form of social processes to get to their underlying causes.

This demand comes out of Marx's insistence on seeing social and historical phenomena not as a jumble of unconnected, unrelated, haphazard occurrences but as embodying some form of rationality and regularity that it is the business of social science to discover. The demand to go beneath the surface of social phenomena meant for Marx an attempt to get past the accidental occurrences to the essential happenings of history. This in turn presupposes that things do not happen haphazardly but follow patterns necessitated by their nature or essences. The nature or essence of a thing may be defined by either that quality in virtue of which the thing is what it is or by its characteristic activity (*ergon*). Those patterns of determination which we find to pertain to the nature of the thing we call its laws. The object of social science is to find the laws of social phenomena.

There is ample evidence that this was Marx's methodology. In the Preface to the first German edition of *Capital*, Marx stated that "it is the ultimate aim of [the] work to lay bare the economic law of modern society."[15] His standpoint is one that views the evolution of the economic formation of society as a process of natural history.[16] The search for laws of social phenomena, for the underlying essence of social processes, is the hallmark of Marx's methodology.[17]

As early as 1837, in a letter to his father, Marx talked of the need for one who wants to understand phenomena to study the objects themselves in their development: "[I]n the concrete expression of a living world of ideas, as exemplified by law, the state, nature and philosophy as a whole, the object itself must be studied in its development; arbitrary divisions must not be introduced, the rational character of the object itself must develop as something imbued with contradictions in itself and find its unity in itself"(MECW, 1:12).[18] In this passage, there is a suggestion that the object

15. Karl Marx, *Capital* (Moscow: Progress Publishers, 1954), 1:20.
16. Ibid., 1:27–28.
17. I have cited the passage from *Capital* first because it is not unusual for some Marxists to argue that the concerns and methods of *Capital* are radically different from those which animated Marx's early writings.
18. Of course, I am reading this passage methodologically, although it contains ontological presuppositions.

of study is integrated, contains within itself the seeds of its own development, and is capable of development. This has methodological implications. Apparently Marx must have taken his injunction very seriously, for later in the same letter we find him reproaching himself for not proceeding in the correct fashion. He had, in his own work, sundered form and content when, "in a philosophical treatment of law, . . . the one must arise in the other; indeed, the form should only be the continuation of the content." By thinking "that matter and form can and must develop separately from each other, . . . I obtained not a real form, but something like a desk with drawers into which I then poured sand" (1:15).[19]

I turn next to Marx's analysis of the debates on freedom of the press (MECW, 1:132–81). Marx argued against members of the Assembly of the Estates who sought to whitewash the latest curbs placed on the press by the king[20] as "a lesser evil than excesses on the part of the press" (1:138) and against those who wanted to prevent publication of the Assembly proceedings. Marx's defense of the freedom of the press was based on the essence of the press. "From the standpoint of the idea, it is self-evident that freedom of the press has a justification quite different from that of censorship because it is itself an embodiment of the idea, an embodiment of freedom, a positive good, whereas censorship is an embodiment of unfreedom, the polemic of a world outlook of semblance against the world outlook of essence; it has merely a negative nature" (1:154). The press has an essence, some attributes that conjointly make the press what it is. These attributes include that of the activity of venting, of airing information to the public, making the public aware of what is going on. This is its justification for being and the standard by which its performance is to be evaluated. Censorship, on the contrary, has no positive attribute; it is defined not by what it brings about but by what it is called forth to preempt; hence its *merely negative nature*. So, freedom of the press is recommended by the nature of the press. Freedom of the press is essential to, and inseparable from, the idea of the press itself. Censorship is to be condemned on account of its contradiction of the nature of the press. (I use "nature" and "essence" interchangeably.) What is the nature of the press?

"The press in general is a realization of human freedom. Consequently, where is a press there is freedom of the press" (MECW, 1:155). Given that

19. See also Marx's discussion on the same theme in his "Doctoral Dissertation," reprinted in the same volume.
20. "The Latest Prussian Censorship Instruction."

the press cannot *be* without freedom, it is obvious that anything which lacks this essential attribute may not be called a "press." For Marx, so much does freedom pertain to the nature of the press that even when the censors think they are combating freedom by curtailing the press, what they are doing is merely combating the freedom of others. In other words, the "unfreedom" of the press is the "freedom" of the censors. "Freedom is so much the essence of humans that even its opponents implement it while combating its reality; they want to appropriate for themselves as a most precious ornament what they have rejected as an ornament of human nature. No man combats freedom; at most he combats the freedom of others. Hence every kind of freedom has always existed, only at one time as a special privilege, at another as a universal right" (1:155). In condemning the censorship instructions, Marx derived the arguments against censorship from the essence of the press itself. No references to possible excesses on the part of a free press would make him concede that there may be a justification for curbing the press beyond those limits generated by considerations of social harmony and prevention of harm to others. What recommends freedom of the press is not that it will have beneficial consequences or that we desire it for any number of instrumental reasons. By the same token, censorship cannot be embraced because it yields good consequences.

Marx argued that it is only by understanding the press from its essence that we can differentiate the bad from the good press. A good press will be a free press; it will correspond to its essence. The freer it is, the better, and that press is best which is freest. It is the "essence, the inner character, which distinguishes the censored from the free press."

If one wants to speak of two kinds of press, the distinction between them must be drawn from the nature of the press itself, not from considerations lying outside it. The censored press or the free press, one of these two must be the good or the bad press. The debate turns precisely on whether the censored press or the free press is good or bad, i.e., whether it is in the nature of the press to have a free or unfree existence. . . .

[T]he generic difference between them is not that they produce individual products of this or that kind; flowers grow also in swamps. We are concerned here with the essence, the inner character, which distinguishes the censored from the free press. (MECW, 1:157–58)

The essentialist bent in the above account is obvious. The press is to be judged not by whether it produces good or bad results, but by how well it realizes its essence in the concrete press. Censorship is bad because it subverts the essence of the press: freedom. The essentialist methodology plays a double role. On the one hand it allows us to identify what the press is and enables us to tell when a particular press is a bad one. On the other hand it also gives us a yardstick by which to evaluate how well or ill the press *in concreto* realizes its essence. When the press *realiter* departs sufficiently from its essence it is a bad press, and when it approximates its essence it is a good press. When it completely lacks this essence it is not a press at all.

Marx's essentialism also guided his critique of the Divorce Bill. The bill was criticized for not really amounting to a reform, for ignoring "the *secular* essence of marriage," for very defective procedure, for lacking "consistency, precision, clarity and comprehensive points of view," and for "severities of a police nature which are contrary to the concept of marriage" and "too great leniency in regard to what are called considerations of fairness" (MECW, 1:307). By far the most serious shortcoming of the bill was that it ignored the essence of marriage, making it easier for a couple to get a divorce by paying heed only to their own, individual wills. Marriage, however, is more than the coming together of two wills. In its essence, it is "the basis of the family" and, for this reason, is of interest to legislators. The legislator should nonetheless reach beyond the whims of the couple; he or she must proceed in accord with the essence of marriage—with what Marx called "the *will of marriage*, the moral substance of this relationship" (1:308).

Any legislation that will regulate marriage must conform to the essence of marriage and cannot depart from this essence without losing its raison d'être. Divorce should not be granted just because the man and the woman so desire. Once a marriage is contracted, on this reasoning, the union is greater than the sum of its parts. Certainly we have the man and the woman. But we also have the family, their children, and their property. Marx was not arguing that marriage is indissoluble. It may be so in its concept.[21] However, the concept of marriage is one thing, its reality is another. No institution "corresponds fully to its concept." Between the concept and its realization lies the play of contingency: accidents may occur that prevent the realization from being adequate to the concept. Real marriage is no different. It follows that real marriage exists. This is irrespective of the fact that the real marriage concerned may have so de-

---

21. "Hegel says: *In itself*, according to the concept, marriage is indissoluble, but only in itself,' i.e., only according to the concept." MECW, 1:309.

parted from its essence that it has ceased to be a marriage. Divorce is a formal recognition that the "marriage in question is a *dead* marriage, the existence of which is mere semblance and deception" (1:309). As in the case of the press, the essence of marriage plays a double role. First, it helps us to identify an existent marriage as an instance, an embodiment of the essence of marriage, *a* marriage. Secondly, it supplies a measure by which we determine whether an existent marriage is worth saving or has irretrievably broken down (i.e., has so departed from the essence of marriage that it is no longer worthy of the name).

There are several other examples one can cite to illustrate Marx's essentialism. His discussion of the human essence both in the *On the Jewish Question* and the *Economic and Philosophical Manuscripts* points to a unifying theme and evaluative criterion for his critique of bourgeois society as well as of his understanding of what the future will be like. If I am correct to regard Marx's methodology as basically essentialist, then some of the usages that we find in Marx and that have remained sources of embarrassment to nonessentialist interpretations of Marxism no longer perplex or bewilder us. Such usages would include repeated references to form and content, essence and existence, necessity and accident, potential and actual, and so on. These have implications for Marxist philosophy of history and of the social sciences that are not addressed in this work. What follows is an explication of Marx's legal rationalism.

IV

Marx's essentialism informed his understanding of law and laws. An essentialist reading, I argue, provides the best interpretation of Marx's legal rationalism and also of the general trend of his thinking on law. Marx distinguished between law and its realization. Just as he insisted that things must be explained and evaluated in accordance with their essences, so too did he maintain that the essence of law must constitute the measure by which we judge and identify laws *realiter*.

The same dualism that we encountered in our account of Marx's essentialist methodology marks his analysis of law. There is objective law, which exists apart from positive law and is the essence of the positive law. Positive laws (legislative enactments etc.) are only the more or less adequate realizations of this objective law, this essence. Their positivity lies in their being enacted. The objective law is their ground, in virtue of participation in which positive laws are laws. Insofar as positive laws depart from this essence, their status as laws is diminished. Wherever they so depart from it that we can say they have severed their links to this essence, we are entitled to say they are not laws. Let us examine Marx's critique of a particular law: the law on press freedom.

Censorship was condemned because it contradicted the essence of the press and was not inspired by this essence. As was pointed out, Marx was not against all regulation of the press. But an appropriate press law will be one that conforms to the essence of the press and punishes departures from that essence. What distinguishes the press law from the censorship law is that the press law has its source in the nature of the press, whereas the censorship law is a curtailment of the essence of the press.

> The press law is a *real law* because it is the positive existence of freedom. It regards freedom as the *normal* state of the press, the press as the mode of existence of freedom, and hence only comes into conflict with a press offence as an exception that contravenes its own rules and therefore annuls itself. . . .
>
> Therefore the *press law* is the *legal recognition of freedom of the press*. It constitutes *right*, because it is the positive existence of freedom. It must therefore exist, even if it is never put into application, as in North America, whereas censorship, like slavery, can never become lawful, even if it exists a thousand times over as a law. (MECW, 1:162)

The essence of the press is freedom—to know, to make public, to inform. Press law does not impede the realization of this freedom; it punishes departures from this essence. Its operation is *post facto*, not preemptive. It punishes what is done; it does not avert action. The press is therefore to be judged by its conformity to an essence external to itself. Obviously, this essence is independent of the positive law. Here an additional element of the methodology emerges. According to Marx, "the legal nature of things cannot be regulated according to the law [obviously reference here is to positive law]; on the contrary, the law must be regulated according to the legal nature of things" (1:227). Similarly, the objective law that the positive law strives to realize is independent of the will of legislators. Quite the contrary, it binds the legislators. Hence Marx's claim that "the legislator, however, should regard himself as a naturalist. He does not *make* the laws, he does not invent them, he only formulates them, expressing in conscious, positive laws the inner laws of spiritual relations" (1:308).

Here, then, are the two elements of Marx's description of law. There is objective law ("the inner laws of spiritual relations"), which the positive law strives to realize; then positive law (the enactment of the objective law), which requires for its identity and rightness, adequation to the objective law. This legal dualism shows a very strong antipositivist bias that surely reduces the plausibility of positivist accounts of the Marxist theory of law.

What is the objective law? I submit that, at this stage, it is Hegel's "natural law of reason." Marx's account of his *point de départ* on this question attests to his appropriation of legal rationalism from Hegel:

> Whereas the earlier philosophers of constitutional law proceeded in their account of the formation of the state from the instincts, either of ambition or gregariousness, or even from reason, though not social reason, but the reason of the individual, the more ideal and profound view of recent philosophy [Hegel's] proceeds from the idea of the whole. It looks on the state as the great organism, in which legal, moral, and political freedom must be realized, and in which the individual citizen in obeying the laws of the state only obeys the natural laws of his own reason, of human reason. (MECW, 1:202)

The law that forms the essence of positive law is the *natural law of human reason*, or *rational law*. Positive laws are merely the proclamation of this rational law. When they incorporate this essence, the rational law, positive laws are what Marx calls "the positive existence of freedom." Following Hegel, the essence of reason is the striving for freedom. Freedom is the essence of humankind. Marx's legal rationalism is tied to his description of human nature. Law is reason coming to know itself. This is why Marx contends that law cannot be repressive measures against freedom. Law embodies reason and reason strives for freedom. "Laws are in no way repressive measures against freedom any more than the law of gravity is a repressive measure against motion, because while, as the law of gravitation, it governs the eternal motions of the celestial bodies, as the law of falling it kills me if I violate it and want to dance in the air. Laws are rather the positive, clear, universal norms in which freedom has acquired an impersonal, theoretical existence independent of the arbitrariness of the individual. A statute-book is a people's bible of freedom" (MECW, 1:162).

Law does not prevent; it commands. Law orients our behavior in the direction of the realization of reason's goal: freedom. Positive laws are no more than the embodiment of this inner character. When positive law falls short of rational law, when it is not the "conscious state law" of "the unconscious natural law of freedom," it "has within it no *measure*, no *rational rule*, for a rational rule can only result from the nature of a thing, in this instance of freedom" (MECW, 1:163). For Marx, therefore, it is legitimate to deny the status of law to positive laws that fall short of the requirements of rational law. Such laws are nonlaws.

Marx's essentialist methodology in law led him to posit a legal dualism: rational law and positive law. In this dualism, rational law is ultimate, being the essence of positive law. This means that for Marx the two elements of this dualism are not of equal importance, nor is one collapsible into the other. This is not a way of thinking that Marx abandoned as he progressed as a thinker. On the contrary, whereas the components of the dualism altered later on, the dualistic account of law did not change in Marx's thought.

The dualistic nature of Marx's account is a principal reason for locating Marxist legal theory within the natural law tradition; the ranking of rational and positive law is another. Moreover, Marx's willingness to deny the status of law to those positive laws which depart from the essence of law qualifies his theory as a variant of natural law. Marx's distinction of law from positive laws will be used to support a critique of interpretations of Marxist legal theory that define law as rules and regulations posited by a constituted authority (e.g., the state) for purposes of furthering the interests of the class that rules in a given society. We shall see presently that Marx was able to criticize positive laws of the Prussian state by refusing to identify law with the positive laws of the state. On the contrary, he adjudged the positive laws to have fallen short of the essence of law and, therefore, to be defective. This trend was not limited to this period of his development.

Marx's dualism is problematic. There is rational law and there is positive law. By virtue of their positivity, positive laws are easily identifiable: they are contained in legal codes, executive orders, and other authoritative enactments of the state. It is not so easy with rational law, the law of human reason for the realization of freedom. Freedom is acting in accordance with dictates of the law of reason. Given that the realization of freedom is said to be the essence of humans, one cannot overemphasize the importance of being able to decipher the law of reason. There is little or nothing to suggest that Marx gave any thought to this problem. But Marx's analysis should not be vitiated by the lack of a suggestion of how we come to know the law of human reason. The plausibility of his analysis is not diminished thereby.

Some commentators have tried to show that the natural law tendency found in Marx was a momentary aberration that he later outgrew. Bob Fine thinks that "in his criticism of classical jurisprudence, Marx did not seek to return to the dogmas of traditional natural law theory—though occasionally he slipped back into this mode—but rather to radicalize the break already achieved by classical jurisprudence."[22] Fine's position is undercut by his own description of natural law doctrines:

> According to natural law doctrines there are at least two different kinds of law: natural and positive. Natural law was supposed to emanate from God or nature or some other moral authority transcending earthly power, while positive (or civil) law is law posited by human beings. . . . It was from natural law that the state was supposed to derive its authority: only those positive laws which accorded with the dictates of natural law were valid; those positive laws which went against natural law were invalid; there was a right to disobey, or even under some circumstances a duty to resist, positive laws which ran counter to those of natural law.[23]

Fine's attempt to distance Marx from the natural law tradition fails for two reasons. First, from the evidence that I have provided so far, Marx did embrace a methodology that is very similar to that of natural law theories. Fine could counter that Marx later abandoned this way of thinking. I shall show in the next chapter, where the theory built on the foundation laid here is fully explicated, that the case for abandonment is tenuous. Secondly, there is nothing in the passage from Fine to show that the natural law tradition as he describes it is not compatible with Marxism. Of course, if the only possible source of natural law is God or some other moral authority transcending earthly power, Marxism and natural law theory will be patently incompatible. But Fine suggests that *nature* could also be a source of natural law. If we can find a conception of nature that would serve as a source of natural law and not transcend earthly power, we could construct a plausible Marxist version of natural law theory. This will be done in the next chapter.

Similar criticisms can be leveled at Paul Phillips, who allows that Marx's early thought on law "has a distinctly natural law cast."[24] Phillips opines that there is a difficulty in maintaining a distinction between "real" and "nonreal" law, a difficulty encountered by any natural law theory. The difficulty is that of "assigning any meaning to a statement that a rule that satisfies the formal criteria of law, e.g. by being a statute duly enacted in the

---

22. Bob Fine, *Democracy and the Rule of Law* (London: Pluto Press, 1984), p. 66.
23. Ibid., p. 19.
24. Paul Phillips, *Marx and Engels on Law and Laws* (Totowa, N.J.: Barnes & Noble, 1980), pp. 6–7.

form laid down by the constitution, and that exists empirically in that subjects and/or enforcement agencies adjust their behaviour in accordance with its norms, is not 'real law.' . . . [This distinction between 'real' and 'nonreal' law] tend[s] to blur the distinction between 'law' as a description of what 'is', and 'law' as a prescription of what 'ought to be.' "[25] According to Phillips, this distinction between what is and what ought to be was one of the main sources of Marx's dissatisfaction with idealist philosophy. The evidence for this claim is taken from Marx's letter to his father of November 10, 1837 (MECW, 1:10–21). "It is not surprising," Phillips writes, "that once [Marx] had broken with that philosophy he should be attracted by a line of thought in which that distinction could be claimed to be 'aufgehoben' (using this term in both of its senses — that of 'abolished' and that of 'raised to a higher level')."[26]

It seems to me that Phillips is simply wrong. If he is right, then we should not expect to find Marx distinguishing law from legislation in subsequent writings. This is not the case. The distinction between essence and appearance, of which the natural law/positive law distinction is only an instance, is a salient feature of Marx's methodology. One wonders what Phillips would say to Marx's critique of the historical school of law, whose fixation on "sources of law" is the object of Marx's ridicule: "The historical school has taken the study of sources as its watchword, it has carried its love for sources to such an extreme that it calls on the boatman to ignore the river and row only on its source-head" (MECW, 1:203). To Phillips's contention that it is difficult to assign any meaning to a statement that asserts that a law that is empirically in force is nonlaw, Marx provides the best rebuttal in the same critique of Hugo: "Hugo's [read: Phillips's] *reasoning*, like his *principle*, is *positive*, i.e., *uncritical*. He knows *no distinctions*. *Everything existing* serves him as an *authority*, every authority serves him as an *argument*" (1:205).

What Phillips and other interpreters like him do not realize is that when we can no longer distinguish between essence and existence, when the two can be said to coincide, the *critical* edge of Marxism is lost or unnecessary. Besides, it is important that Phillips provide evidence for Marx's sublation of the distinction between positive law and natural law. Phillips does not do this because the evidence is simply not there. I conclude that Marx's legal rationalism in the period before the "Kreuznach Notebooks" is principally Hegelian — marked by essentialism in methodology and rationalism in content.

25. Ibid., pp. 9–10.
26. Ibid., p. 10.

V

Marx's legal rationalism has two aspects. The first refers to the locus of law. Legal rationalism in this aspect is the claim that law is the means by which reason seeks to realize its essence: freedom. Law in this sense is what we may call the *law of reason*. This is what Marx meant in those passages where he said that law is the realization of freedom for reason that has come to know itself and to set the laws by which it guides its own activity. This is the law that antedates positive laws. It exists independently of but is realized, however imperfectly, by positive laws. The law of reason serves as a metric with which to measure how well positive law incorporates the essence of law. At the same time, it serves as a source of positive law. In this dimension, the law of reason realizes an essence that is external to it. After all, it is the law *of* reason. Reason itself has a different essence, which is to strive for freedom. Freedom is the essence of human beings. We find, then, that the law of reason is explained by an essence that is more ultimate than it.

Marx also explained law by an essence immanent to it. This brings us to the second aspect of his legal rationalism: the form of law. Contained in the law of reason is the essence of humans. But there is also *reason in law*. That is to say, law, considered as a definite sphere and mode of existence, does have an essence that derives from its own immanent determinations and that accounts for the form of law. This is a corollary to Marx's argument that the human essence that law, as law of reason, embodies is realized differently in different spheres of life, depending on the specific nature of the sphere of life to be considered. The human essence is multifarious and versatile. It manifests itself in the many diverse tasks that humans perform. Over time, however, these tasks themselves develop autonomous, institutional histories that come to define them and limit the scope of expression for participants who come into them later.[27] The sum of these defining presuppositions is what Marx called their "respective natures," and they constitute what he called the "inner rules of [the] life" of such activities. "Freedom of trade is precisely freedom of trade and no other freedom because within it the nature of the trade develops unhindered according to the inner rules of its life. Freedom of the courts is freedom of the courts if they follow their own inherent laws of right and not those of some other sphere, such as religion. Every particular sphere of

---

27. The implications of these histories for the autonomy of law are discussed in Chapter 4 below.

freedom is the freedom of a particular sphere, just as every particular mode of life is the mode of life of a particular nature" (MECW, 1:173).

The natural law of human reason, Marx's rational law, has a nature, or a reason, pertaining to itself which explains its essential features, its structure, which is filled with the material supplied by reason. When Marx wrote that the censorship law "has within it no *measure*, no *rational rule,*" there is a double reference. In the first place, it does not share in the law of reason; that is, it does not represent a positive realization of freedom. In the second place, the law lacks the measure of the nature of law; that is, it is bereft of the reason in law.

Between the law of reason and the reason in law, the first is superior and is the standard by which we measure the adequacy of the second. Reason in law, as well as reason in any other human activity, is the sum of the "inner rules of the activity" concerned. This means that any activity that survives long enough to be the subject of an institutional history and autonomous development is capable of developing, as it were, a nature. This, of course, is without prejudice to what kind of activity it is; that is to say, an activity's nature is indifferent to whether it is good or bad. So, to continue with the examples in Marx's passage quoted above, courts or religion or trade ought to develop in line with the respective natures of the sphere. If this is true, then we can say that stealing, lying, or killing, insofar as each meets the relevant conditions, should follow the inner rules of its respective development. This is where the force of the law of reason can be felt. Freedom, the essence of humans, is the test of the adequacy and worthiness of every activity. Thus understood, activities like stealing, lying, or killing, unless they can be shown to be promotive of freedom, would fall short of what is right and would stand condemned. The measure and rational rule that ultimately determines worthiness of pursuit is conformity with freedom. One direct implication of this standpoint is that a law can meet the requirements of reason in law, be positive, and still fall short of the law of reason. This is why Phillips's reliance on formal criteria is mistaken. In the rest of this section, it will be shown that Marx's analysis of particular laws follows the pattern just sketched. The laws are those concerning freedom of the press, censorship instruction, and thefts of wood.

Marx criticized the three laws that we have chosen for not manifesting the natural law of human reason. The law of reason is the law that reason gives to itself in its striving for freedom. Freedom is acting in accordance with the laws that derive from the natural law of human reason. According to Marx, the law of reason does not issue in "actual preventive laws" (MECW, 1:162). What does he mean by this statement? He could mean that laws are not preventive in the sense in which we might say that the law "preempts" my action. That is, the law does not stop me from acting. Rather, it confronts me after I have acted in contravention of its dictates.

Action is important because it is the medium through which the actor is brought into possible contact, sometimes conflict, with another. Except those who still believe in extrasensory perception and other notorious ways of affecting others through thought, absent action, thought holds no interest for law properly speaking. I can harbor the worst malice toward my neighbor, I can plan in my head the most spectacular robberies, but until I make moves to realize my worst intentions, the law cannot even ascertain which of my innumerable thoughts I might wish to realize. Hence the requirement of external manifestation in action. The inscrutability of thought and our inability to divine thoughts are part of why preventive laws, laws against thought and suchlike, evoke so much unease in us and attract our condemnation. When law does otherwise, it takes away a crucial element of the human essence—freedom. It curbs freedom. But action brings with it responsibility for the consequences of our actions, brings us into potential interference with the spaces of others. Hence we are called upon to exercise due care, to pay attention to the impact of our actions on others. Thought is invisible; action is objective. To the extent that law is the mode of existence of freedom, and freedom requires external manifestation in action, any law that preempts action constricts freedom (MECW, 1:120). When law intervenes to punish me for my thoughts, "my bad frame of mind," what it does is to preempt my action. This should be condemned because freedom, my essence, is principally manifested in my capacity to *act*, to "manifest myself externally."

But the statement that "there are no actual preventive laws" could also mean that laws are essentially *directive* rather than *coercive*. Positive laws serve as guideposts that human actors ought to heed in their actions. "Where the law is real law, i.e., a form of existence of freedom, it is the real existence of freedom for man. Laws, therefore, cannot prevent a man's actions, for they are indeed the inner laws of life of his action itself, the conscious reflections of his life. Hence law withdraws into the background in the face of man's life as a life of freedom, and only when his actual behaviour has shown that he has ceased to obey the natural law of freedom does law in the form of state law compel him to be free" (MECW, 1:162). The censorship instruction and the law on the freedom of the press both fail for falling short of the requirements of the law of reason. Marx's final judgment from this perspective bears quoting in full: "In the press law, freedom punishes. In the censorship law, freedom is punished. The censorship law is a law of suspicion against freedom. The press law is a vote of confidence which freedom gives itself. The press law punishes the abuse of freedom. The censorship law punishes freedom as an abuse. It treats freedom as a criminal, or is it not regarded in every sphere as a degrading punishment to be under police supervision? The censorship law has only the *form* of law. The press law is a *real* law" (1:161).

Marx said that there are no actual preventive laws. We have interpreted this to mean that law allows me to act and only comes into play when my action infringes on the law. However, in the sentence immediately following the claim that there are no actual preventive laws, we are told that "law prevents only as a *command*" (MECW, 1:162). If there are no preventive laws, how can law prevent only as a command? Our two possible interpretations give us a clue as to the possible meaning of the second statement. Law does not prevent me from acting *simpliciter*; it does prevent me (i.e., prohibit me) from acting in certain ways. It is when I have acted in those ways prohibited by law that I become an object for the law's sanctions.

In his analysis of the debates on the Law on Thefts of Wood, Marx also deployed arguments arising from the law of reason. The analysis conforms to the design we have so far examined. But the critique of the wood-theft law introduced an additional consideration: the requirement that there be a convergence of the law of reason with the popular will; that it coincide with the ideas of the people during a given historical period. These are usually contained in *customary rights* when a people have yet to attain the level of consciousness that permits the expression of law in clear, positive laws marked by an impersonal, theoretical existence. The wood-theft law fell short of this requirement of the law of reason by not arising from the popular consciousness of right (customary rights) and by actively ignoring those rights. The new law did not distinguish between gathering fallen wood and cutting wood and appropriating it without the consent of the owner.

For Marx, "the gathering of fallen wood and the theft of wood are essentially different things." In the first instance, he maintained that branches which have fallen off a tree have been organically separated from the tree, whereas in the case of theft the thief effects, by her or his action, the separation. Marx argued that by treating the gathering of fallen wood as a felony, the state created a new crime where there was none and acted against the customary rights of the poor to help themselves to fallen wood. The consequence is that the law classifies as theft "an action that is scarcely even a violation of forest regulations" (MECW, 1:227). Because this was contrary to the people's conception of right, it put the people in a situation where they were forced to see a crime where there was none and to regard the violation of law as a right.

Where the customary rights of the people conflict with those of the aristocracy, according to Marx, only the rights of the people conform to the form of law—it has universality on its side. When customary rights are embodied in positive laws, it is those of the people which ought to be embodied (MECW, 1:231). The customary right of the poor to gather fallen wood was exactly what had been expunged from the new law. This is the nature of the departure from the law of reason, and for this reason the law is a nonlaw. The critique of the wood-theft law places greater emphasis on the inadequacy of this law to the form of law. Here is a good place to consider the second aspect of Marx's legal rationalism: the requirement that laws should conform to the dictates of reason in law.

What Marx called the form of law, the reason immanent to law qua law, is identical to the sum of features that we have come to call the rule of law. The two principal sides of this form are universality and necessity.[28] The new wood-theft law was criticized for conflicting with "the form of universal law" (MECW, 1:231). First, law must be universal. There may be exceptions, but they must be dictated by the nature of the sphere of life to be regulated. Otherwise the laws must apply equally to all who are bound by them. The exceptions must not be in the interests of one class against another. The new law fell short of this requirement, according to Marx. He condemned the censorship laws, too, as the laws of one side against another: "The law against a frame of mind is *not a law of the state* promulgated for its *citizens*, but the *law of one party against another party*. The law which punishes tendency abolishes the equality of the citizens before the law. It is a law which divides, not one which unites, and all laws which divide are reactionary. It is not a law, but a *privilege*" (1:120). When the law becomes a *privilege*, it is subverted from within, because what is supposed to apply to all becomes a weapon in the hands of a few who use it to fight their opponents. At the same time, the object of law changes from that of realizing freedom to one of curtailing the freedom of others. The law suffers an enormous de-form-ity. Secondly, the standpoint of law is that of necessity. Laws are not the product of the whims and interests of individuals or classes. Marx, it should be recalled, had said that legislators do not *make* laws, they only *formulate* them. Law should be derived from the legal nature of things. Positive laws must conform to the dictates of the objective, rational law or, in default, fail to be laws. The Divorce Bill was defective because it did not

28. Again, see Kain, *Marx and Ethics*, pp. 28–29, for a Kantian gloss on this preference.

proceed from the necessary attributes of marriage; the Law on Thefts of Wood failed on the same score for not being the positive expression of rational law as reflected in the people's conception of right (1:232).

There are other elements of the form of law that Marx referred to occasionally. For instance, he required that laws be autonomous of private interests (MECW, 1:245). There should be a clear separation of the accuser from the judge (1:237). "No one, not even the most excellent legislator, can be allowed to put himself above the law he has made" (1:243). Trials must be public, and they must reflect the essence of law. So judges must be unfettered save by the provisions of the law (1:166). Where these conditions are subverted, the consequence is that what should be the realization of freedom is turned into an instrument of private interests. Marx's conclusion on what the wood-theft law meant for the form of law is very clear: "This logic, which turns the servant of the forest owner into a state authority [the accuser is the judge], *turns the authority of the state into a servant of the forest owner*. The state structure . . . is degraded into an instrument of the forest owner and his interest operates as the soul governing the entire mechanism" (1:245).

We have come to the end of our exposition of Marx's legal rationalism. The writings that have been examined are those written by Marx between 1837 and 1842. It is my contention that the concept of legal rationalism provides a unifying theme for these writings and allows us to understand the nature of the changes that occurred later in Marx's thinking about law. In the next and last section of this chapter I examine the reasons for the changes and their nature.

VI

In this section, I will argue that the period between March 1843, when Marx first resigned from the editorship of the *Rheinische Zeitung*, went to Kreuznach, and then to Paris in October of the same year, and spring 1845, when he and Engels completed *The German Ideology*, registers Marx's transition from the legal rationalism of the preceding sections to what I call "legal naturalism." Legal naturalism will be elaborated in the rest of this work. Our discussion of the transition will necessarily be brief. The aim is to set the stage for the subsequent chapters.

If Marx had been no more than a journalist, dissatisfaction with the censorship might not have been enough to force him to rethink some of his ideas. But Marx was also a social critic, a revolutionary democrat, and a legal rationalist. Thus there were sufficient causes to provoke a profound disenchantment with his situation. He had taken seriously the Hegelian thesis of the inherent rationality of the state and the law, and even if he had not actively embraced the inherent rationality of the Prussian state, we do not find in his writings any definite suggestion that the then Prussian state and law were irrational. One could argue that Marx did assume the rationality of the Prussian state and law; and that this assumption illumines his bewilderment at some of the legislative proposals coming out of the Prussian state—proposals that were subjected to withering legal-rationalist criticisms in the texts we have already examined.

A revolutionary democrat and humanist social critic, Marx was quite disturbed by the distress of the peasants of Mosel (MECW, 1:332–58). His analysis of the wood-theft law had also opened his eyes to the overweening influence of sectional interests on the legislative proposals. These had consequences for his legal rationalism. Finally, his engagement with the new law convinced him of the need to supplement his Hegel-derived philosophy of law with an in-depth knowledge of politics and economics. It was against this background that Marx withdrew from public life into his study, first at Kreuznach and later in Paris. There is a fair amount of agreement among commentators concerning Marx's retirement to his study. It is generally agreed that a crisis of theory forced Marx into a retreat in 1843:

[As editor of the *Rheinische Zeitung*] Marx was brought up against the hard facts of reality more sharply than ever. The Prussian state as it actually was could still be measured against the idea of what the true state ought to be. But there was no answer in Hegel to economic questions such as that raised by the debates in the Diet about the wood-theft law or the distress among the wine-growing peasants of the Moselle. Engels wrote later that "Marx always said that it was his going into the question of the wood-theft law and the position of the Moselle peasants that turned his attention from pure politics to economic conditions and thus to socialism."[29]

Marx's own account of this period is perhaps the best support for the argument that his thinking was on the threshold of a transformation. In the 1859 Preface, he stated:

29. Boris Nicolaievsky and Otto Maenchen-Helfen, *Karl Marx: Man and Fighter* (Harmondsworth: Penguin, 1976), pp. 57–58. See also J. O'Malley, "Editor's Introduction," *Karl Marx's Critique of Hegel's Philosophy of Right* (Cambridge: Cambridge University Press, 1982), p. xxvi; Chen Xueming, "An Inquiry into Marx's Early Views on the Philosophy of Law and His Early Legal Thinking," *Social Sciences in China* 4 (1983): 53; Cain and Hunt, *Marx and Engels on Law*, p. 3.

In the year 1842–43, as editor of the *Rheinische Zeitung*, I first found myself in the embarrassing position of having to discuss what is known as material interests. The deliberations of the Rhenish Landtag on forest thefts and the division of landed property; the official polemic started by Herr von Schaper, then Oberprasident of the Rhine Province, against the *Rheinische Zeitung* about the condition of the Moselle peasantry, and finally the debates on free trade and protective tariffs caused me in the first instance to turn my attention to economic questions. . . . When the publishers of the *Rheinische Zeitung* conceived the illusion that by a more compliant policy on the part of the paper it might be possible to secure the abrogation of the death sentence passed upon it, I eagerly grasped the opportunity to withdraw from the public stage to my study.

The first work which I undertook to dispel the doubts assailing me was a critical re-examination of the Hegelian philosophy of law; . . .[30]

When Marx reemerged, the studies he undertook came to represent the abandonment of legal rationalism and the transition to a still inchoate but discernible materialism, a necessary prerequisite to legal naturalism. What is the nature of the transition that Marx's thought underwent during the retreat?

Up to the time Marx resigned his editorship, the source of law for him was reason: law was the natural law of human reason. The positive laws were merely the manifestation of the rational law. In the major work of his stay at Kreuznach we find that Marx's account of the source of law altered. The first faltering steps toward a materialist theory of law were taken in the *Contribution to the Critique of Hegel's Philosophy of Law*. Although he still deployed essentialist explanations (e.g., MECW, 3:29, 57), the essence of law was altered from that of reason to that of material reality—the *mode of life of a people*. There was very little mention of law in the *Contribution*. Marx's doctrine of law, at this stage, was a corollary of his general doctrine of the state.[31] In his earlier position, the state (law) is the product of reason and, at the same time, the vehicle through which reason realizes its goal: freedom. In the *Contribution*, this standpoint came in for serious criticism. Contrary to his earlier position, Marx said: "The idea (Reason) is made the subject and the *actual* relation of family and civil society to the state as its *internal imaginary* activity. Family and civil society are the premises of the state; they are the genuinely active elements, but in specu-

30. Karl Marx, *A Contribution to the Critique of Political Economy*, ed. and intro. Maurice Dobb (New York: International Publishers, 1970), pp. 19–20.
31. O'Malley, "Editor's Introduction," p. xxiv.

lative philosophy things are inverted. When the idea is made the subject, however, the real subjects, namely, civil society, family, 'circumstances, caprice, etc.', become *unreal* objective elements of the idea with a changed significance." The state (law) here is a product of the "multitude in their existence as members of families and as members of civil society." At this point, however, Marx conceded that Hegel had accurately depicted the empirical conditions of the modern state. His criticism was leveled at Hegel's method of exposition. "The difference lies not in the content but in the method of approach or in the *manner of speaking*. There is a double history, an esoteric and an exoteric. The content lies in the exoteric part. The interest of the esoteric part is always that of finding again in the state the history of the logical concept. It is on the exoteric side, however, that development proper takes place" (MECW, 3:8).

The shift in the location of the essence of law, from the *esoteric* to the *exoteric*, set the stage for the next criticism of Marx's legal rationalism. If the family and civil society are the preconditions of the state (law), it is no accident that Marx insists that law exists for people and not that the people exist for law. Law should reflect the life of the people. Democracy is the truth of constitutions, and all concrete states must be judged not by how ill or well they embody reason but by how much they are the incarnations of the people's actual life. Hence the charge against Hegel that he collapsed democracy into the particular constitution of the modern state (MECW, 3:63; cf. 108, 110, 127, 143). Although there is no evidence to suggest that Marx ever identified the Prussian state with the rational state, the discovery that Hegel did aroused considerable opposition from Marx and was one of the reasons he abandoned legal rationalism.

Once the principal element of legal rationalism—law of reason—was subjected to thoroughgoing criticism, it was obvious that the explanation of concrete legal phenomena would have to be altered. Against Hegel's analysis of primogeniture as a determination of the state, Marx countered that primogeniture is merely the manifestation of a deeper essence supplied by landed property. The political constitution, the constitution of the modern state, is the constitution of private property. "*Primogeniture* is merely the *external* appearance of the *inner* nature of *landed property*" (MECW, 3:98). From here on, Marx's analysis took on a more and more materialist hue. The new outlook turned increasingly to political economy for the explanation of social processes. His works written between 1843 and 1845 testify to this direction.

The first work of significance for the theory of law in which Marx's new view was articulated is *The German Ideology*, jointly authored with Engels

between 1845 and 1846. The foundations of social and historical analysis
are anchored in the mode of life of human individuals. The mode of life of
individuals is how and what they produce. "As individuals express their
life, so they are. What they are, therefore, coincides with their production,
both with *what* they produce and with *how* they produce" (MECW,
5:31–32). In production, individuals reproduce themselves and enter into
social relations with one another, the sum of which makes up "civil society." These social relations are determined by the existing productive
forces at all previous stages, and in their turn they provide the condition
for the development of these productive forces. In *The German Ideology*
there is a decisive change in Marx's view of law. Instead of regarding law as
an expression of reason, he now regarded law as expressing the mode of
production. Law becomes an element of the social relations, and the
essence it embodies is derived from the nature of the mode of production:

> This conception of history thus relies on expounding the real process of
> production—starting from the material production of life itself—and com-
> prehending the form of intercourse connected with and created by this
> mode of production, i.e., civil society in its various stages, as the basis of all
> history; describing it in its action as the state [law], and also explaining how
> all the different theoretical products and forms of consciousness, religion,
> philosophy, morality, etc., etc., arise from it, and tracing the process of their
> formation from that basis; thus the whole thing can, of course, be depicted
> in its totality (and therefore, too, the reciprocal action of these various sides
> on one another). (5:53)

There is a noticeable change here in thought and language. No longer is
reference made to reason. Law is no longer judged by its adequacy to reason but by how well it embodies the stage of development reached by civil
society. Law becomes a product of the mode of production and an essential feature of it. Law is the law appropriate to, presupposed by, and conditioned by the nature of the mode of production. Legal naturalism is the
view that the basic law of a given epoch or social formation is that law
which is an essential aspect of the mode of production. The thesis of legal
naturalism, or what is also the Marxist theory of natural law, will be expounded and defended in the next chapter. With the conclusion of the
present chapter we end all references to legal rationalism, and we enter
into the new mode of analysis that Marx embraced from 1845 onward.
    This new mode of analysis which derives law from the nature of the
mode of production forms the basis for the theory of natural law devel-

oped in subsequent chapters. I do not claim that what follows is the theory of law Marx would have written, had he had the time or turned his mind to it. I insist only that this foundation yields a theory of law substantially different from those which have hitherto dominated Marxist discourse about law. Whether it is a better or worse theory will be judged by how well it enables us to make sense of legal phenomena.

2

A Marxist Theory
of Natural Law

I

I aim here to construct a substantive Marxist theory of natural law. I remain faithful to the positions identified in Chapter 1 above but draw upon the body of literature that has accumulated in the Marxist tradition since Marx's death, augmented by insights borrowed from other traditions in both law and philosophy. The hope is that such a theory of law will retain its Marxist pedigree and, more important, advance our knowledge of the nature, evolution, and end of law.

I shall argue that an adequate Marxist theory of law must carve a place for itself in the wide ambit of the natural law tradition. There is a place for Marxism in the natural law tradition, and our chief task in this chapter will be to work out a Marxist theory of law located within that tradition. Before setting out the details of this theory, though, I must dispose of an objection that may easily be deployed by anyone, Marxist or not, who is familiar with the story of the unhappy relationship between Marxism and the tradition of natural law.

It may be asked: What exactly has Marxism got to do with natural law except pour scorn on the latter or try to show that it is an anachronism? In most Marxist writings on law there is a spontaneous, almost elemental, hostility to natural law. First, natural law theory is said to be too diffused and, therefore, of little worth as theory. According to Evgeny Pashukanis, the doctrine of natural law "admits many concrete variations, depending on the historical situation, political sympathies and dialectical abilities of one author or another. This theory admits republican and monarchical tendencies and diverse degrees of democratism and revolutionism."[1] Pashukanis is willing to admit that natural law may accommodate progressive, revolutionary tendencies, but he believes that the fate of the theory is historically determined. According to him, natural law served as a revolutionary banner for the bourgeoisie in its epochal war with feudal society. But since the victory of the bourgeoisie, natural law has become an inadequate tool for understanding reality. In any case, the bourgeoisie in the contemporary period hates to be reminded of the revolutionary past of natural law—a reminder that it finds quite nettlesome as well as threatening to its dominant position in society.[2] Other Marxist scholars have contended that natural law in its current acceptation is conservative of capitalist relations.[3] Finally, Marxists reject one of the basic features of natural law. According to Vladimir Tumanov, Marxism "rejects out of hand the idea of two normative systems—natural law and positive law—functioning in one and the same social system. In one society there can be only one system of law, its base is material."[4] For the preceding reasons, the Marxian pedigree of this theory is not likely to command easy acceptance among Marxists.

The objection, the main outlines of which I just cited, does not have as much merit as its proponents would have us believe. In the first place, spontaneous hostility might be a peremptory and easy way to avert a debate. It cannot be a substitute for one. The proposition that Marxism is incompatible with the natural law tradition can only be the result, not the starting point, of an inquiry. The case for the incompatibility of Marxism and natural law theory, based on a close and presuppositionless reading of both schools is yet to be made. On the contrary, those who have sought to understand the relationship between Marxism and natural law are less dismissive of the possibility of a connection between them.[5] Secondly, every theory, whether in law or in science, is a regulative principle that directs us to look in a particular area for an understanding of given phenomena while it constrains us from looking in some other areas. If a theory starts

---

1. E. B. Pashukanis, *Selected Writings on Marxism and Law*, ed. and intro. Piers Beirne and Robert Sharlet, trans. Peter B. Maggs (London: Academic Press, 1980), p. 97. Incidentally, so does socialism.

2. Ibid.

3. V. I. Tumanov, *Contemporary Bourgeois Legal Thought* (Moscow: Progress Publishers, 1974), p. 269.

4. Ibid., p. 285. I argue later that this viewpoint is mistaken and cannot claim fidelity to the classics that must be the touchstone for those who accept Marxism.

5. For example, see William Leon McBride, "Marxism and Natural Law," *American Journal of Jurisprudence* 15 (1970): 127–53.

out with too restrictive a base it will, to the extent of the restrictiveness, be limited in use and may occlude insights into the nature of the object of inquiry. If Marxism as legal theory starts out by foreclosing whatever insights the natural law tradition may contain in its diverse expressions, it will to that extent be limited in the way I described. Attempts to foreclose an exploration of the Marxism–natural law connection will limit Marxist theory. A Marxist theory of law located within the tradition of natural law, as specified later, can be shown to be more fruitful of explanations of legal phenomena. It can also be shown to be more faithful to the historical antecedents adumbrated in the first chapter of this book.

Marxists alone do not bear all the responsibility for the lack of genuine dialogue with the adherents of the natural law school. Overburdened by their own excess ideological baggage, which predisposes them to an equally elemental hostility to Marxism, natural law theorists have themselves sought to hold the theoretical high ground. One can imagine what consternation and skepticism will greet a title that reads like this chapter's. I should, however, not be understood as sitting on the fence, straddling both worlds. Middle-of-the-road theories are not usually noted for boldness of imagination or attempts at resolving stalemates. I am not a conciliator, and I do not seek to harmonize the two theories. On the contrary, I locate this theory firmly in the Marxist tradition while arguing that, in legal theory, the Marxist theory of law belongs rightly in the natural law tradition as opposed to the school of legal positivism.

For this enterprise to succeed, I must be able to show that the arrival of one more resident will not upset the not so equilibrated relationship among the present occupants of the natural law mansion. I suggest that Marxism shares enough general characteristics of this tradition that its divergences in detail from other theories within the tradition do not suffice to deny it entry.

It is mistaken to talk of *the* natural law tradition. As many adherents of this doctrine will readily concede, there are as many natural law traditions as there are people who profess the doctrine. Thus, A. P. D'Entrèves asserts that "there is really not one tradition of natural law, but many."[6] In "The Case for Natural Law Re-examined" we find the following: "There are, after all, many mansions in the House of the Father; and if all natural law theorists agree on the existence of the ideal law, they have differed, and are bound to differ, in the manner of conceiving and defining it."[7]

---

6. A. P. D'Entrèves, *Natural Law*, 2d rev. ed. (London: Hutchinson, 1970), p. 16.
7. Reprinted ibid., p. 145.

Nonetheless, the diversity of content among the adherents of natural law doctrine does not vitiate the possibility of referring to the natural law tradition. After all, we do consider it sensible to talk of the Marxist or socialist tradition in politics, social theory, or literature even as we allow that not all of the thoughts we put together under this rubric cohere easily.

Any talk about the natural law, or the Marxist, or any other tradition contains an implicit acknowledgment that this identification is made at the most general level only. All that is required is to specify what features are essential to a tradition that offer us a criterion with which to identify and differentiate among its members. What, then, are the essential features of the natural law tradition?[8]

There are three primary features of the natural law tradition. First, *it posits a duality of legal existence: positive law and natural law*. Positive law is often identified with particular municipal legal regimes. Natural law is identified with the ideal legal system which is striving for realization and, being ideal, is desirable and ought to be. In this manner, the natural law tradition acknowledges the division between law that *is* and law that *ought* to be. It allows that the two are logically separate and that one should not be collapsed into the other.[9]

Closely related to the first is the second essential feature of the natural law tradition: *positing a hierarchical relationship between the positive law that is and the natural law that ought to be*. The natural law provides evaluative and justifying criteria for the positive law, and the latter is considered as a more or less adequate embodiment of natural law.[10] Whereas natural law is ultimate and is explanatory of positive law, this does not mean that in all cases of conflict between positive law and natural law, the natural law will prevail. Ordinarily, the natural law ought to prevail. However, in the same way that the positive law may be a less adequate expression of the natural law, the natural law may not prevail because of the play of contingency. Inadequate knowl-

8. In what follows I do not try to summarize the history of the evolution of natural law theory. I have relied mainly on the accounts of D'Entrèves, already cited; H. A. Rommen, *The Natural Law*, trans. Thomas R. Hanley (St. Louis: B. Herder, 1948); and Anthony Battaglia, *Toward a Reformulation of Natural Law* (New York: Seabury Press, 1981).

9. Sergio Cotta, "Positive Law and Natural Law," *Review of Metaphysics* 37, (1983): 268.

10. There is a sense in which the relationship between natural law and positive law is analogous to that which obtains between value and price. Value is ultimate, and price is the concrete expression of value. Price is always a more or less adequate manifestation of value. There is hardly ever a perfect price, but if there is, it will be coterminous with the value of a commodity. By the same token, we hardly ever have a situation in which the positive law perfectly realizes natural law. That is because of the nature of human practice and social action generally.

edge may be one such contingency. Or it may be that the short-term consequences of adhering to natural law precepts are not likely to be pleasant, and those who want to invoke natural law are not certain that they have the wherewithal to handle those consequences. One very good historical instance in which adherents of natural law felt compelled to affirm the supremacy of positive law was in the response of antislavery judges to the Fugitive Slave Law in antebellum United States of America.[11] Thus, while it is a necessary consequence of the superiority of the natural law that it *ought* to prevail, exigencies of practice or considerations of momentary satisfaction can ensure that it does not. The important point to be made is that the natural law is explanatory of the positive law. It provides a measure by which the adequacy, rationality, morality, etc., of the positive law can be ascertained.[12]

The third primary feature of the natural law tradition is its *abridgment of the gulf between what is and what ought to be*. Natural law theorists concede that the "is" and the "ought" are separate and separable. What is predicated of one may not consistently be predicated of the other. Indeed, any attempt to collapse one into the other will wipe out the distinction that is so vital to the plausibility of natural law theory. Yet theorists of natural law sometimes appear to collapse the distinction. This happens when they argue that particular positive laws in some polity are not laws and therefore ought not to be obeyed. The laws ought not to be obeyed because they violate the dictates of natural law and, to the extent of the violation, are not laws. If by denying the status of law to such laws natural law advocates mean to assert that only natural law is law, then of course the distinction between "law that is" and "law that ought to be" is abolished. But there is a more plausible account that one can give of the denial.

When natural law advocates say that a particular law is not law they should be understood as saying something along the following lines: law is a unity of form and content. Formally law is universal and necessary. We identified this as reason in law in Chapter 1. How this form is manifested concretely will be determined by what content is brought into the form. For example, the fact that a law has the form "All eighteen-year-olds shall serve in the armed forces for a period of . . ." does not tell us anything about the nature of the service or what specific assignments the draftees will have to carry out. Suppose the draftees later find out that their service is principally dropping napalm bombs and spraying defoliants on unprotected rural

---

11. For details, see Robert M. Cover, *Justice Accused: Antislavery and the Judicial Process* (New Haven: Yale University Press, 1975), chap. 10.

12. See Rommen, *The Natural Law*, pp. 17–18; D'Entrèves, *Natural Law*, p. 93.

population centers. If the natural law theorist says that individuals *ought* not to obey the law requiring them to report for the draft, he or she should be understood to be talking on at least two levels. What is involved is a conflict of "oughts," and it is perfectly consistent with, if not exactly required by, natural law theory that the ought of the natural law is ultimate and overrides that of the positive law where the positive law is so violative of the natural law which is supposed to give it identity that the latter can be denied the status of law. If our natural law theorist were pressed, he or she would at some point insist that the positive law concerned has only the *form* of law; it does not embody a content consonant with natural law. It lacks the element of the law of reason. If this is true, then the theorist can still maintain the separation of what is and what ought to be.

The natural law theorist has to specify the nature of the relationship between these two separate, logically discrete legal realms. What the natural law tradition asserts is that the natural law that ought to be provides the criteria by which we *identify*, *explain*, and *evaluate* the positive law that is in any society. An adequate account of the justification and obligatoriness of positive law must include reference to the fact that it embodies the natural law. Even though the positive law regime is itself an "ought system," its oughtness is in part traceable to its embodying, however imperfectly, the essence of the natural law. This last feature has oftentimes attracted criticisms from opponents of the theory. Opponents argue that no "ought" can be derived from an "is." Natural law is supposed to be an "ought system" derived from nature, an "is system." Given the logical chasm between "is" and "ought," it is contended, no statements of the first kind can be deduced from statements of the second kind. The numerous attempts at such derivations are generally accused of committing the naturalistic fallacy.

Some versions of natural law theory are vulnerable to this objection. This is especially true of those who talk as if the relationship between natural law and positive law is one of logical deduction, whereby the positive law is deduced as logical consequences from the general theorems of natural law with appropriate middle terms. This is a problematic approach. It assumes that law is a system of logical deductions in which individual legal decisions are deductions from general laws.[13] But such an assumption is wrong. A legal system is open-ended in ways that logical systems are not. In addition, a legal system is an order of practical reason whose elements

13. This approach is not limited to natural law theorists. Hans Kelsen, a very hostile opponent of natural law theories, espouses the same viewpoint. See, generally, Kelsen, *The Pure Theory of Law* (Berkeley: University of California Press, 1967).

are built up over time through repeated findings, struggles, and conflicting interpretations. To construe law as a system of logical deduction is to
misconstrue it. For, as we shall see presently, the relationship between natural law and positive law is more akin to that between a general kind and
its more or less perfect instantiation. Hence we speak of the positive law as
an expression of natural law. Moreover, both kinds of law regulate and are
constitutive of human practice. Since the two are products of practical reason, any attempt to affirm a relationship of logical deduction between
them is apt to generate confusion in analysis. They embody much more
than their formal logical attributes.

So far I have sketched the main lines of the natural law tradition. Of
course different authors in diverse places have put different contents into
the framework of natural law theory. Some have sought it in divine nature.
For example, H. A. Rommen traces the origin of the notion of natural law
as an unchanging and unchangeable law from which all human laws draw
their force to Heraclitus, for whom the *logos* is the underlying reality behind the flux of appearances.[14] For the Romans, however, the natural law
was the rule corresponding to the nature of things. *Ius naturale, naturalis,
natura*, and so on had practical use for them. "They were invoked to provide a basis of rights and duties. But that basis was not of a speculative,
transcendental kind. It can best be described as a quest for the intrinsic
character of a given situation."[15]

The modern theory of natural law and natural rights whose genealogy
we trace to Thomas Hobbes is not directly founded on the divine or the
nature of things.[16] It is the natural law emanating from the nature of humans as rational beings. Thus we identify the natural law of God, the natural law of things, and the natural law of human reason. While all these
diverge in content, my contention is that they share the three main features I have identified. In fact, we may say that a theory of law that lacks all
three features may not properly be called a natural law theory.

II

I have not identified immutability as one of the essential features of natural
law theory. In my judgment, it is not a part of the tradition nor does the tradition require it in order to be what it is. It seems to me that the concept of

14. Rommen, *The Natural Law*, pp. 5–6
15. D'Entrèves, *Natural Law*, p. 33.
16. See Norberto Bobbio, *Thomas Hobbes and the Natural Law Tradition*, trans. Daniela
Gobetti (Chicago: University of Chicago Press, 1993).

"nature" is responsible for the presumption of the immutability of natural law. Those who interpret natural law as an emanation from divine nature may find less room for change in a product of an unchanging source. Even then, given that God does sometimes change his/her mind, there is no reason to believe that (s)he may not, when (s)he so desires, change the character of her/his handiwork. More significantly, it need not be controversial that divinely inspired natural law is merely one among several kinds of natural law. It may be that the immutability that is attributed to natural law more by its opponents than by its adherents is the outcome of an analogical reasoning from the laws of nature. This attribution is a lot more problematic than its proponents and opponents alike seem to think.

Although it can be argued that the laws of nature do not change, it is less controversial, at least since Charles Darwin, to say that nature itself is historical and evolving. In any case, even if it is true that nature and its laws are unchanging, it requires a considerable leap of the imagination to affirm the same of natural law in value theory. There are essential differences between the law of nature and natural law. Natural law is normative, whereas laws of nature are statements of factual uniformities. Hermann Kantorowicz specifies the differences quite aptly:

> These laws (of nature), which down to Newton's time and even later could not be understood except as expressions of the will of a divine "law-giver", describe invariant causal relations or structural conjunctions (of facts, changes, quantities, properties). They impose obligations, not on human conduct but, if demonstrably true, on human intelligence; they are a matter, not of acknowledgment, recognition or approval, but of knowledge, cognition and proof; not sanctions but of consequences; not of authority but of experience; not of conscience but of science; not of duties sometimes obeyed, sometimes disobeyed, but of constant happenings indefinitely repeatable; finally, laws of nature are concerned with what is fully or approximately real (frictionless motion, perfect gas, economic man), whereas rules of conduct (of which natural law is a subset) prescribe a conduct which may or may not be real but *ought* to be real.[17]

Natural law is distinguished by its *practical* character. In Kantorowicz's descriptions each half of the dichotomy referring to natural law can be predicated or required of human conduct, judgment, and deliberation. Probably the most important element of natural law, contradistinguished

---

17. Hermann Kantorowicz, *The Definition of Law* (Cambridge: Cambridge University Press, 1958), p. 25.

from the law of nature, is that it is a matter "of acknowledgment, recognition or approval," attributes that are germane to practice. It is the axiological nature of natural law that is of relevance in and interest to philosophy of law. Being axiological, it allows us to make a choice even as it directs us toward a particular choice rather than another. No one is judged a bad individual for disregarding the laws of gravity; he or she is merely adjudged stupid or ignorant. We may affirm of the laws of nature that they are immutable, but it is erroneous to so affirm of natural law. Opponents of the natural law tradition are apt to collapse the two realms. However, we should not use standards suited to one set of phenomena to understand the nature of a radically different phenomenon. An argument for including immutability among the essential features of the natural law tradition cannot be drawn from an analogy to the laws of nature. Such an argument, if there is one, must come from a consideration of the axiological character of natural law and its status as an emanation from human practice.

In addition, one can argue that immutability has been claimed for natural law more by its opponents than by its defenders. We cannot deny that there are natural law theorists who asseverate that natural law is immutable.[18] But it is false to insist that all natural law proponents do so. Let us for a moment agree that natural law is immutable. It does not follow that natural law, by reason of its immutability, is fully constituted, self-sufficient. For even if it *appears* to be fully constituted in its most general principles, inasmuch as natural law is a guide for practical human conduct and

18. One of the classic statements of this attitude can be found in Sophocles' *Antigone*:

> Creon (to Antigone): You—tell me not at length but in a word,
> You knew the order not to do this thing?

> Anti.: I knew, of course I knew. The word was plain.

> Creon: And still you dared to overstep these laws?

> Anti.: For me it was not Zeus who made that order
> Nor did that Justice who lives with the gods below
> mark out such laws to hold among mankind.
> Nor did I think your orders were so strong
> that you, a mortal man, could over-run
> the gods' unwritten and unfailing laws.
> Not now, nor yesterday's, they always live,
> and no one knows their origin in time.
> So not through fear of any man's proud spirit
> would I be likely to neglect these laws,
> draw on myself the gods' sure punishment.

David Grene and Richmond Lattimore, eds., *The Complete Greek Tragedies: Sophocles I* (Chicago: University of Chicago Press, 1954), pp. 173–74.

human conduct can unfold in numberless unpredictable ways, it remains plausible to suggest that the application of the general principles of natural law to specific cases of human conduct can throw fresh insights into the concept of natural law, take away from or augment its most general principles. This is a point that few natural law theorists deny.[19] At least this much is conceded by Thomas Aquinas: "A change in the natural law may be understood in two ways. First, by way of addition. In this sense nothing hinders the natural law from being changed: since many things for the benefit of human life have been added over and above the natural law, both by the Divine law and by human laws. Secondly, a change in the natural law may be understood by way of subtraction, so that what previously was according to the natural law, ceases to be so."[20]

The concession from Aquinas is significant. First, because it grants that change may come upon natural law. Secondly, he even suggests ways in which natural law may be altered. This concession was forced upon Aquinas by the essence of natural law itself, the most distinctive feature of which is its generality. Were we to admit that natural law is immutable, it would be only in respect of its most general principles. It cannot be applied to concrete cases of human behavior without addition or subtraction. Therefore, the immutability of natural law should not prevent us from examining the mechanics of the evolution of change in law.[21] I conclude that immutability is neither a feature of nor required by a theory of

19. For a recent restatement of this acknowledgment see Battaglia, *Toward a Reformulation of Natural Law*.

20. Thomas Aquinas, *Treatise on Law* (Chicago: Regnery Gateway, n.d.), Dominican translation, p. 69. See also D'Entrèves, *Natural Law*, p. 47; Battaglia, *Toward a Reformulation of Natural Law*, pp. 99–102. In a very interesting paper on legal change in unchangeable law, Haim H. Cohn has shown how change occurs even in divine law. The specific law he examines is the Torah. The Torah is held to have been the product of revelation to the children of Israel by God through Moses on Mount Sinai. As such, it is held to be immutable and unchangeable. Indeed, its immutability is "elevated to the rank of an explicit and binding norm." Cohn, "Legal Change in Unchangeable Law: The Talmudical Pattern," in A. R. Blackshield, ed., *Legal Change: Essays in Honour of Julius Stone* (Sydney: Butterworths, 1983), p. 11. However, the need to supplement the Torah in concrete cases has been satisfied by various strategies that have exploited some of the ambiguities and generalities of the language in which God's injunctions are expressed. Thus the fact that there are other modes of revelation, especially the dicta of his prophets, has been combined with the injunction that "unto him [the prophet] ye shall hearken" in order to justify the exercise of legislative authority by prophets, sages, and elders: "They [prophets, sages, elders, etc.] . . . simply invoked the theory of delegation of legislative power; and their hermeneutical efforts were intended to establish that they and their predecessors had, in modifying and amplifying the Written Law, acted within the authority conferred upon them by the divine law itself" (p. 15).

21. This is done in Chapter 5 below.

natural law. I hope also to have shown that a divine origin is not an essential feature of the tradition.

I have left out of the discussion another common feature of natural law theories: the claim that natural law is an order of practical reason and that law is an ordering of reason. According to Aquinas, "law is something pertaining to reason. . . . Law is a rule and measure of acts, whereby man is induced to act or is restrained from acting: . . ."[22] If this feature is so common, why have I found it necessary to exclude it from an account of the salient features of the natural law tradition? The rationale for exclusion is provided by the fact that the principle of practical reason is part of a larger issue: that of the locus of natural law and its essence. It will become clear in what follows that practical reason is one locus, among several others, that has been suggested for natural law. Besides practical reason, moreover, other elements such as justice and the imperative of self-preservation have been advanced as the essence of natural law.

By electing to identify only the most salient features of the natural law tradition, we recognize only those features which seem to us to define the tradition even if it means neglecting some otherwise important features. Marx, as we saw in Chapter 1 above, at some stage shared the view that law is a certain ordering of reason, even though he later abandoned that view. Instead of focusing attention on practical reason, it is more appropriate to emphasize a deeper commitment shared by natural law theorists: the insistence that law embodies an essence that is external to it and from which it draws its legitimacy (obligatoriness) and identity. Whether this essence is practical reason or the happiness principle is less important.

It can still be objected that by looking at the most general characteristics of the tradition, I have robbed it of its content and, therefore, its specificity. This is an easy charge. Focusing on the most general traits of natural law is the best one can do in the circumstance if we are not unduly and unwarrantedly to take sides with one interpretation of natural law rather than another. The failure to see in the tradition of natural law a multilayered theory whose flexibility enables it to counter many criticisms and constantly renew itself in different climes and times explains the ease with which some claim to have disposed of natural law. The generality of the tradition is not an obstacle to theoretical formulations; it is required for them.

It is not as if one is twisting the tradition to suit one's purpose. Nor is one expanding it needlessly so that one can easily carve a niche for Marx-

---

22. Aquinas, *Treatise on Law*, p. 3. See also J. M. Finnis, *Natural Law and Natural Rights* (Oxford: Clarendon Press, 1980), chaps. 2–5.

ism. By their own admission, those who count themselves within this tradition know well enough that "natural law . . . is essentially a framework law, a skeleton law. It does not ordinarily give us a concrete norm directly applicable to action here and now in the involved situations of actual life. It does not, for instance, tell us which of the many possible forms of laws about property is right in the abstract."[23] Until infused with a new content, in the rest of the present chapter "natural law" should be understood in the manner I have described above.

In the next few sections I argue not only that Marxism is compatible with natural law but that an adequate Marxist theory of law must locate itself in the natural law tradition. Needless to say, the content of a Marxist account of natural law must differ from most other schools within the tradition. The difference is not of a kind that will place Marxism outside the scope of the tradition. At the same time, an interpretation of Marxism in legal theory is needed that will draw on the strengths of the natural law tradition and even on other kinds of legal theory, most notably legal positivism, in an "integrative jurisprudence" without stepping into the snare of eclecticism. The material for such a theory is contained in the original writings of the founders of Marxism. The account in Chapter 1 above provides the textual foundations.

III

Marxist theories of law abound. But because they are mostly dominated by a positivist problematic, they are more appropriately discussed in the next chapter where we examine positive law. In the main they treat law within a general discussion of politics or philosophy of history. They all, in their different ways, accept the base/superstructure dichotomy as the basic schema of the Marxist philosophy of history and description of society. Thus, law is usually discussed as a component of politics or economics and banished to the superstructure.[24] Among the many versions of the Marx-

23. Rommen, *The Natural Law*, pp. 264–65. Also see Battaglia, *Toward a Reformulation of Natural Law*, p. 17.

24. See, generally, M. M. Bober, *Karl Marx's Interpretation of History*, 2d rev. ed. (Cambridge: Harvard University Press, 1962); G. A. Cohen, *Karl Marx's Theory of History: A Defence* (Princeton: Princeton University Press, 1978); John McMurtry, *The Structure of Marx's World-View* (Princeton: Princeton University Press, 1978); William H. Shaw, *Marx's Theory of History* (Stanford: Stanford University Press, 1978); Paul Hirst, *On Law and Ideology* (Atlantic Highlands, N.J.: Humanities Press, 1979); and Melvin Rader, *Marx's Interpretation of History* (New York: Oxford University Press, 1979).

ist philosophy of history dominated by this schema, only Gerald Cohen has deemed it worthwhile to deal with the peculiar problem that law and its cognates present to the base/superstructure interpretation of historical materialism. Moreover, his treatment of law, in a section of *Karl Marx's Theory of History* titled "The Problem of Legality," is novel, if abbreviated. I shall argue that Cohen's very sophisticated account of historical materialism applied to law is, ultimately, inadequate.

The problem of legality is generated by Marx's Preface of 1859. There Marx had written: "At a certain stage of their development, the material productive forces of society come in conflict with the existing relations of production, or—what is but a legal expression for the same thing—with the property relations within which they have been at work hitherto."[25] In the same passage, we are told that the material productive forces plus the social relations of production form the base on which arise a legal-political superstructure and forms of social consciousness. The base determines and conditions the character of the superstructure, and the superstructure corresponds to the base. For a statement of this relationship to be true, the elements of the superstructure must be separate and distinct from those of the base. What we predicate of one may not be applied to the other.

As is obvious from the passage just cited, however, it is plausible to suggest that property relations are at bottom relations of production; that there is an incoherence in the formulation of the base/superstructure dichotomy insofar as the two components of the metaphor are represented as discontinuous with each other and are joined together only in their interaction. This objection has been advanced most notably by H. B. Acton and John Plamenatz.[26] If the economic structure (the sum of the relations of production) is made up of *property* (or *ownership*) relations, then it cannot be separate or distinct from the *legal* superstructure it is supposed to explain.

According to Cohen, there are four positions contained in the explanatory thesis of historical materialism applied to the relationship between the economic structure and the legal superstructure. No more than three of these positions can be maintained consistently:

25. Karl Marx and Frederick Engels, *Selected Works* (Moscow: Progress Publishers, 1969), 1:503–4.

26. By Acton, see *The Illusion of the Epoch* (London: Cohen and West, 1955); "The Materialist Conception of History," *Proceedings of the Aristotelian Society* (1951–52): 207–24; and "On Some Criticisms of Historical Materialism, II," *Proceedings of the Aristotelian Society*, supp. (1970): 143–56. By Plamenatz: *German Marxism and Russian Communism* (London: Longman, 1954) and *Man and Society* (London: Longman, 1963), vol. 2.

(1) The economic structure consists of production relations.
(2) The economic structure is separate from (and explanatory of) the su-
    ·perstructure.
(3) Law is part of the superstructure.
(4) Production relations are defined in legal terms (that is, in terms of
    property in, or . . . *rights* over productive forces).[27]

Obviously, if (2) and (3) are true, then (4) cannot be for reasons that generated the problem of legality in the first place. To remove the inconsistency, Cohen proposes to abandon (4) by providing a way of eliminating
the legal terms from the description of production relations. "The problem, which has two connected parts, is (i) to formulate a non-legal interpretation of the legal terms in Marx's characterization of production
relations, in such a way that (ii) we can coherently represent property relations as distinct from, and explained by, production relations."[28]

Critics like Plamenatz and Acton have accused Marx of confusion and
circularity by his inclusion of law in the superstructure while production
relations (which sometimes *are* property relations) are left in the economic structure. This is because Acton and Plamenatz look at property
relations in an irreducibly legalistic way. They might have seen things differently had they considered that not all production relations are ex- .
pressed in legal form and that not all production relations are property
relations. Cohen seeks to meet these objections by purifying the economic structure of all legalistic references. He wants to argue that law
belongs *entirely* in the superstructure—that when Marx characterizes
production relations as property relations, he means the latter to be understood in nonlegal terms; that all locutions about property relations in .
the economic structure can be couched wholly in nonlegal terms. If
Cohen succeeds, he will have eliminated one of the more enduring and
potent methodological objections to historical materialism. Does he?
First let us examine the proposed strategy.

27. Cohen, *Karl Marx's Theory of History*, p. 218 (I have altered the numbering). In a
more recent formulation we have the following: "(1) The economic structure is the sum total
of production relations; (2) Production relations are relations of ownership; (3) The economic structure is (explanatory of and therefore) distinct from the legal superstructure; (4)
Ownership is a legal relationship." Cohen, "Base and Superstructure: A Reply to Hugh
Collins," *Oxford Journal of Legal Studies* 9 (1989): 95–96. I have stuck to Cohen's original
formulation because the superstructure contains other elements besides law; thus the more
recent formulation's substitution of "legal superstructure" in (3) might give the wrong impression that the superstructure is *strictly* legal.

28. Cohen, *Karl Marx's Theory of History*, p. 219.

Ownership is a matter of enjoying rights. For each ownership right there is a "matching power." Similarly, for every production relation there is a "matching" property relation. By distinguishing production relations from property relations that "match" them, the production relations can be shown to explain property relations.[29] According to Cohen, for every phrase of the form "the right to ø" we can substitute a phrase that denotes a power by dropping the word "right" and substituting for it the word "power":

> If x has power p and power p matches right r, we may say that, roughly speaking, the content of the power he has is the same as the content of right r, but we cannot infer that he also has right r. Possession of powers does not entail possession of the rights matching them. Only a possession of a *legitimate* power entails possession of the right it matches, and only possession of an *effective* right entails possession of its matching power. One might say that the power to ø is what you have *in addition to* the right to ø when your right to ø is effective, and that the right to ø is what you have *in addition to* the power to ø when your power to ø is legitimate.[30]

We have a "power/right" dichotomy. Apparently, power is nonnormative.[31] With the aid of this distinction we can construct *rechtsfrei* production relations that match property relations in just the way power matches rights. In this schema, production relations will be a sort of power relations in which merely the ability to bring about a result is relevant. The desirability or any other normative implication of this ability is irrelevant. Property relations, on the other hand, will correspond to rights, the normative fixing (legitimization) of power relations. Let us consider an illustration Cohen himself uses.

Compare the power situations of a slave and a proletarian. Neither owns any means of production other than the capacity to labor. Unlike the proletarian, however, the slave does not own even his or her labor power. For Cohen, Marx differentiates between the two by pointing out that whereas the proletarian owns his or her labor power, the slave does not. Unlike the latter, the proletarian has the right to withhold it.[32] Why does the proletarian have, while the slave has not, the power to withhold his or

---

29. Ibid.
30. Ibid.
31. "[A] man has the power to ø if and only if he is able to ø, where 'able' is non-normative." Ibid., p. 220.
32. Ibid., p. 222.

her labor power? After all, both may die if they withhold their labor power: the slave by being killed and the proletarian by starvation. One difference, Cohen says, lies in the fact that the withholding slave is liable to be killed outright and the proletarian is not. The critical difference, though, is that the proletarian "may be able to withhold his labour-power from a given capitalist, including his current employer, without fear of death. The slave cannot withhold his labour-power from his particular master and still live."[33]

Why does the proletarian have this power that the slave lacks? It is not because the given proletarian has enough (physical) nonnormative power to assert his or her freedom from individual capitalists. Is it because the proletarian has a *right*? Certainly, the proletarian has a right to withhold his or her labor power. But, on the Cohenian model, this cannot be an *effective right* because the proletarian, ultimately, has to sell his or her labor power to one capitalist or another or face the real threat of starvation. So the proletarian does not have a matching power, which in this case must include alternatives other than (1) surrender to a capitalist or (2) starvation. Anyone familiar with historical relations under capitalism must find this outcome counterintuitive. For we will ordinarily say that the proletarian has an effective right over his or her labor power that is not secured by physical power. The character of this effective right can be seen more clearly when contrasted with the situation of the slave.

The slave may have the physical power, but its exercise is sure to be rendered futile by laws regarding escape, insubordination, and the like. Yet, even in a slave situation, once the practice is implicated in legal norms, slaves are known to have tenaciously insisted on the master's observance of the requirements of law in his exercise of power. Indeed, in such situations the power of the master is inconceivable apart from its legal boundaries. And in the relationship of the proletarian to the individual capitalist and the class of capitalists, the proletarian has an effective right precisely because his or her right is secured by law! The mutual forbearances dictated by law define what powers are operative in appropriate situations. I suggest, then, that the enabling power of the proletarian to withhold his or her labor power is attributable to the *nature* of the structure of rights and entitlements presupposed by and embedded in the framework within which here the slave, there the proletarian operate.

So, why may capitalists not force a withholding proletarian to work? Without doubt, capitalists have the power to coerce proletarian labor. But

33. Ibid., p. 223.

what sort of power is it? According to Cohen, it is nonnormative power to bring about a given result. This is unhelpful, however, because we can identify more than one instance of this power. The "power to ø" might refer to the power of the world heavyweight boxing champion ("heavyweight power," for short) to beat the daylights out of me. Few individual capitalists have this kind of power, in contrast with individual proletarians, who are often better conditioned physically. The power might refer to the ability of the capitalist to coerce an unwilling proletarian to labor. But this is often brought about through the interposition of legally charged institutions like the police, the National Guard, and other paramilitary forces. I am assuming that the capitalists are not interested in bringing about mass starvation among the proletarians. If "power to ø" is understood in the second sense, and the capitalists cannot achieve the desired result without interposing legally charged instrumentalities, then it is at least problematic to suggest that the power of capitalists to ø *is* nonnormative.[34]

The relevant power here is the power of *property* and its *ownership*. Capitalist and proletarian alike recognize, under capitalism, the power of property ownership and what it entails in terms of the property owner's right of use and abuse, and of the capitalist employer's right to the disposal of the employee's labor power under contract.[35] This power is complemented crucially by the *recognition* by the proletarian that ownership is right, and that its enjoyment, abuse, and disposal are deserving of respect. Hence looting is rare in a stable capitalist society, and workers take care of property in their charge. Meanwhile, this complex of rights and recognition is secured by the sedulous cultivation of forms of social consciousness that hold property in awe, that induce in the proletarian a sense of propriety which includes profound respect for the regime of private property. When capitalists resort to "heavyweight power" to coerce proletarian labor, one who is thoroughly acquainted with the presuppositions of capitalism can rightly observe that the capitalists are doing something "wrong" to the proletarians and that the capitalists are not, as it were, "playing by the rules."

34. I am not unaware that capitalists sometimes deploy brutal measures ("heavyweight power") to subdue proletarians. Anyone familiar with the bloody history of the struggle for unionization throughout the world knows this. It is significant, though, that capitalists have routinely cloaked such measures with the authority of law. If nonnormative power were enough, there would be no need for appeal to legal contrivances.

35. See Karl Marx and Frederick Engels, *Collected Works*, published to date: vols. 1–34; 38–47 (New York: International Publishers, 1975–), 5:46, where they say: "[T]he form of property . . . corresponds perfectly to . . . the power of disposing of the labour-power of others." Hereafter cited as MECW.

Capitalism is a distinct mode of production with its own essential features which conjointly make it what it is. One of the essential features of this mode of production is that no individual's labor power may be forcibly appropriated. We would not call a social formation "capitalist" if the labor power of individuals within it were *routinely* coerced. If we did, we would be pressed to admit either that this forcible appropriation of labor power is not genuinely routine or that it has been forced by exceptional circumstances (e.g., war). It is not part of the *presuppositions* of the capitalist mode that its consistent supporters must accept that capitalists may *force* a withholding proletarian to labor. That is to say: even when, as is usually the case, the capitalists have the power (in Cohen's sense) to coerce the labor of proletarians and do so use their power, someone thoroughly acquainted with capitalism's presuppositions (which are not always nonnormative) can rightly observe that the capitalists are "wrong" to coerce the proletarians.

The power that Cohen finds in the proletarian is implicated in the structure of rights and entitlements embodied in capitalism. The positive power of the withholding proletarian is crucially complemented by the capitalist's admission of nonentitlement to the labor power of the withholding proletarian against the latter's personal wishes and desires. That is why the capitalist will not kill the proletarian for withholding his or her labor power even when the capitalist has the "heavyweight power" so to do. After all, right is a relational concept and notoriously involves implicit or explicit respect, or at least recognition, by others. In the case of the withholding proletarian, the power to withhold is a product of a preexisting right to her or his labor power respected by, or at least recognized by, others (including capitalists). It is not accidental that the quintessential relation between the capitalist and the proletarian is embodied in a contract, a form of agreement to which the dialectic of subjectivity and mutual recognition is indispensable. The worker–capitalist relationship cannot be understood outside this structure of rights and entitlements. If this is true, then Cohen may not have given us "*rechtsfrei* powers," because the powers he talks about are inseparable from right. *Rechtsfrei* descriptions cannot accommodate the sense of right and wrong that is a constitutive element of the capitalist–worker relationship.

Cohen does not deny this conclusion. He admits that law and ideology play a part in the genesis and maintenance of production relations.[36] In a reply to a similar criticism from Steven Lukes that norms are indispensable

---

36. Cohen, *Karl Marx's Theory of History*, p. 223.

to power, Cohen introduces a crucial distinction which, on one hand, clarifies his argument but, on the other, undermines it: "To achieve clarity in this matter, one must distinguish between a *non-normative concept of power*, and a *concept of non-normative power*. I recommend the first concept, not the second, and much of Lukes's critique depends on his having confused the two. . . . What I call 'powers' are not essentially non-normative (in Lukes's sense of not being supported by norms) but simply not essentially normative, and I have no difficulty in admitting that, *in the standard case*, 'norms . . . are* what enables' people to exercise powers. . . . My claim is just that what norms enable are not themselves norms."[37]

These passages contain a significant concession, some of whose implications Cohen does not anticipate. It is stated differently in a more recent reply to another critic: "In *the standard case*, people have the economic-structural powers they do *because* they have the legal rights they do."[38] The problem has to do with how we explain the character of the relation between powers and rights. Cohen offers an *externalist* explanation. The rights are what they are not in virtue of any intrinsic features of the production relations that explain them but because they sustain the economic structure made up of the production relations. I suggest that Cohen's description is inadequate for understanding the phenomenon of law under capitalism.

In affirming that rights are indispensable in "the standard case," Cohen concedes the insufficiency of power. And for ordinary folk and even for members of the ruling class who live under a capitalist regime, this right is the most important game in town. That is why capitalists do not routinely resort to "heavyweight power" to achieve their ends. Quite the contrary, serious, concerted, and sustained efforts are made by intellectuals of the ruling class and by the rulers themselves to show that theirs is not only a regime of rights, but that it is *the* right regime.

The constitutive relevance of rights, their overarching importance as well as their specific coloration, is part of what distinguishes capitalism from other modes of production. The importance of this characteristic is brought out more clearly by the fact that power and its impact may be indistinguishable under different modes of production. The "power to ø," where ø is "make the proletarian starve," is indistinguishable from the power that the lord had under feudalism to make the serf starve. An outsider observing both phenomena can report only that the proletarian and the serf died from the power of x in the one case and y in the other, where

---

37. Cohen, "Reply to Four Critics," *Analyse & Kritik* 5 (1983): 215.
38. Cohen, "Base and Superstructure," p. 96.

x and *y* are capitalist and lord, respectively. Such an observer can nonnormatively describe that an individual *x* or *y* has the power to ø when it is the case that ø-ing occurs every time *x* or *y* makes the required moves. To this extent we have to concede that Cohen's case against Acton and Plamenatz is successfully put. But this will be a quite anemic description. It would leave out the distinctive elements of each situation. In both cases, it may fail to apprehend what H. L. A. Hart has called "the internal aspect" of the legal relation.[39] It is not inconceivable that in the feudal situation the serf might have had the power to gain access to the land despite the lord's opposition. But had the serf exercised this power, the lord would have been able to secure the assistance of his fellow lords and their forces to assert his right and keep the serf out. Conversely, had he expelled the serf in violation of mutual agreement, he might actually have attracted the hostility of his fellow lords for *wronging* the serf concerned. Additionally, a serf who was so wronged would likely challenge the *power* of the lord and summon the assistance of those people and institutions which were interposed between the lord and the serf and which denied the lord's "heavyweight power" of its salience in the serf–lord relationship. It turns out that, outside of "heavyweight power," the lord's "power to ø," where ø is "requisition the serf's labor," is not susceptible of *rechtsfrei* description. And when it is, it fails to capture the complexity of the relationship. Similar considerations apply to the capitalist–worker relationship.

This sense of right,[40] of propriety of social arrangements, is what undergirds the *acceptance* of these arrangements, even by those who are in subaltern positions. Any description, no matter how elegant, that fails to capture this sense of right held by the powerful and the powerless alike, cannot be adequate. When Cohen claims that he does not subscribe to "a concept of non-normative power" but affirms "a non-normative concept of power," he might have clinched the argument with Acton and Plamenatz, whose concern was with what is *descriptively* possible. But this is a pyrrhic victory. In focusing narrowly on the problem of description, Cohen managed to evacuate the categories of historical materialism of any real-life content.

His schema is inadequate for another reason. Those who are implicated in the relevant production relations of capitalism would include a reference to some norm in their account of why it is not within the nonnormative, "heavyweight power" of capitalists to kill workers, even when they are able to do so. In the first place, the nonnormative power is not the power

---

39. H. L. A. Hart, *The Concept of Law* (Oxford: Clarendon Press, 1961), chaps. 4 and 5.
40. More will be said about this in Chapter 4 below.

that counts. Secondly, and more important, the right-based power does not merely *enable*, it *constitutes* and *defines* capitalist relations.

If the foregoing is true, then it is inadequate to affirm only a functional relation between a mode of production and its structure of rights and entitlements. As I shall argue presently, the structure of rights that is indispensable to capitalism is indispensable in more than a functional sense. Whereas many structures of rights might promote the stability of the mode of production or the development of its productive forces, some are *constitutive* of the mode of production itself. For instance, Nazism was responsible for huge leaps in the development of productive forces in Germany and to that extent could be regarded as functional to capitalism. The same could be said of apartheid in South Africa. But a capitalist analysis can conclude that Nazism and apartheid and their appurtenances violated the structure of rights constitutive of capitalism.

By his insistence that *rechtsfrei* descriptions are possible and that we can purify descriptions of production relations of all normative references Cohen is led, by a different route, into the same kind of error made by those who, like Acton and Plamenatz, assert that production relations, being property relations, are legal relations. Cohen, on the contrary, asserts that no production relations are legal relations and that property relations can always be expressed in a *rechtsfrei* manner. But, as I have argued, although some production relations can be described in a *rechtsfrei* manner, some cannot be described adequately without reference to right. From the fact that it is possible to describe some production relations in a *rechtsfrei* manner, it does not follow that no production relations are property (i.e., legal) relations.

It can be argued, and I so argue in subsequent sections, that there are specific production relations which are expressed as property relations and that such property relations constitute law which is of a different kind from the law found in the superstructure. I call this the *natural law of the mode of production*. Meanwhile, I hope I have shown in this section that although there can be nonnormative, *rechtsfrei* descriptions of the relations of production, they are inadequate. We turn now to the Marxist theory of natural law, or sociolegal naturalism.

IV

Natural law has been sought for everywhere but where it is likely to be found: in society. As was pointed out at the beginning of this chapter, Marxist theory of law will benefit from reappropriating the natural law tradition. It is now time to redeem that pledge.

Cohen's solution of the problem of legality rests on the contention that no relations of production are legal relations—that whenever production relations appear to be legal relations, or when Marx spoke of production relations as if they were legal relations, we can render such references *rechtsfrei*. As I have argued, however, and as Cohen too concedes, social relations of production are not always *rechtsfrei*. The challenge is to distinguish between one kind of production relations and another, to determine which production relations are legal and which are not. This approach is not without foundation in Marx's own writings. At various places in his writings are several key passages, some of which support the functionalist gloss Cohen and others place on them, and others of which have to be understood in *essentialist* terms. When understood in essentialist terms, such passages speak of a necessary, not an accidental, connection between certain modes of production and certain production relations that are legal. I shall be presenting some of these passages in a moment, and they will supply us with the necessary warrant for a Marxist variant of natural law. The key is to be found in a proper understanding of the concept of *mode of production*.

There are at least three different meanings of the "mode of production" in Marx: (1) the *material mode*, which is how individuals work with their productive forces, what material processes they set in motion, and the forms of specialization and division of labor among them; (2) the *social properties of the production process*, namely its purpose, the form of the producer's surplus labor, and the means of exploiting the producers; (3) the *totality of the material and social properties of the way in which production is carried out*.[41] In his account of Marx's philosophy of history Cohen, by his defense of the primacy thesis, seems to employ "mode of production," in the first sense, more often than not. In this chapter, unless otherwise specified, I am using "mode of production" in the third sense.

Marx, as noted, used "mode of production" in all three senses: none is privileged. We must establish the sense involved in each case. By interpreting some occurrences of "mode of production" in Marx in the third sense, we are more likely to make intelligible Marx's contention in many areas of his writings that the material mode of production, or mode (1), is always found with a certain mode of cooperation, or mode (2). The unity of mode (1) and mode (2) is mode (3). The issue between Cohen and me is that he excludes law from his iteration of the social relations of production, or mode (2) and I propose to include law therein. It is pos-

41. These three meanings were identified by Cohen, *Karl Marx's Theory of History*, pp. 79–84.

sible that Cohen does not want to exclude law completely. In his book
and in many other writings on the Marxist philosophy of history and
legal theory, there is an equivocation about the word "law" which hides a
crucial distinction that ought to be made. Often when law is excluded
from the social relations of production, law is meant to be *legislation* (i.e.,
positive law). This interpretation is suggested by the fact that law is frequently understood to follow fact; legitimization comes *ex post facto*. That
this is Cohen's manner of exclusion is supported by his claim that law is
one of the instruments by which power can be sustained. Many who affirm that no legal relations are production relations similarly have in
mind the positive law. In different ways, the same theorists say that the
law in the superstructure is a formalization of (nonnormative) power relations or production relations in the base.

As evidence I have cited in Chapter 1 attests, for Marx, the concept of
law is not exhausted by legislative and other authoritative enactments.
Marx made the point clearly: "The legislator, however, should regard himself as a naturalist. He does not *make* the laws, he does not invent them, he
only formulates them, expressing in conscious, positive laws the inner laws
of spiritual relations" (MECW, 1:308). The import of this passage is that
what the legislators enact as positive laws is not a product solely of their
consciousness or will. The "inner laws of spiritual relations" serve as a
source of positive lawmaking as well as a constraint on the will of legislators. Recall the distinction I made in Chapter 1 between *law* and *positive
laws*. Positive laws are not independent or purely the products of willful activity. What Marx initially referred to as "inner laws of spiritual relations"
he would later identify with the indispensable elements of what I am calling mode (3). I cite for support texts written at a later stage of Marx's
work: "Since the state is the form in which the individuals of a ruling class
assert their common interests, and in which the whole civil society of an
epoch is epitomised, it follows that all common institutions are set up with
the help of the state and are given a political form. Hence the illusion that
law is based on the will, and indeed on the will divorced from its real
basis—on *free* will. Similarly, justice is in its turn reduced to statute law"
(5:90). Elsewhere he wrote:

> The material life of individuals, . . . their mode of production and form of
> intercourse, which mutually determine each other—this is the real basis of
> the state and remains so at all the stages at which division of labour and pri-
> vate property are still necessary, quite independently of the *will* of individ-
> uals. These actual relations are in no way created by the state power; on the

contrary they are the power creating it. The individuals who rule in these conditions—leaving aside the fact that their power must assume the form of the *state*—have to give their will, which is determined by these definite conditions, a universal expression as the will of the state, as law, an expression whose content is always determined by the relations of this class, as the civil and criminal law demonstrates in the clearest possible way. Just as the weight of their bodies does not depend on their idealistic will or on their arbitrary decision, so also the fact that they enforce their own will in the form of law, and at the same time make it independent of the personal arbitrariness of each individual among them, does not depend on their idealistic will. (5:329)

In the above passages there are suggestions that I essay to develop here. As in the earlier writings of Marx examined in Chapter 1 above, there remains here a basic commitment to an objective normative structure that (1) is independent of the will of legislators, (2) constrains the will of legislators, and (3) requires of positive laws that they conform to it. The affirmation of a necessary connection between the mode of production and form of intercourse in the second passage is not accidental; it survives in Marx's descriptions of complex modes of production. And it is the form of intercourse that he will later identify with social relations of production, or what I am calling mode (2). Modes of production (1) through (3) conjointly represent one component of our theory of legal naturalism. There are others.

Marx repeatedly asserted that some elements are indispensable to a mode of production. Cohen has interpreted such allusions to indispensability in functionalist terms. But as I have argued above, a functionalist gloss on them is not the only possible or plausible one. They are eminently suited to essentialist interpretation. Consider the following passage:

It is furthermore clear that here as always it is in the interest of the ruling section of society to sanction the existing order as law and to legally establish its limits given through usage and tradition. Apart from all else, this, by the way, comes about of itself as soon as the constant reproduction of the basis of the existing order and its fundamental relations assumes a regulated and orderly form in the course of time. And such regulation and order are themselves indispensable elements of any mode of production, if it is to assume social stability and independence from mere chance and arbitrariness. These are precisely the form of its social stability and therefore its relative freedom from mere arbitrariness and mere chance.[42]

42. Marx, *Capital* (Moscow: Progress Publishers, 1959), 3:793.

To affirm only a functionalist interpretation of the above passage is to tell a partial story. The regulation and order that are parts of some modes of production are not merely requisite for the stability of the mode concerned; they are *constitutive* of the mode in the following sense. The mode is defined by the requisite regulation and order: it is what it is, in part, in virtue of its possession of this regulation and order, and it would not be what it is in the absence of this order and regulation. The order and regulation form a subset of (social) relations of production, or mode of production (2). Elsewhere Marx had called these social relations of production "a productive force." He writes: "It follows from this that a certain mode of production, or industrial stage, is *always* combined with a certain mode of cooperation, or social stage, and this mode of cooperation is itself a 'productive force.' " (MECW, 5:43; my emphasis). The positing of a necessary connection between a mode of production (1) and its mode of production (2) occurs very frequently in Marx's writings. The question to be answered, in light of the preceding, is whether or not some of these necessary relations are *legal*. If they are legal, then they will constitute the structure of rights *natural* to the given mode of production: they will give us the *natural law* of the mode of production.

Social relations of production make up the mode of production (2). Marx variously referred to mode (2) as "form of intercourse," "division of labor," "form of commerce and consumption," "civil society," "mode of cooperation," or "form of property." These relations involve individuals and groups and, sometimes, things (e.g., productive forces). The comprehensive nature of mode (2) is evidenced by the fact that Marx placed in it *all* relations in which individuals interact with one another. And he insisted that the superstructure merely formalizes officially these relations which arise in the emergence and subsequent evolution of mode of production (3). So expansive is Marx's conception of social relations that he characterized historical human nature in terms of them. These relations are the *form*, the organizing principle of the mode of production; they give the mode of production its specific identity, its principle of differentiation from other modes. In recognizing this expansive conception of social relations of production, we can begin to make sense of passages like the following:

What is society, irrespective of its form? The product of man's interaction upon man. Is man free to choose this or that form of society? By no means. If you assume a given state of development of man's productive faculties, you will have a corresponding form of commerce and consumption. If you assume given stages of development in production, commerce or consumption, you will have a corresponding form of social constitution, a corresponding organization, whether of the family, of the estates or of the classes—in a word, a corresponding civil society. If you assume this or that civil society, you will have this or that political system, which is but the official expression of civil society. (MECW, 38:96; cf. 5:355)

Those "forms of social constitution," "forms of intercourse," "civil society," are indispensable precisely because, without them, the mode of production (3) will be missing an essential ingredient. And the official, superstructural recognition of these constitutive social relations is parasitic upon these social relations. I argue that there is a subset of social relations that are legal and necessary to or constitutive of the mode of production (3). These conjointly form the natural law of the relevant mode. The natural law of a mode of production is that regime of law which is essential to its constitution, is discoverable in its operation, and provides the outer limits of possible positive laws within it. Admittedly, this is a very general, vague characterization. But that is the most we can claim, given the framework character of all natural law. It obtains content and specificity from *historical* modes of production and the practices that unfold within them.

The elements that conjointly form the natural law are natural because they form part of what makes the given mode of production what it is. Without this set of relations, apprised of the full determinations of the given mode of production, we will be right to conclude that the given mode is really not what it is said to be. This subset of the social relations of production is attributable to the nature of the mode of production. Of course, once we bring in reference to nature, we are talking about something that persists over time, is definitive of a thing, and supplies the essence shared by all things of that kind which enables us to affirm of them that they are instances of that kind of thing.

In capitalism, for example, there are some defining traits which conjointly constitute the *nature* of capitalism, and we will ordinarily call "capitalist" a society that shares enough of these traits to permit us to call it an instance of "capitalism." The question of whether the nature of capitalism encompasses some species of law is one that an analysis of capitalism would resolve. If there is some species of law that is part of the nature of capitalism, then, we can say that a capitalist society which lacks this law is not really a capitalist society. In such a case the law is a necessary part of the capitalist mode of production.

The necessity here is more than an empirical one. The necessity is not merely accidental; it is *essential*.[43] If it were merely accidental, it would be wrong to suppose, as Marx did, that "every form of production creates its own relations, form of government, etc. In bringing things which are organically related into an accidental relation, into a merely reflective connection, [bourgeois economists] display their crudity and lack of conceptual understanding."[44] One hastens to add that it is not only bourgeois economists who are guilty of this charge. Marxist interpretations that suggest that the ruling class is free to legislate what it likes insofar as it serves its purpose are equally guilty.

If there are legal relations of production that are indissolubly linked with the material mode of production, then we must be cautious in accepting any interpretation that banishes law to the superstructure. Marx in some passages locates the state, law, and property rights in the superstructure; in other passages he locates them in the base. For instance, when Marx says that "law is only the official recognition of fact" (MECW, 6:150) or when he speaks of "the illusion that law is based on the will . . . —on *free* will" (5:90), I suggest the reference here is to positive law (including, principally, legislation). Not so when he says: "Under the patriarchal system, under the caste system, under the feudal and guild system, there was division of labour in the whole of society according to fixed rules. Were these rules established by a legislator? No. Originally born of the conditions of material production, they were raised to the status of laws only much later" (6:184). Here I interpret the reference to rules as being to law or a system of rules constitutive of the various social formations he mentioned. The fact that he says they were raised to the status of laws later lends support to such an interpretation inasmuch as technical rules are not normally, if ever, raised to the status of laws.

The confusions that Marx's procedure generates could, in some measure, be removed or at least mitigated if law and rights are in certain respects superstructural and in other respects structural.[45] Law that is structural is what I call "natural law." This is not a mere verbal shuffle. The transformation is very significant. By disambiguating "law" we will ap-

43. This is by no means a logical necessity—although it approximates one if the problem were to be expressed in terms of definitions. We need not resort to such desperate measures. The concept of, say, "capitalism," is one that is capable of many determinations which it is the task of analysis to differentiate. Our claim is that such an analysis *plus* knowledge that hindsight avails us of the essence of capitalism through its historical development should give us a richer account of capitalism than a bare definition could ever do.

44. Marx, *Grundrisse*, trans. M. Nicolaus (New York: Vintage, 1973), p. 88.

45. See Rader, *Marx's Interpretation of History*, p. 36, for a similar view.

propriate for Marxism one of the salient features of the natural law tradition: the *duality of legal systems.*

Legal relations are *"social, societal* relationships, like all relations between men and men. All questions that concern the relations of men with each other are therefore also social questions" (MECW, 6:321). Social relations arise from the activities of human individuals in society in the production and reproduction of their lives. From the time that human beings made the transition from being solely gatherers of food to conscious producers, production has always been "a definite form of activity of these individuals, a definite form of expressing their life, a definite *mode of life* on their part" (5:31). From the start, production has always been accompanied by the division of labor within which the development of the productive forces takes place and which is itself conditioned by the level of development of the productive forces. The key to the development of law, for Marx and Engels, lies in the evolution of the division of labor. "The various stages of development in the division of labour are just so many different forms of property, i.e., the existing stage in the division of labour determines also the relations of individuals to one another with reference to the material, instrument and product of labour" (5:32). A superficial reading of the passage just quoted might suggest that the emergence of "the relations of individuals to one another" is consequent upon the division of labor. An alternative, and for us, deeper reading would indicate that it is not the *technical* division of labor that is at issue but the *social* division of labor involving the distribution of control over the material, instrument, and product of labor. With this conception, I intend to argue that the form of property is at the same time a structure of rights, entitlements, privileges, duties, immunities, and the like. What is law about if not rights, entitlements, and the like? But not every form of property is expressed in legal forms.

At that stage of development which was closest to the transition from food gathering to cultivation it will be wrong to talk about law, because the form of property was "tribal property [which] corresponds to the undeveloped stage of production, at which people [live] by hunting and fishing, by cattle-raising or, at most, by agriculture" (MECW, 5:33). There was little or no differentiation, there was a mass of uncultivated stretches of land, and the social structure was barely more than a collection of families. The principle of individuality had not made its appearance. Certainly there was individuation, but individuality as a principle of distribution was, in the main, absent. Notions of *mine* and *thine* could be said to be similarly absent. In short, we are painting the picture of an era in human history that Hegel has called the period of "undifferentiated substantiality." At this stage of development every attempt is made to eliminate difference. Could one talk of "rights" in an era when there is a systematic, even if inarticulate, effort to obliterate difference? How can one speak of private property in land or other things when the stress is on group solidarity as the prerequisite for collective survival? It stands to reason that in such a situation the division of labor will be quite primordial and we can deny that it has any form of property. Even if it does have a form of property, it is highly unlikely that this would be expressed in legal forms.

We could say, then, that law is not present in every social formation. Similarly, we can speak of natural law without positing an eternal law valid in all times and places. Law is a product of social differentiation occasioned by the increasing sophistication of the division of labor brought about by development of the productive forces, an increase of population, the growth of wants, and the extension of external intercourse. The foregoing might do as an account of the emergence of law. But we still have to say what law—natural or positive—is.

V

Law is a structure of rights, entitlements, duties, privileges, immunities, and the like ("structure of rights etc.," for short) that regulates and directs the relations in society (1) between an individual or group and another individual or group and (2) among individuals and groups with reference to the material, instrument, and product of labor. There are two levels, then, at which law directs and regulates the relations in society. First, between one individual or group and another. At this level, law prescribes the bounds of reciprocal expectations between two individuals or groups: namely, what one individual may do to or with the body, mind, and other attributes that pertain to the individuality of another without infringing that individual's personal space and incurring some unpleasant consequences. Second, between one individual and another with reference to the material, instrument, and product of labor. At this level, law prescribes the limits of mutual expectations among individuals with respect to what one may do to or with another's material, instrument, and product of labor once it is determined who has what. Law sometimes takes part in the determination of who has what.

This description of law leaves out most of the articles of faith underlying so many definitions of law, such as sanctions, coercion, or legislative authority. Most of these items, in my view, are incidental to law and are not essential. Sanctions are only consequences of infringement; even if law does not have coercion behind it, it will not stop being law. I admit that it may be ineffective. But what law *is* is a different question from how it is enforced.

Sanction theories of law tend to ignore the fact that what is essential to law is that it prescribes behavior and provides for consequences to follow when its prescriptions are infringed. These consequences are not always in the form of sanctions. For instance, if I refuse to have the required number of persons present when I authenticate my will, the consequence is that the act itself will be null. There are those who will argue that nullity is a sanction. This view has been subjected to withering criticisms, and I do not know of many theorists who still subscribe to it.[46] Furthermore, it is plausible to assert that in a stable society it is unlikely that more people will appeal to the sanctions behind law as their reason for obeying particular laws. On the contrary, more people will likely cite the fact that it is law and that it embodies, however inadequately, what is right.[47]

If sanctions are an essential part of law, then why are they invoked only when the prescriptions of the law have been breached? Most important, no amount of sanctions will make people believe that they are restrained by law if the only thing the law has going for it is sanction. It seems to me that it is the aim of every legal system to exact obedience from those it binds without the aid of sanctions. Finally, we might concede that in class societies in which the ruling class has yet to achieve hegemony, it is difficult to separate positive law from sanctions. Such a situation, however, would likely be considered as a less than desirable state of affairs. Therefore, whereas sanctions may be essential to the enforcement of law, they are not an essential feature of law. Despite the noninclusion of sanctions in our characterization of law, the definition at least satisfies the general characteristics of law identified by Kantorowicz. It holds that law is prescriptive, that the rights it embodies are describable in terms of legal duties imposed on private parties or public authorities, and that its prescriptions can be divested of their hypothetical character and individualized through their application to the concrete conduct of individuals.[48]

46. See the critique by Hans Oberdiek, "The Role of Sanctions and Coercion in Understanding Law and Legal Systems," *American Journal of Jurisprudence* 21 (1976): 71–94.

47. Although we do not have enough empirical research yet, social-scientific studies of the obligation to obey the law have come up with evidence that a sense of the rightness of law and a feeling of obligation to it is a principal reason that people give, when asked, for obeying the law. See, for example, Tom R. Tyler, *Why People Obey the Law* (New Haven: Yale University Press, 1990), pt. 2.

48. Kantorowicz, *The Definition of Law*, p. 38.

It can be urged against our definition that it is too broad. How, on our definition, do we distinguish law from any system of rules that directs and regulates? As it stands, there is hardly any difference between law and the rules of a game or of etiquette. And what about codes of religion and the like? The criticism is plausible only because it does not take cognizance of the conditions we identified for the existence of law. Law is a historical phenomenon that emerges at a definite stage of human history. Etiquette and other social rules did regulate a subset of social relations before law emerged. So did the rules of religion. It is significant that in highly differentiated societies in which religious rules regulate and direct social relations of the kind we have specified, the relevant subset of religious rules resembles law more than any other subset and, under Christianity, was named canon law, and under Islam, shariah. In such circumstances, the rules embodied rights, entitlements, privileges, duties, etc. Whether the rights etc. involved were supposed to have been enjoined by God or by reason matters very little.

We have described law in the most general terms, concentrating on the most essential features of law. We have also asserted that the emergence of law is historical. As a most general phenomenon law needs to be embodied in concrete laws of specific social formations for it to guide human conduct. History has been marked by definite stages of development of the division of labor and productive forces. In Marxist theory these stages are epochs in which some mode of production or another is dominant. In fact, the epoch is identified by its dominant mode of production. It is within these modes of production, otherwise called "social formations," that various species of law are realized. Given that modes of production differ from one historical stage to another, it follows that law will be differently realized in different modes of production insofar as they contain within them the existence conditions for law. Law is not embodied in the same way in every social formation in which it is present.

The definite form of law necessitated by a given mode of production is the natural law of that mode of production. The structure of rights etc. that is constitutive of any mode of production in the way I have described it is the natural law of the mode. The key word here is "constitutive." What is it to say that a structure of rights etc. is constitutive of a mode of production? It definitely does not mean a structure of rights that is most functional for the mode of production or one whose nonrecognition in the positive laws of a society would lead to social dysfunction. What is constitutive of a mode of production is not what is most functional for its operation. For example, a particular law might be functional for a mode of production in the short term and be dysfunctional over the long haul. Once we introduce the short-term/long-term distinction, we are faced with a fresh problem: that of determining how short and how long the short term and the long term are. Moreover, let us suppose that two policy options in a mode of production are equally promising functionally. There may still be a need to choose between them if we have reason to believe that *one is recommended more strongly by the underlying principles informing our social and political practices*. That is to say, one option might be closer to the natural law of the social formation. It is for these reasons that being "constitutive" is not the same as being "functional." Apartheid was for a very long time functional for South African capitalism: it secured for white South Africans a standard of living comparable to those of the most technologically advanced countries in Europe and America. Nevertheless, one could still do an internal critique of the South African system based on solid capitalist principles, especially those respecting the individual's proprietary rights over his or her labor, the mobility of labor, or the right to freedom of association that undergirds the practice of trade unionism.

When we say that a structure of rights etc. is constitutive of a mode of production we mean that that structure of rights etc. is one of the *essential* elements of the mode of production. Any description of the nature of that mode which fails to mention that structure will be incomplete. If the mode lacks the requisite structure, it will not be what it is supposed to be. To the extent that South Africa's capitalism under apartheid lacked some of the features identified above, we should adjudge it a less adequate realization of the concept of capitalism. Let us recall here some of the discussion in Chapter 1 above.

At section III of that chapter, we said that Marx deployed essentialist explanations. Like other social phenomena, a mode of production has both essential and accidental attributes. For instance, it is part of the essence of every mode of production that it will include humans, raw materials, and instruments of production. This is the mode of production in its most general and essential aspects. Whether a mode of production is feudal or socialist is an accident. When we limit our discussion to, say, the capitalist mode of production, the emphasis shifts from the essence of the mode of production *simpliciter* to that of the *capitalist* mode of production. The accidental attribute in this connection would refer to whether it is monopoly-capitalist, competitive-capitalist, industrial-capitalist, neocolonial-capitalist, and so on.

The essence of a mode of production is either that quality in virtue of which the mode is what it is or its characteristic activity (*ergon*). When the mode is missing its essential element(s) we deny that it *is* what it is sup-

posed to be. We will, for example, deny that a mode of production is capitalist if it forbids the ownership of private property, makes profitmaking
illegal, and decrees that commodities shall be produced only for use, not
for exchange. Between a mode of production that is sufficiently complex
and differentiated to foster law and its structure of rights etc. there exists
the same relationship as that between a thing and its essential attributes.
To say, therefore, that a structure of rights etc. is constitutive of a mode of
production is to affirm one or both of two things: (1) the structure of
rights etc. is one of the criteria of *identity* of the mode of production; (2)
the same structure gives us a *yardstick* by which to measure how well or ill
the positive laws in the relevant societies realize the natural law of the
mode of production concerned. By the same token, law that is constitutive
of a mode of production is not merely one that is promotive of the development of the mode—it will, of course, be that—but one that has a role in
defining the mode. When the positive laws depart radically from the constitutive law of a mode, they shall be bad laws; when they approximate it,
they are good laws. When they completely lack any of the features of the
constitutive law, they are not laws at all. Every time we think of a mode of
production that is sufficiently differentiated and complex in the manner
specified above, we must think of it with its natural law. The character of
this natural law is determined by the other elements in the rich totality that
a mode of production is: the material productive forces; the social, nonlegal (e.g., managerial) relations of production.

The natural law of the mode of production provides the foundation for
the positive law of each society. It is the law that positive law seeks officially to express. It is the law that legislators seek to formulate in conscious
positive law.[49] Being the foundation of positive law, the natural law of the
epoch provides the limits of possible, efficient, and rightful positive law of
the epoch. It is in this sense that all forms of voluntarism, Marxist or not,
are inadequate. Voluntarism is inadequate because there is a sense in which
it is true to say that lawmakers—the state, legislators, judges, etc.—really
do not *make* laws if by "make laws" is meant that law is a product mainly
of the interests or will of those we call "lawmakers." Rather, in most cases,
they merely formulate them.

"Lawmakers" formulate law because they ultimately have to operate
within specific or specifiable limits imposed by the natural law of the given
mode of production in which they are located. For example, if a social formation is feudal, no matter how determined the legislators are they cannot

---

49. How this proceeds will be fully explicated in Chapter 3 below.

make or implement laws that will guarantee capitalist commodity production and exchange, or liberty, equality, etc. Bourgeois civil law is not possible where the equality of commodity owners is not a fact. This does not mean that human ingenuity cannot think up laws that differ essentially from those necessitated by the natural law—that is, by the structure of rights etc. inherent in the social formation in which the thinking occurs. The point is that unless the practical means are at hand or are feasible such laws cannot be enacted.

Incidentally, the argument in the preceding paragraph brings out one of the features of natural law: *it is objective law that exists apart from and independently of positive law*. This objective law is the essence positive law tries to embody; it is the ground of positive law. In his legal-rationalist phase Marx located this objective law in reason. From 1845 onward the locus of this law shifted to the mode of production. The distinction between law and laws is one of the principal theses of legal naturalism. Marxist legal naturalism shares it with other theories of natural law.

There can be more or less conformity between the natural law of a social formation and its positive law. Many factors may be responsible for this variance. First of all, there is considerable opacity in the natural law which results from the fact that we are not here establishing patterns of determination in infinitely repeatable physical-natural regularities (as in physical science). We cannot put society under the microscope. The natural law of an epoch is not a deliberate, articulate creation of the human will. For the most part, it arises spontaneously from the usages that develop in everyday life, centrally those which form around production of material life. So, a fair amount of our knowledge of the social formation comes *ex post facto*, from some of what we know of the history of human societies. The most important factor is perhaps the extent to which the individuals in a society understand the dynamics and possibilities of their social structure. If they possess an ample understanding of the nature of their social formation or mode of production, they are less likely to formulate positive laws that are out of concurrence with the natural law of their mode of production. Moreover, if the individuals also happen to believe that their social formation has a lot to recommend it and very little to be disapproved of in it, they have reason to want to preserve it.

Natural law is an axiological system. It is a system of norms. This characteristic distinguishes it from the natural laws of physical science. Being an axiological system, it prescribes the norms of acceptable conduct, obligations, duties, and mutual forbearances in respect of the issues that fall within the structure of rights etc. concerned. However, natural law shares one significant attribute with the natural laws of physical science: it is objective; that is, it is independent of human will. Natural law exacts obedience in the same way that physical laws do. For example, capitalist natural law must be observed in a capitalist polity if its laws are to remain capitalist and the society itself wishes to realize as much of its capitalist potential as is possible or desirable for it. If people living in, say, a capitalist society believe that their social formation has a lot to recommend it and very little to be disapproved of in it, and if they want it to survive or be improved, they must pay heed to capitalist natural law when they work out their positive laws. The objective, independent character of natural law becomes quite significant when one considers the situation of a ruling class under, to continue with our example, capitalism.

In the objective, independent character of capitalist natural law is contained the real limit on the actions of the ruling class. In this sense, natural law performs a regulative role. If the ruling class understand that theirs is an example of the capitalist mode of production and they hold beliefs approbative of their society, they may not make positive laws that contradict the norms of the natural law of capitalism. If they lack adequate understanding of what capitalism entails or if they are interested in committing class suicide, they can make positive laws that are violative of the norms of capitalist natural law.

There is no need to probe the grounds of the belief concerning what recommends a social system to its supporters. It is sufficient that this belief grounds the effort to express in positive laws as much of the norms of the natural law of the social formation as is practicable. The content of such a belief must include a presumption of the following sort: that the society concerned should ensure near-optimum conditions for its members to enjoy their holdings, make individual life plans, and strive to realize those plans. Law, state, and other social relations must incorporate this presumption in their purpose. Thus, even though law may be used by one class to oppress another, it does not for that reason follow that law exists only as a weapon of one class. To be sure, positive law can be, and often is, used to oppress. But when it is used to oppress, it must at the same time exclude arbitrariness, internal contradictions, or inconsistencies if it is to make that oppression appear to be legitimate. Except in a complete tyranny, even a class law must work within the limits imposed by the structure of rights etc. it embodies.[50]

50. See E. P. Thompson, *Whigs and Hunters: The Origins of the Black Act* (London: Allen Lane, 1975), for a discussion of how tenacious this sense of justice can be in a specific case. The question of whether there are senses of justice other than the one mentioned here has been deliberately left open. More will be said about this in Chapter 4 below.

Those who accept the rightness of the natural law of their epoch can be expected to try to realize in their positive laws the closest possible approximation to the natural law of their epoch. At the least, they will act to prevent from coming into being those positive laws which are likely to undermine or even destroy what they accept as the foundations of their social formation. This is the *conservative essence* of every natural law. When other members of a society, outside the ruling class, also accept that the existing positive legal order incarnates the best possibilities of the natural law of their epoch, they should be expected not to question, much less to seek to change, the extant social order. Whether they are aware of it or not, they thereby accept the natural law that grounds their positive legal system. Most legal positivists fall within this category. They do not question the natural law foundation of their positive law, or they assume that the positive law needs no further grounds save that offered by validity and due process. Obedience to law, therefore, can stem from two sources: (1) awareness of and belief in the value of the natural law foundations, or (2) unawareness of other possibilities even when there is an awareness that something is wrong with the existing social order.

There are people so taken by their belief in the good qualities of their society and its operation that they see it as the best of all possible worlds. Such people are not interested in change. Others believe there is nothing eternal or permanent about the natural law foundations of the existing regime of positive law. A subgroup among these might want to see their positive law approximate more and more closely the norms of the existing natural law. Those who fall within this category will likely choose the path of reform. Still others, believing that the society has little to recommend it and a lot to disapprove of in it, might seek to change the social system for what they consider a better one.

People in this last group can be expected to make demands for a positive law regime that they know, or have reason to think, will generate consequences that are potentially or actually destructive of the existing social structure, including its natural law. By seeking to generate consequences potentially or actually destructive of the natural law foundations, it is clear that they have, or should be understood to have, given up any commitment to the existing social order. So long as they embrace the legitimacy of the existing social order they cannot overthrow it: there is no reason to overthrow it. We are not assuming that people who want to build a new social order have or should have a lien on the truth or privileged access to the riddle of history. They *can* make such claims, but they do not have to.

In fact, they may be quite fuzzy in stating what the new social order will look like. All that is required is that they be sufficiently dissatisfied with the existing social system and believe that there are no further possibilities for positive development within it.

VI

It does not follow from the Marxist theory of natural law that championing natural law is intrinsically conservative or revolutionary. In Marxism, natural law provides the essence in the social structure which the positive law embodies. Our theory, then, satisfies the first salient feature of the natural law tradition.

Secondly, the natural law of an epoch provides evaluative and justifying criteria for the positive law. The positive law embodies the natural law in ways that will be specified in Chapter 3 below. The natural law is explanatory of the positive law and provides a measure by which the adequacy, rationality, justness, etc. of the positive law can be ascertained. For example, when a particular positive legal enactment in a social structure does not violate the norms of the natural law of the epoch, it is just; when it does violate those norms, it is unjust. Marx writes:

> To speak here of natural justice . . . is nonsense. The justice of the transactions between agents of production rests on the fact that these arise as natural consequences out of the production relationships. The juristic forms in which these economic transactions appear as wilful acts of the parties concerned, as expressions of their common will and as contracts that may be enforced by law against some individual party, cannot, being mere forms, determine this content. They merely express it. This content is just whenever it corresponds, is appropriate, to the mode of production. It is unjust whenever it contradicts that mode. Slavery on the basis of capitalist production is unjust; likewise fraud in the quality of commodities.[51]

In the above passage, there is a hint of what I have tried to develop: namely, that contained in the production relationship of, say, capitalism, is a structure of rights etc. that makes both the conversion of a proletarian to a slave and fraud in the quality of commodities unjust. Why is this so? Be-

---

51. Marx, *Capital*, 3:339–40; also MECW, 6:319.

cause capitalist production is premised on the freedom of everyone equally to dispose of their labor power as they see fit, slavery on the basis of capitalist production is violative of the essence of capitalism which includes the freedom just mentioned. Fraud in the quality of commodities is likewise unjust because the exchange relationship is based on the understanding that equivalents are being exchanged, whereas fraud in the quality of commodities is precisely a negation of what the exchange of equivalents is all about. This is quite apart from the fact that fraud in the quality of commodities might produce dysfunctions in the operation of capitalism. The essence of capitalism is the real source of the limits on capitalist power suggested in my criticism of Cohen's discussion of the difference between a slave and a proletarian.

A partisan of capitalism who operates within its structures can condemn particular laws of the positive legal system for violating the natural law norms of capitalism. Thus, we can explain the difference between the municipal legal systems of the United States of America and apartheid South Africa as "better" (in the case of the U.S.A.) or "worse" (in the case of apartheid South Africa) approximations of the natural law of the capitalist mode of production, once it is agreed that part of the structure of rights etc. inherent in capitalism is that the labor of a proletarian should not be coerced and that labor contracts must be a meeting of the free wills of the contracting individuals.

Our theory of natural law enables us to explain the diversity of positive municipal legal systems that are all grouped together under the same category. Whereas national, racial, geographic, and other peculiarities may affect the positive laws, all social structures that are identical must share the natural law of their mode of production. No geographic peculiarity, for example, will enable a capitalist society to make laws outlawing profitmaking and still retain its capitalist nature. Partisans of capitalism ought to, and can be expected to, fight to abrogate such a law for being unjust.

Not only does natural law provide an evaluative criterion for positive law, but it provides a reason for acting or not acting to change or preserve a given regime of positive law. That is how and why natural law can be a rallying cry of reactionaries and a battle theme of revolutionaries. There is nothing odd about this once it is realized that what the natural laws of the two parties have in common is only form and not content. Lastly, then, the Marxist theory of natural law bridges the "is" and the "ought." Positive law is the actualization of the natural law which those who operate the social system will strive for if they have adequate knowledge of the dynamics and possibilities of their social formation and are not deflected by consid-erations of momentary self-interest.[52]

Natural law offers a guide to action which differs from that of positive law. As a framework law, natural law is a guide to action designed to enact its precepts into positive law. An awareness and acceptance of the natural law of a social formation enjoin a duty to act to bring about its positive im-plementation. It would be counterintuitive to know what the natural law requires, to accept that it is worth bringing about, and yet do nothing when the opportunity offers itself. But there may be a question of whether or not there is a more ultimate duty to *bring about* natural law within a given social formation. Such a question is unwarranted.

First, as I have pointed out, natural law is not a product of human de-liberation or choice. It is part of the inheritance we receive when we are born into and become functioning members of a society in which natural law is a presence. Certainly, as intellectuals in our society or savants of our epoch, we may become explicators of the natural law and its presupposi-tions. So, we do not pick and choose our natural law, although we can choose whether or not to work for its realization. We cannot introduce natural law into a social formation in which law is absent.

Secondly, the question assumes that natural law can exist outside spe-cific social formations. This assumption represents a throwback to theories of natural law that affirm transhistorical, timeless natural law. So far in this work I have tried to repudiate such variants. For they are apt to be with-out content, almost trivial. An injunction to do good and shun evil, a pre-cept of immutable natural law, does not tell us what "good" is and what "evil" is. What good or evil is cannot be understood outside specific con-figurations of human practice, usually represented in different types of so-ciety. "Thou shall not kill" does not by itself tell us what are permissible or impermissible killings. After all, natural law theorists all recognize the right to self-preservation which includes a right to kill an aggressor who puts one's life in jeopardy. Each society/social formation will have to for-mulate—in light of its understanding of human nature, knowledge of so-

52. This statement needs to be qualified. In a revolutionary situation, in which the posi-tive legal system of a society has been overthrown but the new social formation is in the mak-ing, we might have a new positive legal system that has little in common with the natural law of the still more-or-less dominant mode of production. Even then, one would insist that there must be some degree of presence of the requisite natural law for the positive law concerned to be effective. For instance, the New Economic Policy in the former Soviet Union was founded on continued state control over the commanding heights of the economy. A good contrast is offered by the French Socialist efforts in 1981 to enact positive laws to direct the economy after a socialist fashion while the basic capitalist structure remained unaltered.

cial processes, even divine inspiration—the boundaries of the injunction "Thou shall not kill." These are the elements that make for the historicity of natural law and the play of contingency in its realization. An attempt to affirm a timeless natural law is bound to lose sight of this important characteristic of natural law theories.[53]

What I have just said does not preclude the positing of a different kind of duty. There may be a duty to strive to bring about better and better social orderings, where the best possible social ordering is one in which human beings are enabled to realize their human potential as fullly as possible, limited only by the constraints of physical nature, human and material.[54] One can say that Marx does affirm such a normative standard of human and social evolution.[55]

It is pertinent to discuss the problem posed by the historicity of natural law. If natural law is relative to social structures, are there evaluative criteria that are not epoch-bound by means of which we can criticize the natural laws of various epochs? If there is no other possibility under capitalism beyond the natural law inherent in it, then why should we vilify the capitalist mode of production for being unjust, especially in its juridical aspects? It is obvious that if we believe a capitalist society has more to recommend it than to be disapproved of in it, then no reason for criticizing the natural law foundations of capitalism can be found within capitalism itself. The same applies to any mode of production we care to consider.

At the point where we allow that the natural law of capitalism is too limited for purposes of making the world better and improving the human condition, we already put into question the claim of capitalism and its defenders that it is, comparatively, the best social formation. We may conclude that it is not. Once we do this, we have renounced capitalism and can be said to be striving to realize a better social formation. At this level we no longer quibble over particular laws. We are involved in a struggle to bring into existence a new social order, complete (if such be necessary to it) with a new natural law.

This is an epochal struggle in which two or more conceptions of society contend for supremacy: supporters of one no longer feel bound by the dictates of the laws of the other. There is already in motion the process of re-

53. See also Battaglia, *Toward a Reformulation of Natural Law*, pp. 102–4.

54. There is contained in our statement a latent conception of human potential that will exclude some potential as not being *properly* human and, therefore, not worthy of realization.

55. I shall have more to say about this in Chapter 6 below. William Leon McBride holds a similar view; see his "Marxism and Natural Law," p. 138.

pudiation of a whole social order *and* its natural law. This could be impelled by a significant failure of the social formation to deliver on some of its promises or by a failure of the ruling class to observe its own laws such that the other classes are moved to question the legitimacy of the social order as a whole. We are talking of conditions that generally proliferate on the eve of social revolutions.

So long as enough people in a given society believe that there is more to recommend their kind of society than to be disapproved of in it, they are unlikely to call into question the natural law foundations of the society. Some who are opposed to the social formation might be willing to concede that it has a lot to recommend it, even though they wish to replace it with something else that is even more commendable. Insofar as this attitude persists, we can be sure that whatever disagreements there are will be over the positive laws and how well they approximate the essence of the natural law.

As soon as many people, or at least a preponderantly influential few, call the natural law into question, the disagreement can no longer be resolved within the boundaries of the extant natural law and the social formation of which it is a part. It is then a question ultimately of one vision of society winning out over another. Often, those who are seeking to overthrow the present social order will appeal to the possible emergence of a new order that will do everything they accuse the one they wish to overthrow of not doing. In short, they are likely to insist that the claim of, say, capitalism to being the best mode of production, comparatively speaking is false or unsupportable.

Such people might sometimes appeal to a notion of duty on the part of people who are appropriately placed to bring about the best possible social arrangement. However, this duty cannot be derived from the current prevalence of any mode of production. Anyone who does not admit the *prima facie* justification of such a duty cannot be convinced by any argument. The presence of such a duty may be ranked as one of the features all human societies have in common, unless one can visualize a stage of human evolution where further changes for the better are superfluous. To those who may want to argue that such a transhistorical "natural law" is foreign to Marxism I reply only that it does not seem so to me.[56] Even if it is, no damage would be done if Marxism were to embrace such a duty. There are implications for human action in such a commitment, and some of these implications will be expounded in Chapter 6 below. A little antic-

56. See ibid., p. 139.

ipation is in place here, though. I take only one example: law. Except among those who fetishize law and who believe that no social order is possible without law, historically law has occasioned great discomfiture among social theorists and utopian thinkers, who tend to look upon law-based order as making the best of a bad situation. Law is not and has not always been looked upon as an unqualified human good. And in ordinary life, law is regularly seen as a weapon of last resort in those relations on which we place the highest premium. Thus, a society without law remains a desirable alternative to a litigious society. To the extent that this is true, then so long as such a society is feasible, we ought to strive to bring about non-law-based social ordering.

VII

I end the present chapter with a sketch of Marx's own advocacy when he was arraigned on charges of calling on citizens to resist forcibly attempts to collect taxes. Most of Central Europe had witnessed revolutions in 1848 which, although they failed, had wrung concessions from the various European monarchies. Marx and Engels had interpreted the revolutions of 1848 as episodes in the march of the bourgeoisie to consummate its rule over Europe's societies. Marx's advocacy is contained in the speech he gave in his own defense at what has come to be known as the Trial of the Rhineland District Committee of Democrats (MECW, 8:323–39).[57]

Marx's own advocacy lends itself to a natural law interpretation. First he tried to show that the Crown itself did not have any legitimacy for charging the accused—that the Crown had violated the rules of its own laws (positive laws in this case).

Gentlemen of the jury, if this action had been brought *before* December 5, I could have understood the charge made by the Public Prosecutor. Now, *after* December 5, I do not understand how he dares to invoke against us laws which the Crown itself has trampled under foot.

On what does the public prosecution base its criticism of the National Assembly and of the decision on the refusal to pay taxes? On the laws of April 6 and 8, 1848. And what did the Government do on December 5, when it on its own authority granted a Constitution and imposed a new electoral law on the country? It tore up the laws of April 6 and 8, 1848.

---

57. The trial was held on February 8, 1849. Marx's coaccused were Karl Schapper and Karl Schneider II.

These laws are no longer valid for the supporters of the Government, so why should they still be valid for the opponents of the Government? (MECW, 8:323)

Marx, in the above passage, "accepted" the legitimacy of the existing law. He accused the Crown of having made a new law without regard to the laid-down procedures which, apparently, included approval by the National Assembly. By not making the new law in accordance with the laid-down rules, Marx argued that the Crown has violated its own rules. If the Crown was right to make a new law unilaterally, then the old law was no longer valid and could therefore not be used to bring charges against him. If, on the other hand, the Crown was wrong, then it did not possess the legitimacy, having infringed the law itself, to charge him with committing a crime. He addressed the jury further:

The Crown has made a revolution, it has overthrown the existing legal system, it cannot appeal to the laws it has itself so scandalously annulled. After successfully carrying out a revolution one can hang one's opponents, but one cannot convict them. They can be put out of the way as defeated enemies, but they cannot be arraigned as criminals. After a revolution or counter-revolution has been consummated the annulled laws cannot be used against the *defenders* of these laws. That would be a cowardly pretence of legality which you, gentlemen, will not sanction by your verdict. (MECW, 8:324)

So far, Marx has situated himself on the ground of the laws passed by the National Assembly in April 1848. Their validity was not at issue. We have nothing yet on which to base a legal-positivist protest. Then comes the next stage of the defense: what I interpret as the appeal to natural law. "But let us leave aside the formal aspect, gentlemen. What was the United Diet [National Assembly]? It represented old, decayed social relations. It was against these relations that the revolution was directed. . . . The Diet was overthrown together with the old monarchy. . . . The Diet represented primarily big landed property. Big landed property was indeed the foundation of medieval, *feudal society*. *Modern bourgeois society, our* own society, on the other hand, is based on industry and commerce" (8:326).

According to Marx, it was not enough to deny the validity of the law under question as he did in the first part of his defense, important though the formal aspect may be. Apparently, even if the law under which he and his codefendants were charged had met the formal requirements for validity and their prosecutors had proceeded in accordance with the dictates of reason in law, Marx was prepared to question the legitimacy of the entire legal system by raising questions about its natural law. Few would deny that the nineteenth century was the period when the political victory of the economically dominant bourgeoisie was being brought to conclusion. For Marx, the United Diet was the official expression of "old, decayed social relations." The revolution of the 1848 (and others) had repudiated the old mode of production and its structure of rights and entitlements—its natural law—and had confronted it with a new mode of production and its concomitant structure of rights and entitlements—a new natural law, as it were. Hence his argument that since bourgeois society rests on completely different foundations and on an altered material mode of production, it had to seize political power for itself; to wrest it from those who represented the interests of the "foundering society and whose political power, in its entire organization, had proceeded from entirely different material relations of society." The fact that the old society was foundering was the origin of the revolution.

"How then," Marx asked, "was the idea conceived to allow the United Diet, the representative of the old society, to dictate laws to the new society which asserted its rights through the revolution?" (MECW, 8:327). Here we have a classic appeal to natural law. I take Marx to be appealing to the structure of rights, entitlements, etc. that has emerged with capitalism (8:313–14, 327, 328).[58] The natural law of the old society had died with it. Positive laws (e.g., the laws of April 1848) made by a United Diet whose legitimacy was founded on the natural law of the old society were no longer valid or applicable. The revolution had introduced the possibility of a new and (to those who believed like Marx) better society with, in this case, a different (and likewise better) constitutive natural law. Any attempt to force the newly emergent society to operate within the ambit of the defunct natural law is, in this case of transition from feudalism to capitalism, to hinder trade and industry and set the stage for "*social crises*" which come to a head in "*political revolutions*" (8:328).[59]

58. Cf. *Hegel's Political Writings*, ed. Z. A. Pelczynski, trans. T. M. Knox (Oxford: Clarendon Press, 1964), pp. 243–44.

59. Hegel had similarly warned Württemberg against attempting to stop the march of progress at the beginning of the nineteenth century: "The picture of better and juster times has become lively in the souls of men, and a longing, a sighing for purer and freer conditions, has moved all hearts and set them at variance with the actuality [of the present]. . . . The passage of time and the postponement of the satisfaction of these hopes can do no more than purify the longing and separate out its genuine and false elements; yet time can but strengthen the urge towards what satisfies a genuine need; the longing will penetrate all the

Although Marx has not explicitly employed natural law terminology, I
think the defense we have been considering can plausibly be interpreted as
a natural law defense. It posits a duality of legal systems: it grounds the nature and legitimacy of positive law in deeper structures lying at the heart
of the mode of production and uses the latter to judge the appropriateness
of the former. It assumes that the natural law of an epoch cannot survive
the death of its epoch. At the point where the adherents of an old,
foundering society confront the partisans of a new and promising society,
it cannot be a case of political conflict between two parties standing on the
ground of *one* society. In such a struggle, no juries, no courts can decide.
Here are the terms in which Marx described the struggle to the jury at his
trial: "What took place here was not a political conflict between two parties within the framework of *one* society, but a *conflict between two societies*,
a social conflict, which had assumed a political form; *it was the struggle of
the old feudal bureaucratic society with modern bourgeois society*, a struggle between the society of *free competition* and the *society of the guild system*, between the society of landownership and the industrial society, between the
society of faith and the society of knowledge" (MECW, 8:335).

Marx's advocacy secured an acquittal for all three men. Maybe members
of the jury had been infected by the spirit of the newly emergent society.
That is not important, though. What is significant are the terms in which
the advocacy was conducted. I have presented a natural law interpretation.
The stridency of the submission was not the stuff of which sentimental appeals are made. I have concluded on this note only to show that Marxist
natural law is not just good in theory, it is employable in practice. In fact,
the account I have given may enable Marxist lawyers to operate within
positive legal systems, perhaps even struggle for reforms within them
without actively contributing to the survival of the natural law that forms
the basis for such positive laws.[60]

---

more deeply into men's hearts as a result of the delay; it is no casual dizziness which passes
off. Call it a fit of fever if you like, but it is a fit that ends only in death or after the diseased
matter has been sweated out. It is the still healthy force's effort to expel the disease. . . . How
blind they are who may hope that institutions, constitutions, laws which no longer correspond to human manners, needs, and opinions, from which the spirit has flown, can subsist
any longer; or that forms in which intellect and feeling now take no interest are powerful
enough to be any longer the bond of a nation." Ibid.

60. Perhaps good Marxists can be good lawyers after all. See Tom Gerety, "Iron Law:
Why Good Lawyers Make Bad Marxists," in J. Roland Pennock and John W. Chapman, eds.,
Marxism: Nomos XXVI (New York: New York University Press, 1983).

3

Laying Down the Law:
The Positivization
of Natural Law

I

This chapter fulfills the promise made in Chapter 2 to explicate fully the nature of the relationship between natural law and positive law in particular epochs. More specifically, I intend to tell a story in this chapter: the story of the emergence of positive law and of positive legal systems from natural law. The story will be told against the background of the assumption that laying down the law in any named or nameable society is, in the main, the positivization of the natural law of the social formation of which such a society is an instance.[1] What has to be done, therefore, is to give an account of the nature of positivization, the processes of positivization or strategies of lawmaking, why positivization is always a partial realization, and so on.

My conception of positive law does not differ radically from many that one will find in the literature. There is agreement that positive law is the law that *is* in a given society; this is a good part of its positivity. In addition, the law that is is a product of more or less *conscious* human action. Also, it is generally conceded that the law that is, as a consequence of more or less conscious human action, (1) is so regarded by those whom it binds

1. I use the term "society" to describe particular societies, such as England in the sixteenth century or Japan in the twentieth. I reserve the expression "social formation" to describe the compendium of social and technical practices in a given epoch that cut across specific societies (e.g., capitalist social formation). Capitalist social formation may refer to nineteenth-century England or twentieth-century Taiwan. Both are instances of the capitalist social formation even as they remain different and discrete societies.

and (2) commands general acceptance or at least widespread acquiescence. The positive law in any particular society, then, is the total system of more or less consciously adopted rules, regulations, procedures, and other similar enactments that exists in a given society, is generally regarded as binding by its members, and is widely accepted or acquiesced in by them. In what follows, I describe some key attempts to construct a Marxist theory of law inspired by positivism. I try to show why they are inadequate. Then I present a new account of the origins of positive law based on legal naturalism. Finally, I describe the strategies for positivization of natural law.

II

Marxist theorists of law are fond of positivism. But this is not the positivism that one finds in non-Marxist philosophy of law. For instance, with the exception of interpretations of Marxist legal theory that draw their inspiration from legal positivism associated with H. L. A. Hart and Joseph Raz,[2] Marxist legal positivism is usually preoccupied with law that is. It does not pay much attention to the sources thesis that is one of the fundaments of contemporary positivism.[3] Nor does it concern itself with the many distinctions and procedural requirements that equally characterize positivism. On the contrary, Marxist positivism accepts as law whatever the ruling class in a given society posits as law. As I shall show later in the present chapter, variants of Marxist positivism are incapable of apprehending some of the most interesting questions about law. That is because the focus on positive law tends to make short work of the problems of the origins of the positive law itself.

Existing Marxist theories of law can be grouped under three general categories: economism, class instrumentalism, and *legal ideologism*. Although there are some differences in emphasis, all focus on positive law and do not seek deeper aetiologies for law beyond that offered by vague references to the needs of the economic structure, the problem the ruling class wishes to solve, or what best serves the interests of the rulers. The concern with positive law is what sets these interpretations apart from Cohen's theory considered in the last chapter.

Economism. Economism is the view which holds that law is a superstructural reflection of the material or economic base of the social formation.[4] Law

2. E.g., Hugh Collins, *Marxism and Law* (New York: Oxford University Press, 1982).
3. See Joseph Raz, *The Authority of Law* (Oxford: Oxford University Press, 1979).
4. I am aware that there are other meanings of "economism." Usually the term is used as a megacategory to describe all theories in Marxism that locate the origin, nature, and func-

is said to be determined by, and to correspond to, the dominant mode of production; that is to say, it expresses in legal form the relations of production extant in a given society. This interpretation posits a relation of determination between the material base (made up of the forces of production) and the economic structure (made up of the relations of production, on the one hand, and the legal, political, etc. superstructure on the other). While the more sophisticated version of this interpretation grants that the superstructure does affect the base, it is argued that the ultimate determinant influence in the relationship lies in the base.

For those who accept economism, support for their interpretation is drawn from Karl Marx's famous 1859 Preface:

> In the social production of their life, men enter into definite relations, that are indispensable and independent of their will, relations of production which correspond to a definite stage of development of their material productive forces. The sum total of these relations of production constitutes the economic structure of society, the real foundation, on which rises a legal and political superstructure and to which correspond definite forms of social consciousness. The mode of production of material life conditions the social, political and intellectual life process in general.[5]

We have seen Cohen's attempt to purify the economic structure of legal relations and to show how historical materialism, properly understood, must consign law to the superstructure. Long before Cohen, Karl Renner had tried to articulate the implications for law of this passage.[6] I propose to consider a more sophisticated (by the standards of the time) and arguably more rigorous formulation of the economistic problematic offered by Evgeny B. Pashukanis in 1924.[7] Pashukanis saw more than most of his

---

tion of law in what generally is called the "economic structure" of society. See Colin Sumner, *Reading Ideologies* (London: Academic Press, 1979), p. 247. Another view affirms a strong historical determinism under which the economic base determines everything else in the social formation. Economism of this sort reaches its apotheosis in a political strategy that borders on fatalism: there is no need for revolutionary activity; once the economic structure changes, the ideological structure will change, too. All we have to do is wait for the economic base to alter. This is not the understanding of economism I wish to consider.

5. Karl Marx and Frederick Engels, *Selected Works* (Moscow: Progress Publishers, 1969), 1:503.

6. See Karl Renner, *The Institutions of Private Law and Their Social Functions* (London: Routledge & Kegan Paul, 1949).

7. E. B. Pashukanis, *Law and Marxism: A General Theory*, ed. and intro Chris Arthur (London: Ink Links, 1978; London: reprint Pluto Press, 1983).

contemporaries the limits of class instrumentalism (discussed below), which regarded the law as an instrument of class oppression and reduced the law to the articulate will of the ruling class. He also argued, against the current, as it were, that Marxists should examine law in its specificity and should come up with appropriate abstract theoretical categories peculiar to law. The fruit of his theoretical labors is what has come to be known as the *commodity exchange theory of law*.[8]

At the outset, Pashukanis called for a richer description of law. Ironically he ended up with a highly schematic and narrow conception of law. Taking his cue from Marx's discussion of exchange relations in *Capital* (vol. 1, chap. 2), Pashukanis sought to do for the theory of law what Marx accomplished for the study of political economy: to generate sufficiently abstract concepts which at the same time retain enough concreteness to enable us to employ them with respect to specific social phenomena. Marx had written that: "the wealth of those societies in which the capitalist mode of production prevails, presents itself as 'an immense accumulation of commodities,' its unit being a single commodity." The centrality of commodity production, then, is part of what marks out society as capitalist. Hence the study of capitalist political economy must begin with what Marx called "the analysis of a commodity."[9] Pashukanis writes: "The basic juridic abstractions, which are produced by the development of juridic thought, and which are the closest definitions of the legal form, in general reflect specific and very complex social relationships."[10] Just as capitalist society incarnates the most advanced form of commodity production, so does bourgeois law embody the most advanced species of legal form. The abstractions of the theory of law are artificial. But there is no doubt that "very real social forces are hidden behind these abstractions."[11] Even though they are abstractions, they are not the product of arbitrary thought processes. What, then, are the "very real social forces" behind legal abstractions? The answer places Pashukanis in the economist orbit: "It is only with the advent of bourgeois-capitalist society that all the necessary conditions are created for the juridical factor to attain complete distinctness in social relations."[12]

8. For a discussion of Pashukanis's theory, see Isaac D. Balbus, "Commodity Form and Legal Form," in C. E. Reasons and R. M. Rich, eds., *The Sociology of Law* (Toronto: Butterworths, 1978).

9. Karl Marx, *Capital* (Moscow: Progress Publishers, 1954), 1:43.

10. E. R. Pashukanis, *Selected Writings on Marxism and Law*, ed. and intro. Piers Beirne and Robert Sharlet, trans. Peter B. Maggs (London: Academic Press, 1980), p. 43.

11. Ibid., p. 45.

12. Pashukanis, *Law and Marxism*, p. 58.

Why was there no law but merely "embryonic legal forms" in precapitalist social formations? Because, says Pashukanis, the societies were not sufficiently differentiated for law to come into its own as "objective norm" and "legal power."[13] This is so because production for exchange—the defining trait of capitalist commodity production—had not become dominant. When it did, the legal form reached full bloom with it. The legal form is a juridical expression of the commodity form; legal relations are reflections of economic social relations (viz., commodity exchange relations). The destiny of the legal form, therefore, is indissolubly linked to that of the commodity form. The death of the latter must in the course of time lead to the demise of the former. Pashukanis explains why the law (along with the state) must wither in the fullness of time which will be inaugurated with the socialist revolution.[14]

Pashukanis's advance, both over his contemporaries and even some recent offerings, lies in the fact that he rescued law from the voluntarism that the class-instrumentalist interpretation foists upon it. Even though the dominant class may introduce "clarity and stability into the structure of law," argues Pashukanis, it does not create the premises for it; the latter are rooted in the material relations of production. "The development of law as a system was not predicated on the needs of the prevailing power relations, but on the requirements of trading transactions with peoples who were precisely not yet encompassed within a unified sphere of authority."[15] On Pashukanis's thesis, law is a product of necessity imposed by the requirements of commerce. But how the commodity form transmutes into the legal form is to be sought in the activities of the state and its ruling class. Positive law, then, would be an emanation from a complex state called upon to moderate the antagonisms of a society of atomized individuals brought together by the exigencies of commerce. The theory does have real limitations. Some it shares with other versions we shall be considering presently. Others are peculiar to it.

First, if law belongs entirely in the superstructure and there is no legal content in the economic structure, and if one affirms that law derives from the base, we must explain the notion of derivation we have in mind. If it is meant to be a logical derivation, I suggest that is impossible—for the simple logical commonplace that no amount of nonlegal premises without at least one legal premise can generate a legal conclusion in a valid derivation.

13. Ibid.
14. I shall say more about the withering away of law in Chapter 6 below.
15. Pashukanis, *Law and Marxism*, p. 95.

There is evidence to suggest that those who deploy the base/superstructure metaphor mean the relationship to be empirical and that the derivation of law is meant in a practical-empirical sense.[16] However, theorists who assert this practical-empirical derivation must specify how exactly such a derivation takes place in practice.

Secondly, if legal relations are mere legal expressions of nonlegal social relations, we have to explain why they express themselves, or are expressed, in legal form and not, say, in religious form. What is it about the legal form that so well suits it to express specific economic relations? A proponent of economism might rejoin that these social relations are sometimes expressed extralegally, that it does not make any difference whether the expressions are legal or religious. To this we should reply that it makes a lot of difference how these relations are expressed. For one thing, it cannot be denied that some modes of expression are more appropriate and more efficient than others. In highly complex societies, even when religion is used to secure holdings, this has often been done through the medium of law. Canon law under the Holy Roman Empire is a prime example of such a phenomenon. However, if law is best suited to regulate some spheres of life in highly complex societies, our opponent might claim that the cause must be sought within the economic structure. If law is generated by the severe clash of interests among classes and individuals in the economic structure, it is conceivable that some form of law is generative of those conflicts. If this is true, then we are back to where we started from: we have to explain why some relations of production are expressed in legal form. The legal-naturalist answer is that particular economic structures have law as a constitutive element; they will not be what they are if they are missing this element. Thus, the relevant relations are necessarily legal, not accidentally so.

Finally, sometimes there is a discontinuity between economic relations and their legal expressions. That is to say, there is sometimes a non-isomorphism between economic and juridical relations within the same social formation. Economism can explain only a little of this nonisomorphism. In transitional periods between epochs, when an old order is dying out and a new one is struggling to be born, this lack of fit is most poignantly illustrated in the presence of several competing legal systems—a kind of legal-systemic bonapartism—in which no one legal system is dominant. Economism breaks down at such a development and is thereby limited in

16. See, in general, John McMurtry, *The Structure of Marx's World-View* (Princeton: Princeton University Press, 1978), chap. 7.

its applicability. These and other problems discussed below have made economism less appealing as a theory of law in contemporary circles, Marxist or not.

Class instrumentalism. In *The Communist Manifesto*, Marx and Engels wrote that "the history of all hitherto existing society is the history of class struggles."[17] Society is divided into classes, and law is one of the instruments of class domination in specific situations where the legal form has emerged. As usual, the authority appealed to is Marx and Engels. The following statement from *The Communist Manifesto* is often cited: "The executive of the modern State is but a committee for managing the common affairs of the whole bourgeoisie" (MECW, 6:486). And in *The German Ideology*, we are reminded that "[The State] . . . is nothing more than the form of organization which the bourgeois are compelled to adopt, both for internal and external purposes, for the mutual guarantee of their property and interests. . . . [The] State is the form in which the individuals of a ruling class assert their common interests" (MECW, 5:90). For those who see the statements just quoted and others similar to them as an authority for instrumentalism, there is a direct line from the state to law. The legal system is an integral part of the state; it is merely another channel through which the ruling class ensures its dominance. Laws are no longer reflections of the mode of production; they are the contraptions by which the ruling class subordinates the lower classes while masking the brutality of its rule.[18]

According to Jangir Kerimov, law is a peculiar phenomenon of class society. In a society divided into two broad classes of owners and nonowners, where the owners are in a position to exploit the nonowners, "the owner class organizes itself into the state, which acts as an instrument for exploiting, suppressing, and fighting the less fortunate classes. The law is also used to that end."[19] Citing for support the passage in *The German Ideology* where Marx and Engels assert that the ruling individuals are bound to give their will a universal expression as the will of the state—as law—

17. Karl Marx and Frederick Engels, *Collected Works*, published to date: vols. 1–34; 38–47 (New York: International Publishers, 1975–), 6:482. Hereafter cited as MECW.

18. A class instrumentalist can insist that he or she can always discern the class dimension of every law we might care to say does not embody any obvious purpose of the ruling class. Such a move will be self-defeating. For even a class instrumentalist must concede that some laws are not motivated by class interests. Otherwise, there will be no boundaries for the theory, and every instance will be converted to a proof. I do not know of any class instrumentalist who makes this move to save his or her theory.

19. Jangir Kerimov, "The Marxist Conception of Law," in "Social Sciences Today" Editorial Board, *The Marxist Conception of Law* (Moscow: Progress Publishers, 1980), p. 6.

Kerimov concludes that "the basic category characterizing the essence of law is will or, to be more precise, class or state will."[20] Hence his definition of law: "law is the will of the ruling class vested in the state and expressed in a system of universally obligatory norms aimed at regulating social relations in the interests of this class and relying for its realisation on the state's power of enforcement."[21]

Vladimir Tumanov, too, avers that "law in a class society is always the same—it is a system of rules established or sanctioned by the state."[22] Less extravagant in his explication of this definition, he concedes that while the law is a product of state activity, the state is by no means unfettered in its lawmaking activity. Pointing out that the foundation of the law is always material, Tumanov is able to contend that Marxism is distant from legal positivism because, for Marxism, the state is restricted by the basic principles of the existing socioeconomic system. However, the attempt to distance Marxism from positivism is vitiated by the following: "Developed legal systems do not emerge automatically from the socio-economic and political conditions and relations, but are a result of class-conscious and volitional activity determined by these conditions and relations based on the utilization of state power. Naturally, in this class-conscious and volitional process of lawmaking politics and political interests play an essential role."[23]

One should not deny that the ruling class does sometimes subvert the law for its purposes. Nevertheless, it is wrong to believe that this is the only thing the law does. It is even doubtful that this is what it does in the main. A class-instrumentalist account cannot adequately explain those situations in which the law embodies no obvious purpose of the ruling class or those in which the object of the law runs counter to the identifiable interests of the ruling class.[24] Those who accept this version have many possible rejoinders.

They might argue that the palpable concessions in the circumstances I described are mere sops to the subaltern classes and do not vitally affect the fundamental interests of the ruling class. Or they might argue that such concessions are wrung out of the ruling class by the subaltern classes, that they are granted by the ruling class in order to pacify the latter. It is also possible that the ruling class might inefficiently calculate its self-interest or that cer-

20. Ibid.
21. Ibid., p. 11.
22. Vladimir Tumanov, " 'Natural Law' and Legal Positivism as viewed by Marxism," ibid., p. 14.
23. Ibid., p. 24.
24. See the discussion in Collins, *Marxism and Law*, chap. 2.

tain politically powerful factions might sacrifice in their own interest the interests of the rest of the class. In other words, the concessions I referred to might be products of inter- and intraclass contradictions in a given society. If all this is true, the rejoinder will have considerable force. But is it true?

For it to be true, our opponents must attribute to the ruling class a cognitive competence that just is not possessed by anyone. It is easy to see that the instrumentalist account is ruling-class-centered. Everything seems to depend on what the ruling class does or does not do. The ruling class grants concessions, the ruling class recognizes that it has to make concessions, the ruling class calculates its self-interest, and so on. This is not to suggest that the ruling class and its members never act in their own interest. However, the way class instrumentalists explain it, to know what concessions to grant and what not to grant, when to go ahead and when to hold back, it seems that the ruling class must be capable, conceptually at least, of foreseeing even the longest-term consequences of its actions. After all, in an analogous case in ethics, deficient knowledge has always been held against the possibility of an efficient utility calculus. It never happens that the ruling class is in a position, even conceptually, to undertake the task attributed to it by class instrumentalism. To suppose otherwise is to give ammunition to Karl Popper, who foists a conspiracy theory on Marxism.[25]

What the class instrumentalists ignore is that most of us, including the ruling class, are hampered by a huge epistemological blind spot that confers ample significance on the unintended consequences of our actions. Furthermore, the class instrumentalists are wont to forget Marx and Engels's caution in *The German Ideology* that the bourgeois "are compelled to adopt"; this caution imports an element of involuntarism into the development of law. In his discussion of the Factory Acts, Marx made it clear that the laws regarding factory protection were not promulgated by the English ruling class out of any voluntary concessions to the working class.[26] On the contrary, the necessity for the acts was thrust upon the ruling class in England by the requirements of capitalist production as it had then developed.[27] Where the ruling class recognizes the need for conces

25. See, in general, Karl Popper, *The Poverty of Historicism*, 2d ed. (London: Routledge & Kegan Paul, 1960). Also see Popper, *The Open Society and Its Enemies* (London: Routledge & Kegan Paul, 1974), esp.2:94–99.

26. Marx, *Capital* vol. 1, pt. 4, chap. 15, § 9.

27. "But if, on the one hand, variation of work at present imposes itself after the manner of an overpowering natural law, and with the blindly destructive action of a natural law that meets with resistance at all points, Modern Industry, on the other hand, through its catastrophes imposes the necessity of recognising, as a fundamental law of production, variation of work, consequently fitness of the labourer for varied work, consequently the greatest pos

sions, it is important to stress that such a recognition entails a necessity imposed by contradictions in the social formation. Such a recognition is often forced by the agitations of the subaltern classes or results from new knowledge of the structure of rights etc., of the social formation. Thus, an adequate explanation of ruling-class responses and their consequences must include reference to the limited cognitive competence of the ruling class, the role of unintended outcomes of deliberate actions, contradictions in the social formation, divergent interests within and outside given classes, and so on.

It is necessary to caution that our argument is not intended to demonstrate the falsity of instrumentalism or to show that it cannot give useful explanations in legal theory. Nor do we purport to show that law cannot be an instrument because the ruling class is forced to adopt it. It is plausible to say that law is an instrument that ruling classes are compelled to adopt. This manner of speaking should serve as a corroboration of our argument that the ruling class is not unconstrained in its choices. It does not support the ruling-class-centered view presented by class instrumentalism. We must be wary of accepting a theory of law that gives the impression that the law is a product of the will or interest of the ruling class. The history of legal development shows that, even under the most unstructured orders of privilege, there were specific limits on the ruling-class will that could not be breached without inducing in those over whom they rule a feeling that justice had been trampled underfoot.

Legal ideologism. What is sometimes referred to as the hegemony of law or the ideological nature of law[28] I am calling "legal ideologism" merely for verbal symmetry. In this more sophisticated version of class instrumentalism, law is still seen as a weapon in the hands of the ruling class. But the ruling-class-centered view of the class instrumentalist is modified here in a view that argues for some measure of autonomy for law construed as a body of discourse. The coercive dimension of law is less emphasized: law does not ride roughshod over the subaltern classes. On the contrary, law

---

sible development of his varied aptitudes. It becomes a question of life and death for society to adapt the mode of production to the normal functioning of this law. . . . What strikes us, then, in the English legislation of 1867, is, on the one hand, the necessity imposed on the parliament of the ruling classes, of adopting in principle measures so extraordinary, and on so great a scale, against the excesses of capitalistic exploitation; and on the other hand, the hesitation, the repugnance, and the bad faith, with which it lent itself to the task of carrying those measures into practice." Ibid., 1:458, 464.

28. See Sumner, *Reading Ideologies*; Paul Hirst, *On Law and Ideology* (Atlantic Highlands, N.J.: Humanities Press, 1979); and Collins, *Marxism and Law*, chap. 4.

contains an ample *dirigiste* element. The ruling class does not secure obedience to its rule by brute force. Rather, it educates the consent of the governed in such a way that the lower classes come to view the rule of the ruling class as "right rule," obedience to which and acquiescence in which should be exacted and given. Like the state, law is a kind of "educator," the harbinger of a species or level of civilization. It is an "ideological formation" (Sumner's phrase), the aim of which is to consummate the hegemony of the ruling class over the rest of society. According to Sumner,

> the law . . . objectively is a collection of ideologies, sanctioned in the correct manner by the institutionalized executors of social power, which define the socially permissible modes of social intercourse. It is distinguished from ordinary ideology by its political backing. It is distinguished from politicians' speeches and policies by the fact that it has received political backing in the manner laid down by custom or constitution. It is distinguished from administrative decisions not by due process or rights of appeal but by the fact that it expresses approved rules of conduct in a general form and by the fact that these rules have been agreed upon in the proper manner by the proper persons in power. What counts as the "proper" mode of law-creation is, of course, itself a matter in the control of the powerful.[29]

Sumner believes that his definition will cover stateless societies since he does not presuppose a state. It accommodates judge-made law, subordinate legal systems, and inoperative or unenforced rules, for all these are either properly sanctioned ideologies or come from executive agents of social power or operate by permission of the social power–holders. For the origins of law, we must look to "the power bloc behind the legislation, the nature of the problem this bloc wants to solve, the ideologies in which this problem is perceived and understood, and the political opposition to the proposed legislation. Law is a hybrid phenomenon of politics and ideology: a politico-ideological artefact."[30]

Sumner focuses on the positive law in any society. Because law, for him, is superstructural, its generic origin lies at the base, the economic structure of the social formation. As a superstructural phenomenon, law is a product of the activities of the ruling groups in society. It is plausible to claim as he does that only properly sanctioned ideologies can be called law. This means that law is not just a product of the will of the ruling class. It is also less contentious to claim that the origins of the positive law

29. Sumner, *Reading Ideologies*, pp. 266–67.
30. Ibid., p. 267.

can be traced to the power bloc behind its promulgation. That is to say, law is inseparable from politics. But Sumner's account remains ruling-class-centered. For, ultimately, the substitution of consent for forcible obedience and of hegemony for coercion does not get rid of the central role assigned to the will of the ruling class. Law is the set of ideologies sanctioned by the ruling class, who also decide what will be " 'proper' modes of law-creation."[31]

Legal ideologism merely puts class instrumentalism under a thicker layer of verbiage. Law is a "politico-ideological artefact." It remains, in the last instance, the weapon of a class and class fractions. It is still "geared to the creation, definition and maintenance of power relations. As such it is only one weapon within a whole armoury."[32] Legal ideologism does not represent much of an improvement over class instrumentalism. If we can show that a class instrumentalist need not emphasize the coercive dimension of law, there is little or no difference between legal ideologism and class instrumentalism. This is an important flaw, because those who assert the ideological nature of law wish to distance themselves from class instrumentalism. So far, we have considered the specific problems pertaining to each of the three attempts at constructing Marxist theory of law. It is time to discuss the problems they share.

III

(1) The idea of conscious or volitional activity is central to the accounts in the preceding section. That is why I think they are voluntaristic. One of the most intractable problems voluntarism confronts in legal theory is that it attributes to lawmakers more competence at deciphering the hieroglyphics of social practice than is warranted by the evidence. It is true that we can point to several instances of volitional legislation in highly complex societies. It is equally true that many such instances are near hits; often, they are absolute misses. Thus, a theory like that advanced by Sumner—which holds that the origins of law always relate to the nature of the problem the ruling power bloc wants to solve, the ideologies in which this problem is perceived, and the political opposition to the proposed legislation—supposes that the actors in these situations can be held to know what the problem is and to disagree only about the solution. In many instances, however, the analytical task is complicated by the fact that the dis-

31. Ibid.
32. Ibid., p. 268.

agreement is really about the nature of the problem; there are as many conceptions of the problem as there are ideologies through which to perceive and understand the problem.

(2) The story of law as the enacted will of the ruling class or as the compendium of the ruling ideologies tends to give the impression that the rulers in the relevant societies are able often enough to come to a consensus as to what the law ought to be. This is an exaggeration. Members and factions of the ruling class frequently have to struggle among themselves over *what the law ought to be*. In other words, even as Marxist interpreters seek to distance themselves from talk about what the law ought to be, municipal legal systems are marked by differing understandings of what the law should be and in what direction it ought to evolve. This susceptibility to contestation is not limited to the ruling class; the subordinate classes are not to be left out in the struggles over the law. I limit myself to the ruling class in this discussion.

Members of the ruling class are not always in agreement about what positive law should be. In advancing different conceptions of the law, each faction tries to draw legitimacy from its own account of what is best for their society, what the extant structure of their society requires, and why or how the suggestions of the opposition, if accepted, will undermine the foundations of a social system that they all cherish. For example, few people will deny that Franklin D. Roosevelt was no less committed to the survival of capitalism than Herbert Hoover.[33] Yet, FDR and Hoover disagreed vigorously about what capitalism could accommodate by way of governmental legislative programs with respect to social policy. Each believed that his own prescription expressed what was best for capitalism and what the capitalist social formation enjoins. In a speech in September 1932, Roosevelt had this to say concerning the growing tendency to monopoly in American capitalism:

---

33. A much scaled-down version of their struggle over the evolutionary direction of the American social system was manifested in the U.S. presidential elections of November 1992. The background was very similar. American capitalism was in a crisis brought on by a severe recession. A key focus of debate in the campaign was what to do to resolve the crisis: there was a basic disagreement about what the right direction was for the American economy and society. Then-candidate Bill Clinton kept talking about an active role for the government/state in lifting the economy out of the recession and, what is more, in dealing with the many crises of the polity. President George Bush ridiculed such a role as a proposal to "grow government." He preferred to trust in the power of business, unfettered by excessive government, to lead the charge for economic recovery, and he relied on various nonstate institutions to resolve the social crisis. As in the Hoover–Roosevelt case, neither candidate questioned the relevance or legitimacy of capitalism as the best way of life.

Put plainly, we are steering a steady course toward economic oligarchy, if we are not there already. Clearly, all this calls for a reappraisal of values. . . . The day of enlightened administration has come. . . .

Every man has a right to his own property, which means a right to be assured, to the fullest extent attainable, in the safety of his savings. . . .

In all thought of property, this right is paramount; all other property rights must yield to it.

If, in accord with this principle, we must restrict the operations of the speculator, the manipulator, even the financier, I believe we must accept the restriction as needful not to hamper individualism but to protect it.[34]

Unless one were to suggest that Roosevelt was a closet socialist, it is obvious from the excerpts that he was not yielding on the basic commitment to individualism and property ownership that capitalism presupposes. In fact, he did not want to admit that he was making a tactical move: a short-term loss for a gain in the long term. He insisted that curbs on monopoly were meant to protect private property and individualism. In his first inaugural address, he cited the crash of 1929 to underscore his belief that unrestrained speculation on the stock exchange was inimical to the healthy development of capitalism.

Ranged against Roosevelt on the opposite side were the Republicans. I cite here excerpts from a speech by Herbert Hoover in October 1936:

Through four years of experience this New Deal attack upon free institutions has emerged as the transcendent issue in America. [Railing against Roosevelt's New Deal as a form of creeping communism, Hoover went on:] .

During my four years [Hoover was president when the crash of 1929 occurred] powerful groups thundered at the White House with these same ideas. . . .

I rejected the notion of great trade monopolies and price-fixing through codes. That could only stifle the little businessman by regimenting him under the big brother. That idea was born of certain American Big Business and grew up to be the [National Recovery Act].

I rejected the schemes of "economic planning" to regiment and coerce the farmer. That was born of a Roman despot 1,400 years ago and grew up into the [Agricultural Adjustment Act].

34. Franklin D. Roosevelt, "Speech to the Commonwealth Club, September 23, 1932," in Richard Hofstadter and Beatrice K. Hofstadter, eds., *Great Issues in American History*, rev. ed. (New York: Vintage, 1982), 3:341–42.

I refused national plans to put the government into business in competition with its citizens. That was born of Karl Marx.

I vetoed the idea of recovery through stupendous spending to prime the pump. That was born of a British professor. . . .

I rejected all these things because they would not only delay recovery but because I knew that in the end they would shackle free men.[35]

On one level, these excerpts from the speeches of Roosevelt and Hoover indicate a fundamental rift in understanding between members of the same ruling class ostensibly committed to the same pattern of social ordering. One can argue that such disjunctures in ruling-class understanding are rare exceptions and that they do not critically threaten to undermine the social formation or upset its institutions. This is true to some extent. For the presence of such discrepant perceptions is crucial to explaining why one faction's understanding of what the social formation requires triumphs over that of another. In situations of struggle between the ruling and the subordinate classes, the lack of a consensus within the ruling class often has implications for the eventual outcomes of such struggles. For example, a Supreme Court decision that weighs in on the side of freedom of contract against the power of the state to promulgate social policy legislation respecting the health of working persons, as in *Lochner v. New York*, may portend failure or serious difficulties for a working class that wants working hours to be regulated.[36] Moreover, a legal theory that asks us always to relate legislation to the problems that a ruling bloc seeks to solve is likely to break down when confronted with the lack of a straightforward description of those problems by the members of the ruling class.

On another level, the fundamental rift in understanding may be premised on divergent interests among various factions of the same ruling class. The divergence of interests among ruling factions may be occasioned by a misreading by one or more factions of the hieroglyphics of social process. Quite often, though, the divergence reflects basic contradictions in the social formation itself. The contradiction of class interests

35. Herbert Hoover, "Speech on October 30, 1936," in Hofstadter and Hofstadter, eds., *Great Issues*, 3:350–51. The divisions were not just between politicians. The Supreme Court was busy throwing out one piece of New Deal legislation after another because, it held in most of the cases, the legislation violated diverse provisions of the U. S. Constitution: from the right to private property to the freedom of contract to the protection of states' rights. See the division in the Court in *U.S. v. Butler et al.*, 1936, excerpted in Hofstadter and Hofstadter, eds., *Great Issues*, 3:352–62. See also Robert G. McCloskey, *The American Supreme Court* (Chicago: University of Chicago Press, 1960), chap. 6.

36. See 198 U.S. 45 (1905), in Hofstadter and Hofstadter, eds., *Great Issues*, 3:254–60.

might be, to borrow a phrase from Jürgen Habermas, "a contradiction of system imperatives."[37] Capitalism is rife with such contradictions of system imperatives. I cite a few: the unregulated operation of the free market might imperil the investments of many people, put their retirement savings in jeopardy, and scuttle their old-age plans; the freedom of association might in its operation overcome the right to private property; the right to freedom of assembly frequently runs into conflict with the assertion of the right to private property. In the contest between Roosevelt and Hoover, then, discrepant perceptions could have arisen from the situation to explain why Hoover insisted the market should be left unrestrained, in spite of the depression, and why, at the same time, Roosevelt maintained there was a need to regulate the market as a precondition for the survival and further development of capitalism. A singular focus on the ruling class and its activities is likely to obscure the importance of the problems just identified.

(3) There is the problem of "gaps" in the positive law. Gaps are omissions in the positive law, owing either (a) to an unawareness of the need for a particular area of activity to be brought within the ambit of the law or (b) to the advance of social and material processes yet to be acknowledged by and taken account of in the law. In contemporary advanced-capitalist societies, for example, the problem of possible deleterious consequences from the proliferation of computer technology has revealed gaps in the laws of several countries, and these are now being rectified by new legislation. The new legislation is designed to cope with new forms of theft ("hacking"), invasions of privacy, and similar activities generated by the widespread use of computers.

---

37. Jürgen Habermas, *Legitimation Crisis*, trans. Thomas McCarthy (Boston: Beacon Press, 1975), p. 26. Claus Offe has argued that the present conflicts between conservatives and progressives regarding the fortunes of the welfare state in advanced capitalist countries is a reflection of "a contradiction of system imperatives" in monopoly capitalism. See his *Contradictions of the Welfare State*, ed. John Keane (Cambridge: MIT Press, 1984). Conservative critics argue that the welfare state discourages investment because it imposes a heavy burden of taxation and regulation upon capital. Also, they argue, it is a "disincentive to work" because it grants to workers claims, entitlements, and collective power positions that hamper productivity in a way that market arrangements would not. The Left, on the other hand, argues that the welfare state is "(1) ineffective and inefficient; (2) repressive; and (3) conditioning a false ('ideological') understanding of social and political reality within the working class" (pp. 149–57). According to Offe, this debate ignores the basic contradiction of monopoly capitalism which necessitates the welfare state: "The contradiction is that while capitalism cannot coexist *with*, neither can it exist *without*, the welfare state" (p. 153). The discrepant perceptions within the ruling class might be owing to the fact that there are contradictions, or at least tensions, in the social formation itself.

Some will say that gaps are functional to the system. Or it may be that a class-conscious ruling class has yet to become aware of gaps in the law. This nonawareness can be attributed to the lack of systemic dysfunctions as a consequence of the gaps. None of the authors we have examined displays any awareness that the existence of gaps in the legal system poses problems for their theories. Or if they are aware, they have chosen to ignore the possibility that gaps can exist.

(4) Marxist positivism ignores custom and judicial usage. Of course, Marxist positivism might contend that customs are endorsed by legislation or that they can be regarded as part of the law insofar as the ruling class tolerates them. To be sure, such a reply would be unsound because ordinary people who obey such laws and use the relevant customs as reasons for action and as justification for applying social sanctions will refer neither to the say-so of the ruling class nor to its legislation: for ordinary people, acceptance of custom is a matter of antiquity and efficacy. Writing about custom in English law, C. K. Allen points out that "in the main, with [certain] exceptions . . . , *if a custom is proved in an English Court by satisfactory evidence to exist and be observed, the function of the Court is merely to declare the custom operative law*. In other words, the custom does not derive its inherent validity from the authority of the Court, and the 'sanction' of the Court is declaratory rather than constitutive."[38]

It could be, a positivist might rejoin, that over time the declarations of the courts would seem more and more the products of deliberate intervention. To that extent, customs would begin to resemble legislation. And, in that case, customs that are declared law by the courts can be explained by the willed, class-conscious activities of the ruling class—all we need do is show that those who preside over court proceedings are either themselves members of the ruling class or are acting on behalf of the ruling class. We should reply that an emphasis on the later influence of willed activities of the courts ignores the fact that at the time when particular customs are first declared in law, their authority, as Allen points out, predates their recognition by the courts. Their genesis, too, does not lie in the willed activities of a class but is spontaneously generated and later fixed in use. That is why the courts' recognition is only declaratory and not constitutive. Inasmuch as it remains true to say that the authority of customs in law is not a matter of recognition by courts, a theory of law built on the willed or class-conscious activities of a class is not adequate to explain customs and their participation in the positive law.

38. C. K. Allen, *Law in the Making*, 7th ed. (Oxford:Clarendon Press, 1964), p. 130.

(5) How do we explain the diversity of legal regimes in a given social formation? Take capitalism for instance. The capitalist mode of production has mutated over time. It has engendered diverse positive-legal regimes in history. Limiting ourselves to the contemporary world, we observe that Japan, the United States of America, France, and South Africa are all capitalist countries; each is an instance of the capitalist social formation. We call their legal systems "capitalist legal systems." But the positive legal regimes differ in details from one country to another. Whereas there used to be laws in South Africa and in the United States that impaired the ability of a black person to enter into a contract, such a restriction will *prima facie* not be entertained by the present-day U. S. judiciary. Whereas the law in Japan allows the state to organize and regulate business through the Ministry of International Trade and Industry, and the law in South Africa used to allow the government to commandeer any industry and run it, the U. S. legal system does not permit such interference (except perhaps in time of war). Nevertheless, despite acknowledged radical differences in the positive legal regimes of these countries, we still call them "capitalist legal systems."

Our insistence on calling them capitalist legal systems is best explained by the fact that each of these countries possesses enough of the definitive characteristics that a genuine capitalist legal system must have if it is to be called "capitalist." From the ample knowledge we have of the capitalist social formation, we can construct an adequate concept of a capitalist legal regime. By using the concept we construct, we can explain the diversity of legal regimes as the result of the partial understanding people have of the possibilities contained within their social formation, an understanding that, perforce, must be shaped by their knowledge of social forces, their history and customs, the class struggle, and so on. A theory of law that sees law as a class-interest-inspired politico-ideological artifact may be able to explain the diversity of legal regimes in terms of the divergent understandings of various ruling classes. I am not so sure it can explain the unity that underpins this diversity.

A ruling-class-centered theory cannot explain the underlying unity because, at best, it asserts a functional relationship between the positive law and the relations of production it legitimates. For all we know, the only limitation on the positive law is that it has to be functional for mode of production (2). On the contrary, it was contended in Chapter 2 above that the positive law is what it is because it embodies an essence that is external to it and from which it derives its identity. On a functional account, the positive law could be different from what it is in a given society so long as it is functional. On a legal-naturalist view, the positive law cannot be, in any significant sense, other than it is insofar as it is *the* positive law of *the* relevant social formation. The necessity of the connection between natural law and positive law supplies the basis for a more adequate explanation of the unity of diverse legal systems.

To explain the unity, one must suppose a more deterministic relationship between the nature of, say, the capitalist social formation and people's understanding of it. Put in this manner, it is not simply a question of the ruling class fashioning the law that happens to be capitalist in its essence. Rather, it is that, whoever the lawmakers may be, if they know that theirs is an instance of the capitalist formation and they believe that capitalism enables the fulfillment of the myriad social, political, and economic aims of their society, they must orient their lawmaking activities toward the realization of a legal regime adequate to the concept of capitalism. Whatever false starts, errors, etc. they make will be attributed by Marxists to the relative opacity of social forces, limited knowledge of their history, and so on. This procedure already means we have abandoned the view that only positive law exists and have substituted a variant of dualism, which affirms the existence of both positive law and natural law, discussed in Chapter 2 above.

(6) Theories of law that require the state for lawmaking will eliminate from legal theory all talk of law in all social formations that either have no state in them or cannot have a state in them. For instance, it will take a considerable expansion of the concept of "state" to put it at the source of customary law. This is so for the same reason we cannot say that customs, at their origins, are creations of class-motivated activities of any group in society. Recognition by the state or the courts is declaratory, not constitutive, of the authority of customary law.

Furthermore, in those societies in which class formation has not crystallized, class conscious, state-mediated law will necessarily be absent. We should not for that reason alone conclude that they have no law. By such *a priori* forbearances, research could only be stunted.[39] For insofar as each theory is also a regulative principle, it stops movement in every direction it excludes from having any interest for research. What is required in each instance is to examine the society, see whether it fits the description of any

---

39. For discussion of some of the baneful consequences of an *a priori* exclusion of so-called nonstate societies from the study of law, see T. O. Elias, *The Nature of African Customary Law* (Manchester: Manchester University Press, 1956), esp. chaps. 3 and 4, and John L. Comaroff and Simon Roberts, *Rules and Processes* (Chicago: University of Chicago Press, 1981), esp. chap. 1.

of the social formations we have encountered in history, scan it for law and law analogues. The assertion that a society is without law will then be the outcome, not the commencement, of a research program. By writing non-state societies out of its schema from the outset, Marxist positivism limits its range.

(7) Positivism rarely discusses the problem of the obligation to obey the law. Being ruling-class-centered, it asserts that the law is actuated by class interests and by the functional necessities of mode of production (2). It seems to assume that, at least for the members of the ruling class, not only do they obey the law, but they *ought* to obey the law. It is a problematic assumption.

It is a fairly straightforward empirical matter whether or not members of the ruling class and others within a society obey the law. What is not susceptible of easy ascertainment is whether or not members of the ruling class and others within a society have an obligation to obey the law. The interesting questions generated by the issue include the following: What is the nature of the obligation involved, assuming we affirm that members of a society have an obligation to obey the law? Why do they have this obligation? That is to say, what is the basis of the obligation to obey the law? These questions are seldom posed by Marxist theories of law. They are important nevertheless.

If asked why members of a society have an obligation to obey the law, we should expect positivists to insist that the question must be asked in more specific, class-relative, terms. This is so because in a society divided into hostile classes, in which some are rulers and others are ruled, we cannot speak of a general obligation to obey the law. Let us, for a moment, go along with this distinction between the obligation of the rulers and that of the ruled. Our theorists would contend that the ruling-class members have an obligation to obey the law. What is the nature of this obligation?

The obligation that the ruling class or any other group in society has to obey the law cannot be solely a legal one. It is trivially true to say that everyone has a legal obligation to obey whatever is a law. When questions about the obligation to obey the law have arisen, however, they have often been held to require answers that refer to obligation which is required over and above the fact that what is to be obeyed is law. In other words, the basis for the obligation to obey the law must be *extralegal*. I have substituted "extralegal" for the more prevalent designation of this obligation as *moral* because what is important is that the obligation not be *legal*. Whether it is moral or rational or any other quality is something that can, and will, be determined at a different time. The question then becomes:

Do members of a society have an obligation to obey the law over and above that provided by the fact that it is law? Consistent with their account of law and laws, we should expect the theorists we are discussing to answer in the affirmative.

What is the basis of the obligation to obey the law? Basically the answer to the present question requires an analysis of what is contained in the notion of an extralegal obligation to obey the law. One possible answer is that ruling-class members have an obligation to obey the law because they make the law and because the law, in the main, serves their interests. It is assumed that these interests include that of ensuring the survival and healthy functioning of their social formation. After all, the members of the ruling class have the interests they do, by and large, because they are located in particular spaces within the social formation.[40] When one adds their belief that their social formation, of which the law is a part, has more to recommend it and less to disapprove of in it, it would appear that their obligation to obey the law is indisputable. But is it? A closer analysis indicates it is not.

From the fact that members of the ruling class make the law it does not follow that they ought to obey the law. Otherwise it will be absurd to speak of a lawmaker disobeying the law. No matter how odious it might be, there is nothing absurd about lawmakers themselves breaking the law they have made. Of course, this claim might be based on a further premise that one ought to obey laws that one has made and that serve one's interests. What happens when, as a result of some of the divergences in perceptions and interests among members of the ruling class, some members deny they have an obligation to obey the law because they have not had any hand in making it?

One possible response is that such persons do not have to be actively involved for them to be regarded as parties to the making of the law. Another is that exemptions should not be granted on the basis of particular laws once the individuals concerned admit that they are party to the mak-

40. No distinction has been made between members of the ruling class and those whom they employ to operate the machinery of government, economy, and other spheres of life in society. The distinction can and ought to be made in some situations. They are treated together here because the distinction between the *ruling* and the *governing* groups is not required for the point to be made about obligation. The distinction is important where what is to be explained is whether someone who works in government (e.g., a civil servant) has an obligation to obey the law, especially when the individual concerned takes the job merely to earn a living and does not make any serious commitment to the norms of the social formation. For our purposes, members of the ruling class include those who run the machinery of government etc. as decisionmakers.

ing of the bulk of the law. Responses of this sort would tend to exclude those who are not within the ruling class from having any obligation to obey the law. In addition, the requirement of passive or tacit involvement in lawmaking would raise new problems of how that involvement is established and what is the threshold at which noninvolvement stops and active involvement begins. A better principle is needed to explain the obligation to obey the law of the members of the ruling class.

There are many elements that could conjointly make up such a principle. It might be pointed out that the positive laws, as a whole, are promotive of beneficial consequences for the greatest number of people in the society. Put in general terms, there is an obligation to obey the law if and only if the law ensures the greatest amount of beneficial consequences for the greatest number of people. Incidentally, this principle can be appealed to both by the ruling class and by those outside it. The principle requires an appropriate attitude toward it on the part of those who are supposed to live by what it enjoins. The requisite attitude is one of a positive disposition to want to do what the principle enjoins and to refrain from doing what it prohibits. For us to say that people should have the requisite attitude toward the law is to say that they know the law, that they can discern the weight of the principle, what it means, and so on in appropriate circumstances.

For all of the preceding to occur people must *accept* the law. They must exhibit what was identified in Chapter 2 above as "the internal aspect" of law. The extralegal obligation to obey the law is therefore a conjunction of (a) the law's content (i.e., the consequences it generates) and (b) the acceptance of those whose obligation we are talking about that the consequences which the law promotes are worth having and that the law indeed promotes or appears to promote those consequences. Thus, someone has an obligation to obey the law when he or she accepts that the consequences the law promotes are worthwhile and accepts that the law does promote, or appears to promote, those consequences. Although it does not follow deductively that someone who accepts the law ought to obey it, few people will deny that the fact of acceptance supplies grounds for a reasonable presumption that an accepter would be expected to obey and to cite as reason for his or her action, in appropriate circumstances, his or her acceptance of the law.

What is it to accept the law of a given society? A distinction was made in Chapter 2 between the external aspect and the internal aspect of a legal system. General obedience to law in a society is enough for us, speaking from the external aspect, to assert that the law in that society is obeyed and that its members have an "obligation" to obey the law. When the matter is considered in its internal aspect, it concerns members who are not only bound as a matter of empirical fact by the law, but who also *feel* bound by it and cite its injunctions as reasons for their actions. In the following discussion our primary concern is with this internal aspect.

William McBride describes the notion of acceptance quite well: " 'acceptance' may designate either (a) a long-term, perhaps life-long, perhaps highly unreflective, dispositional attitude towards a legal system or (b) an act of choice (here, of a legal system as one meriting allegiance) occurring at a given time, though surely capable of being repeated at any other given time, or (c) any of the gamut of shorter-term dispositions or long-term series of acts of decision and choice that may be regarded as intermediate possibilities between the extremes of (a) and (b)."[41] McBride's description is very appropriate for our purposes. It covers a wide range of possibilities in its three designations. In addition, it allows for temporal shifts in the texture of acceptance and its form. For example, in a stable society where the foundations of the law are not contested, a member of the ruling class is likely to accept the law in sense (b), whereas a civil servant who is simply doing his or her job might at one point accept in sense (a) and at another in sense (b). On McBride's construal of acceptance, even a revolutionary might have, at an earlier time, accepted in sense (a) when he or she was just growing up, in sense (b) when he or she has come to the stage of having reasons for obeying the law beyond trivial legal ones, and in sense (c) when he or she has begun to have doubts about whether the conditions for acceptance still stand but has yet to repudiate the law's foundations.

Using the notion of acceptance as the basis for the obligation to obey the law gives us better explanations for why people obey the law, in the main. A legal system that commands widespread acceptance will need sanctions only for those few (relative to the population) who break the law. The fact that more people obey the law or, at least, do not disobey the law than disobey it is supportive of the assertion that acceptance is more important for the obligation to obey the law than, say, sanctions or force or fear.

"Acceptance" also offers us a tool with which to explain the obligation to obey the law of someone who is not an official or a member of the ruling class. Most ordinary people who advert their minds to the law elect for obedience because, except in situations of a breakdown in the legal system,

41. William Leon McBride, "The Acceptance of a Legal System," *The Monist* 49 (1965): 383.

they too accept, in the senses specified by McBride, the law. So long as they exhibit this attitude toward the law we can expect that breaches of law, fundamental disagreements over the law, and similar phenomena will be kept to a minimum.[42]

Nothing we have said so far should preclude the presence of other reasons for obeying the law. One reason that people obey the law might be that they are afraid of the consequences of disobedience. If this is a principal reason why people obey the law, it ought to follow that they will break the law when there is no chance of being caught and suffering the unpalatable consequences. It is also possible that people do not think about obeying or not obeying; they just act, thinking of the law only when they run afoul of its prohibitions. Needless to say, these other reasons for conforming to the law can be adduced by people irrespective of class affiliation.

We shall, in a moment, discuss the reasons for accepting the law in a society. Briefly put, most people who choose to obey the law or who feel that they have an obligation to obey do so because they believe, even when their beliefs are unreasonable, that their society has many agreeable qualities and the law, in the main, embodies a substantial proportion of those qualities.[43] Indeed, this acceptance might explain why so few people, under normal circumstances, break the law and why the law commands the respect of rulers and ruled alike. Theorists who dwell on the activities of the ruling class are liable to ignore this dimension of the acceptance of a legal system. Marxists should not talk as if law does not contain class-neutral, power-conferring rules or does not without exception guarantee safety of life and limb in society. The problem is not that

42. For an account of the role of acceptance in compliant behavior, see Tom Tyler, *Why People Obey the Law* (New Haven: Yale University Press, 1990), chaps. 3–5.

43. One is struck by the ease with which those who affirm an obligation to obey the law invoke the fact that the law, by and large, embodies many commendable qualities of the social order and, for that reason, is deserving of, or at least can be presumed to deserve, people's obedience. Here is an example: "In contrast to the view that almost any destabilization of established authority is a necessary medicine for a diseased society, I start from three more conservative premises. First, that flawed as it is by substantial injustices and deep irrationalities, our society is still one of the best that human beings have managed to create. Second, the light of history affords no assurance that rapid, radical change will better social conditions. Third, the destabilizing force of widespread disobedience is, therefore, not a good to be embraced but a harm to be feared." Kent Greenawalt, "Promise, Benefit, and Need: Ties That Bind Us to the Law," *Georgia Law Review* 18 (1984): 728. See also Bernard P. Dauenhauer, "On Strengthening the Law's Obligatory Character," *Georgia Law Review* 18 (1984): 824–25, 833, 834; David Luban, *Lawyers and Justice* (Princeton: Princeton University Press, 1988), chap. 11; and Laurence H. Tribe, *God Save This Honorable Court* (New York: Random House, 1985), p. 96.

law is sometimes an inconvenience to the ruling class but that, most of
the time in a stable society, the gulf between the interests of the ruling
class and the settled law can be considerable.[44] The really difficult task
for the Marxist theory of law is to explain the multidimensionality of law
when its class bias is evident. That is precisely what class instrumentalism and legal ideologism are not equipped to do. They cannot give the
necessary explanation until the terms in their theoretical inventory have
been increased.

IV

In the rest of this chapter, I propose to show how legal naturalism helps us
meet some of the challenges highlighted from (1) through (7) in the preceding section. The key lies in the explication of positive law and how it is
adapted from natural law. We have seen that positivism works with a
monistic idea of law and cannot find a source for positive law beyond the
say-so of the ruling class or the nonlegal requirements of the economic
structure. By contrast, legal naturalism, with its notion of natural law inherent in the social formation, provides a more solid anchor. Let us take as
an illustration the issue discussed in section III (7) above: obligation to
obey the law.

Usually, when this problem is raised it is with respect to the positive law.
Does one have an obligation to obey the positive law in a particular society? The basis of the obligation is the acceptance by an individual or group
of the law in that society. What are the conditions for the acceptance of a
legal system? According to the theory being developed here, people accept
the legal system of their society because they believe, even though their beliefs may seem unreasonable, that their society has many agreeable quali-

---

44. The more entrenched the rule of a class is, the more stable the society is. For the en-
trenchment of the rule of a class means that its view of the world is the dominant one in the
society and that those whom it rules look upon that rule as, in the main, right and deserving
of their obedience or acquiescence. The importance of this point will become clear when we
discuss the issue of obligation to obey the law. For the present, note that part of what it
means for the rule of a class to be entrenched is that while it holds sway in society, the distinction between what is motivated by class interests and what is required by the general interest is difficult to draw. As Antonio Gramsci has pointed out, a class can begin to feel secure
in its dominance when it has succeeded in making its interests into the general interest or, at
least, has succeeded in getting those whom it rules to believe, even when they are wrong to
believe so, that what the dominant class does is done in the general interest. See *Selections
from the Prison Notebooks*, ed. and trans. Quintin Hoare and Geoffrey Nowell Smith (New
York: International Publishers, 1980), p. 161.

ties and that the law, in the main, embodies a substantial proportion of those qualities. This is where the relevance of natural law comes out clearly.

Quite often, when the question of the obligation to obey the law comes up, there is already an admission that the law requires some extralegal justification. Although I cannot argue for the claim here, those who affirm that there is an obligation to obey the law insist not infrequently that theirs is a good society—at least, comparatively speaking. They try to show that the law, by and large, does express some of the commendatory qualities their society has. They conclude that a person who wishes to be exempt from the obligation to obey the law must show that the particular law involved either does not adequately express some of the most cherished aspects of their society or is an outright violation of them.[45] If the individual concerned admits that the society is a good one but that a given law breaches the norms enjoined by the society, he or she might resort to civil disobedience. This move in itself will be a big concession to the claim of the basic goodness of the society. The refusal to obey a given law might even be a way of persuading the members of the society to bring their law into phase with the basic goodness claimed for it. Suppose, however, that the person denies that it is a good society and that the legal system as a whole embodies the evil that inheres in the society itself, it is not clear to me that anyone who accepts the legal system in the way we have described would be inclined to engage in an argument with our objector.[46]

The natural law of a social formation is that structure of rights etc. which is constitutive of the social formation. In those social formations with law, when those who uphold the obligation to obey the positive law appeal to the qualities that recommend their society and when they affirm that the law embodies those qualities, however inadequately, they should

45. It is striking how much of contemporary Anglo-American philosophy of law is dominated by idealized constructs of American political culture and legal history. Additionally, theorists routinely appeal to the superiority of the American way of life or the mode of social ordering prevailing in the United States as their justification for using it as the foundation for their theoretical endeavors.

46. This last point is very important, although it cannot be pursued here. Consider the inability of proslavery and antislavery forces in the antebellum United States to reach any agreement on the merits/demerits of slavery. As the consensus over the legitimacy and applicability of natural law unraveled—a consensus that had enabled antislavery forces to eke out a few victories in the courts despite the Compromise of 1850, embodied in the Fugitive Slave Law—antislavery forces became less inclined to concede that preserving slavery was an acceptable cost for saving the Union. Many came to feel that any compromise with slavery was unacceptable. For details see, Robert M. Cover, *Justice Accused: Antislavery and the Judicial Process* (New Haven: Yale University Press, 1975).

be understood to be saying that the positive law embodies this constitutive structure. That is to say, if the positive law does not violate the dictates of the natural law, and one does not question or fundamentally disagree with the dictates of the natural law, one has an obligation to obey the law.

For example, in a capitalist social formation, one of the constitutive rights of an individual is the right freely to dispose of his or her labor as he or she desires. This is one of the constituent elements of capitalist natural law. We have greater warrant to assert this now than people did at the dawn of the capitalist era. We know more now than they did then, and there is little doubt that we can construct a more adequate model of capitalism and its presuppositions than we could, say, a hundred years ago. In the light of our historical experience, we can say that most people who accept the positive laws of various capitalist countries could be said to believe that this freedom to dispose of one's labor as one sees fit is one of the principal commendable qualities of their society. They can be expected, therefore, consistent with this belief, to resist positive laws that *systematically* assail this freedom. The members of the ruling classes, too, are unlikely to promulgate laws violative of this freedom. One reason they will not do so is that dysfunctions will occur in the system. A more important reason, though, is that laws systematically eroding the right to dispose of one's labor freely, in conjunction with other laws similarly violative of other rights that are constitutive of capitalism (e.g., freedom of contract), will surely undermine the identity and, eventually, the legitimacy of the capitalist social formation. This is so because laws guaranteeing freedom to dispose of one's labor are not merely functional for capitalism; capitalism requires them to be what it is.

Our proposed solution will be effective, however, only if the dictates of the relevant natural law are susceptible to unproblematic ascertainment. This is seldom the case, though, because there are disagreements over what exactly the dictates of the natural law are. Yet, so long as there is agreement on what the natural law dictates are, the problem of the obligation to obey the positive law is amenable to easy solution in the manner specified above. To eliminate the possibilities of divergent subjective understanding of what the dictates of the natural law are, I argued in Chapter 2 that the natural law should be located in the social formation as one of its constitutive elements. It is likely to be easier to secure convergence on the nature of capitalism than to harmonize the several subjective conceptions of natural law that are abstracted from history and society.

If our theory stands, if one accepts the natural law of a social formation—that is, if one is committed to the rightness of the social ordering it entails, and one does not contend that the positive laws derogate in any radical manner from what natural law commends—then one has an obligation to obey the positive law. "Acceptance" is a crucial element in the obligatoriness of law. The acceptance of the positive law is predicated on the noncontestation of the natural law dictates that provide the foundation. So long as this foundation remains unchallenged, one can reasonably expect that any disagreements over the positive law will be contained within the framework of the structure of rights, entitlements, etc. constitutive of the existing social formation. This is the situation in a stable legal system. Under these conditions, it should not be surprising to find that when disagreements over positive law occur, the disputants always appeal to the natural law postulates of their social formation.

By way of illustration, it is not a rare occurrence to find that in struggles to organize unions under capitalism, the capitalists appeal to their right to freedom of contract and the workers emphasize their right to freedom of association, both of which freedoms are inherent in the structure of rights etc. constitutive of capitalism (i.e., the natural law of capitalism). So long as both parties believe that their goals are realizable within the framework of capitalism, they are likely to accept, or at least acquiesce in, judgments that try to harmonize these conflicting rights and create some balance in the social formation. It is a fact that the ruling class comes out the winner more often than not. Nevertheless, inasmuch as the ruled believe either that there are no better alternatives or that no matter how often they lose, the chances are still there for them to change the situation, they are not likely to challenge the natural law foundations: they will remain firm in their acceptance of, or acquiescence in, the legal system. They are not likely to question their obligation to obey the law. In a situation where the natural law remains uncontested, its normativity supplies the grounds for the obligation to obey the law. There is an obligation to obey the law if we "accept" the natural law of the social formation in the manner specified above.

It will be noticed that we have been talking about the obligation to obey law, understood as a legal system. What of the obligation to obey specific laws? What has been said so far applies also to specific laws and the obligation to obey them. However, a qualification is needed. For someone who accepts the legal system but who has to answer the practical question of whether or not to obey a particular law, our theory offers an answer that can serve as a guide but that may not necessarily determine an outcome. Indeed, it will be odd for us to find an individual who exhibits the attitude of acceptance but who consistently, at every opportunity, disobeys every law of the system. We would say of such a person that he or she has not really accepted the law or has not understood what acceptance entails. The reason for obeying or disobeying law and laws in society must ultimately be derived from extralegal considerations to be supplied by the nature of society, from general principles of social ordering based on some conception of what we are and what most conforms to it. Such an ultimate ground goes beyond the narrow confines of a theory of law and may therefore remain unstated in a theory like ours. It surely has a role to play in general social theory, which is beyond the scope of our work.

It might be objected that the requirement of acceptance introduces a subjective element into the concept of natural law. This objection supposes that objective arrangements are right or wrong in themselves, irrespective of how human beings think of and about them. The position adumbrated in the preceding paragraph does not suggest that acceptance alone constitutes the criterion by which we judge the rightness or wrongness of any social ordering. There is nothing in legal naturalism to deny that objective arrangements may be right or wrong objectively. It is possible that some objective arrangements are subjectively right (i.e., human beings see them as right) even when they are wrong objectively (i.e., wrong, regardless of the fact that they have been chosen by humans). Few people would deny that it was wrong of Nazis to have murdered millions of Jews or of American slaveholders to have held blacks as chattel. Needless to say, the basis for affirming the wrongness of the acts mentioned is most likely to be supplied by some assumptions about human nature and about what arrangements best conform objectively to the requirements of our nature. Whether these assumptions are supplied by theological or secular considerations is for the moment immaterial.

Human choices are relevant to the rightness or wrongness of objective arrangements. For human behavior is not merely consequent to these arrangements; it sometimes plays a role in how they are constituted. Human agency and its diverse manifestations are simultaneously the subject and object of these arrangements. Moreover, we have to be careful when we assert that human choices are irrelevant so as not to fall into the error of some species of natural law theory which maintain that there are some precepts which hold true *sub species aeternitatis*. As was made clear in the preceding chapter, I do not accept this point of view; nor do I concede that natural law theory requires any such assumption for its coherence. On our theory we can admit that some objective arrangements are objectively right or wrong while we maintain that human choices are not only relevant, in specific instances, but are what makes them right for us. The relevance of human choices means that what is objectively right or wrong will change in the course of time as human choices change.

So far, we have examined the problem of the obligation to obey the law as it applies to both natural law and positive law. There is a sense in which it is inapt to ask whether there is an obligation to obey the natural law of an epoch. The natural law exists independently of our desires, wishes, or preferences, although it is a product of human actions. It sets the limits of the possible range of positive laws within a social formation. So construed, we do not speak of obeying it; rather, we speak more appropriately of observing it. Once we know it, we can ignore it only at our own peril. The natural law here has more relevance to the task of positivization, or laying down the law, than it has to specific human conduct. It is more incumbent on the legislator to take cognizance of it than it is of the ordinary members of society.

In legal theory, too, knowledge of the natural law of our social formation brings to our notice the limits of lawmaking within the formation. Although we can exercise many options, the range is not boundless. For example, a generalized situation of laws that abolish private property, render profitmaking illegal, eliminate the freedom of contract, etc. will not merely undermine a capitalist society; it will convert its nature to a non-capitalist society. We cannot change the natural law of a social formation in the same way we can change our positive laws; we either learn to live with it (i.e., accept the social formation of which it is a part) or overthrow the social formation and, with it, its natural law. The task remaining is to describe how the natural law of an epoch gets realized *in concreto*. This is done in the next section.

v

Once it is granted that the natural law of an epoch is the ultimate source of the positive law and of the latter's obligatoriness, we should be guarded in saying that the ruling classes, or whoever else lawmakers may be in a specific society, make law. It is more appropriate to say that they *formulate* law. This qualification is necessary because I do not wish to fall into the same errors I have gone to great lengths to point out: lawmakers do not make law insofar as lawmaking is taken to mean a free, unrestrained or partially restrained exercise of will. Why may we not say that lawmakers make law except with the caveat I have suggested?

We may not because, in formulating the law, lawmakers are hampered by what I call an epistemological blind spot. Our perception of things always comes up against some degree of opacity. The situation in social cognition is not much different from what happens in the cognition of natural processes. Only the phenomena yield themselves immediately to us. To get to the essence behind the appearance requires more theoretical and practical effort. We should thus be less sanguine in accepting the self-images of any age. What this means in legal theory is that we should be less eager to admit that the ruling class is better able than other sectors of a society to decipher the hieroglyphics of social reality. On the contrary, we should always bear in mind that the ruling class, no less than the subordinate classes, sometimes lives in the world of the "pseudo-concrete." Of course, the ruling class does sometimes have the edge. Often it can call on the labors of the savants of the epoch—sociologists, economists, historians, philosophers, political scientists—to decipher the hieroglyphics of social process, and it can formulate policies accordingly. The task of the theorist is to reach beyond the appearance to get to reality—the unity of the phenomenon and the essence. In the present case, we should go beyond the positive law to the grounds of it. Legal naturalism asserts that deeper etiologies are possible for the positive laws in a society beyond what is supplied by the will and interests of the ruling class. Voluntarism, which is the opposite of this view, insists that the law is a product of the machinations of a power bloc behind the law, the nature of the problem this power bloc wants to solve, and so forth.

We do not deny that class will and interests have a role to play in the positivization of natural law. In fact, they are indispensable to it. Natural law is quite abstract, and human agency is the medium through which it is concretized. The ruling class has the responsibility of ruling. Thus, its members have a crucial role to play in the positivization of natural law. The process is bound to be marked by the will and interests of the class that undertakes it. In addition, it is possible that, with the progress of human society, the scope of willful social ordering will be widened and a better knowledge of the sociological laws operative in society will increase the degree of convergence between what we do and what our social formation requires. The possibility is part of the promise of postrevolutionary socialist and communist society. It does not appear that there will ever be a time when human beings will be able effectively to eliminate the gap between essence and appearance.

In light of the abstractness of the natural law of a social formation and the opacity of social processes, we should not be surprised that there is sometimes a noticeable discontinuity between the discernible natural law and the positive legal regimes in a social formation. Indeed, we should be more surprised that such discontinuities are not more widespread than they are. Added to this is the character of the sphere of positive law itself. The sphere of positive law is the realm where capriciousness, interests, blind alleys, false starts, and numerous other contingencies come into play. If we may call the realm of natural law one of "necessity," we may in similar vein call the realm of positive law one of "freedom." The sphere of natural law is one of constraints, limits, determinism. The limits of the epoch set the limits of the natural law even as the natural law is part of what makes the epoch what it is. Within these limits, the scope for lawmaking can be wide or narrow. In an emergent social formation the scope will necessarily be wide and can even include a large possibility of progressive legislation. For example, the history of capitalist legislation from its beginnings has witnessed a wide body of progressive legislation (relative to feudalism) which in our day has eventuated in the welfare state. The more mature a social formation is and the more its inherent possibilities are realized, the narrower the scope for progressive legislation is likely to be. So the assertion that the natural law sets limits must not be understood in a negative sense only. The limits sometimes indicate a direction in which progress could be made. Unless the epoch is transcended, its natural law cannot be set aside.

Things are quite different with the positive law. Human agency can fashion whatever positive laws its wildest, unrestrained imagination may suggest to it. A crazed tyrant, for example, can decree that people should not eat forthwith, or that men should write with their teeth. However, one could interpret legal history as showing that, in whatever age and place, human beings can be said to have, in the main, striven to fashion positive laws in accord with the natural law of their epoch, limited in their achievements only by the insufficiency of human knowledge and understanding of operative social forces, divergent interests, and similar contingencies.

If legal naturalism is correct, or at least plausible, if the lawmakers in a particular society know the requirements of the natural law of their social formation, and they are not subversives, they will strive to realize these requirements in their positive law.[47] The lawmakers' commitment to their

---

47. By contrast, subversives like Marx might know the requirements of the natural law of their social formation. In the interim they may, without contradiction or inconsistency, applaud the progressiveness of their epoch while insisting that a better mode of social ordering is possible. Marx had no difficulty speaking approvingly of the capitalist mode of production in comparison with the feudal mode of production, even as he savagely condemned the former for its many defects.

way of life is inseparable from a disposition to seek to realize the inner laws of their social formation in its purest expression. Consequently, a better explanation—better than that offered, for example, by class instrumentalism—for why the ideas of the ruling class are the ruling ideas might be that the rulers have, by virtue of their location in the social formation, the burden of ruling thrust on their shoulders. Even when they try not to, the objective requirements of their social situation impel them to legislate in accordance with their view of the world, their construction of reality, effected through the prism of their class affiliation, in the main.

By emphasizing the deterministic influences on the ruling class, the urge to class reductionism is diminished and the pressure of class instrumentalism is reduced in Marxist legal theory. The regulatory, coordinative, and other functions that the ruling class is made to perform on behalf of the whole society can be subverted to serve narrow class interests. But the ruling class, any ruling class, that pushes such interests to the fore does so at the peril of losing the confidence and consent of the subaltern classes. Hence, even when the ruling class is pursuing the narrow interests of its members, it must continue to cloak its pursuits in the rhetoric of general interest. Its claim to legitimacy does not rest on the undisguised pursuit of narrow class interests; rather, it is founded on the promise to cater to the interests of, if not all members of the society, at least the majority of them.

A positive legal regime is constructed within the limits imposed by the natural law of the social formation. A ruling class that has at its head individuals and factions who possess ample understanding of the operation of the social forces in their social formation, and who are not deflected by narrow factional interests, is likely to be more enlightened in its legislative practices and less likely to get into too many blind alleys and false starts in making positive laws that will ensure the smooth unfolding of the determinations of their social formation. A ruling class that has limited understanding, and is riven with internal contradictions, will be less enlightened. The fact that there can be divergences in the knowledge situations and interests of different factions of a ruling class suggests that the notion of struggles within the class must be taken seriously.

In a social formation that has survived and stabilized over time, the struggle among its ruling-class elements will not be very pronounced, and the discrepancies in their knowledge situations and factional interests will not be profound. On the other hand, in an emergent or newly emerged social formation, the divergences between the factions of the ruling class will be more profound and less amenable to harmonization. One can cite the fierce struggles among various factions of the ruling class in France in the middle of the nineteenth century which Marx so brilliantly analyzed and chronicled in *The Class Struggles in France, 1848–1850*, and *The Eighteenth Brumaire of Louis Napoleon Bonaparte*, or the equally vicious, sometimes violent, struggles in England between the landed gentry and the emergent bourgeoisie over factory legislation and unionization, meticulously reported and analyzed by Marx in the first volume of *Capital*. Struggles over the law within the ruling class are not bourgeois misrepresentations but real divergences in both the understanding of the class and the imperatives of the social formation which are more adequately explained in legal-naturalist terms.

So far, it has been argued that the ruling class, or whoever gets to lay down the law in a society, is determined and circumscribed in its actions by the natural law in the social formation. The next stage of the argument is to outline the modes of laying down the law: the *mechanics* of positivization.

VI

Marxist legal theory tends to emphasize legislation as the main means by which positive law comes to be. But the process of positivization is much more complex and multifarious. Legislation is only one mode within the mechanics of positivization. Instead of "legislation," I would like to substitute the omnibus category of *practice*. Why "practice"?

The notion of law without human beings interacting, infringing on one another's personal space, violating one another's entitlements, either as individuals or organized in groups, is meaningless. Even when law is natural law, we should not forget that it is a consequence of human action. It is no less a human artifact for being natural. As a human artifact, law—created as natural law and positive law—is the result of both conscious and unconscious practice. I have chosen the concept of "practice," therefore, because it supplies the needed flexibility to accommodate different modes for laying down the law. Whereas the practice that generates the natural law is relatively *spontaneous, inarticulate* and, sometimes, even *unconscious*, the practice that gives us the positive law is more or less *conscious, articulate* and somewhat *directed*. By adopting practice as the midwife of the process of positivization, I can accommodate the many modes of laying down the law that rarely appear in Marxist legal theory: custom or customary law, legislation, judicial usage, precedent, administrative lawmaking, etc.[48] All of the modes just enumerated are no more than instances of practice.

---

48. In what follows, my debt to non-Marxist jurisprudence will be obvious.

Legislation. Among the many strategies of laying down the law, legislation can be regarded as the most conscious, the most articulate attempt at realizing the natural law *in concreto*. We may regard legislation as every legal rule established by direct action of the lawmaking organs of the given society. In contemporary capitalist societies, the lawmaking organ is the state acting through the government: namely, the executive and the legislature. In other kinds of social formations the components of the lawmaking organs will be different: under feudalism, law was mostly made by monarchs and lords; in slaveowning societies, by the assembly of the slaveowners (as in ancient Greece) or the emperor (as in ancient Rome).

Legislation has received the most attention from Marxist legal theory and, in my opinion, the overemphasis on the will of the ruling class can be attributed to this concentration on legislation. It is possible to see in many legislative enactments the articulate and not-so-articulate will of the ruling class. But it is fallacious to hold that legislation always bears the stamp of its class origin. From what was said concerning the role of interests in the making and administration of the law, we can reasonably aver that in the majority of cases legislation must aspire to perform the coordinative, regulatory, and policing functions of society and present itself as the best means of accomplishing this task. It is true that the ruling class is limited in its aspiration by the constraints of its class interests and the refraction of its vision of what is best for the society. Yet, the generality, impersonality, and universality of legislation is not an accidental property. It is the realization of reason in law. Needless to say, reality can always mock the aspiration, but it is wrong to say that the aspiration is nonexistent. Sometimes it is difficult to separate the two. Where the aspiration bears the stamp of its class origins, it is only incidentally so. Just because legislation is not synonymous with class will, it does not follow that law is a "catalogue of [the] interests" that produce it.[49] This will underplay the strength of the class interests of the rulers and will give the wrong impression that every interest counts for the same in legislation. The fact is, *contra* Friedman's statement, some interests do predominate.

Legislation can take various forms. We should distinguish between (1) the programmatic enactments of the lawmaking organs (e.g., the Constitution), which specify the general norms by which citizens shall live, the terms of the relationship between rulers and ruled, and the limits of governmental power, and (2) the orders that the executive arm passes without

49. Lawrence M. Friedman, *The Legal System* (New York: Russell Sage Foundation, 1975), p. 150.

reference to popular institutions for the more mundane administration of the society's day-to-day affairs. The orders must satisfy the requirements of the programmatic provisions to be valid and obligatory. In those societies which are instances of the capitalist social formation, there is a hierarchy among the various strategies of laying down the law. Usually legislation is at the head of this hierarchy. All other strategies of laying down the law are subordinate to it.

The reason for the subordination, in my view, is to be found in the fact that legislation is the most conscious, most articulate, and most directed strategy for laying down the law. A society that is constituted within a stable social formation and that has a vast store of accumulated knowledge about deciphering the hieroglyphics of social process is more likely to trust its conscious enactments than it is likely to trust the spontaneous order of customs etc. In fact, the course of legal development can be fruitfully interpreted as a long march toward bringing more and more elements of social reality under conscious human control.

Judicial usage. Once legislation is enacted, one mode of laying down the law is completed and another is set to commence: judicial usage. I have adopted the term "judicial usage" rather than the more prevalent "precedent" because I think the latter term is too narrow to describe the source of judicial lawmaking. Judicial usage is not only less conscious and less articulate than legislation, but it is also given to disclaimers and disavowals in its development. That is to say, judges are not wont to admit that they lay down any laws, and such a tendency toward self-effacement sometimes makes this particular mode appear haphazard and inarticulate, even nonexistent. Moreover, legislation is deliberate creation; usage is only vaguely so.

It does not make a difference whether we are talking of common-law legal culture or one typified by a civil code. In non-common-law legal cultures, the laws in the Civil Code do not apply themselves. Law application is analytically distinct from lawmaking. Law application is meant to bring the general principles of the law to bear on particular cases. There is always room for judges, in a way to be discussed presently, to be involved in lawmaking.

One of the most heated controversies in contemporary jurisprudence concerns the question of whether or not judges make law or merely apply the existing law as may be found in legislative enactments (statutes, orders, etc.), customs, or the common law (in some jurisdictions).[50] The details of

50. See H. L. A. Hart, *The Concept of Law* (Oxford: Clarendon Press, 1961), chap. 7, and Ronald Dworkin, *Taking Rights Seriously* (Cambridge: Harvard University Press, 1978), chaps. 2 and 3.

this controversy are not germane to my concerns in the present chapter. Those who say that judges do not make law insist that judges do nothing more than apply the existing law to the case at hand. Those who say that judges do make law insist that laws are by nature "open-textured"[51] and that the meanings of statutes etc. are not always, or even usually, univocal. In situations where the judge is faced with ambiguities, equivocations, and gaps in the law, he or she legislates, using his or her discretion to resolve the given case.[52]

Legal naturalism recognizes that judges are active participants in the business of laying down the law. The effective execution of the law's coordinative, regulatory, and policing functions requires predictability and relative stability of expectations which will enhance the ability of those whom the law binds to order their lives in the hope that the law will not spring any surprises on them. One way by which this hope is fulfilled is through the institution of precedent: the expectation that the law applier will not be capricious and will treat cases alike that are similar in significant respects.

It is precedent and the crucial role it plays in law application that turns law application into a mode of lawmaking. Furthermore, legislative enactments cannot embody all the possible instances of whatever it is that they regulate. Thus, in specific instances, the law appliers must determine whether the case at hand is an instance of the general type with which a particular law is concerned. Their decisions, via the institution of precedent, hold implications for subsequent decisions that other law appliers will make with respect to similar cases. The implications are stronger the higher up a law applier is in a hierarchy of law appliers. Even when the decision of a particular law applier is not binding on others, the others can be expected to take judicial notice of the decisions of their peer.

Many jurists have written about how the process of judicial usage unfolds. According to C. K. Allen,

It must never be forgotten that the Judge has to review every precedent cited to him, not as a precise formulation of a general, abstract rule of law (like an article of a code), but as a concrete application of, or as an argument in favour of, some real or supposed rule of law. We say that he is bound by the decisions of higher Courts; and so he undoubtedly is. But the superior Court does not impose fetters upon him; he places the fetters on

51. Hart, *The Concept of Law*, chap. 7.
52. For criticism, see Dworkin, *Taking Rights Seriously*, p. 31.

his own hands. He has to decide whether the case cited to him is truly apposite to the circumstances in question and whether it accurately embodies the principle which he is seeking. The humblest judicial officer has to decide for himself whether he is or is not bound, in the particular circumstances, by any given decision of the House of Lords.[53]

And Benjamin Cardozo, in his classic *The Nature of the Judicial Process*, wrote: "We do not pick our rules of law full-blossomed from the trees. Every judge consulting his own experience must be conscious of times when a free exercise of will, directed of set purpose to the furtherance of the common good, determined the form and tendency of a rule which at that moment took its origin in one creative act."[54] In his book on legal reasoning, Lief H. Carter has not only argued that judges take part in laying down the law, but he asks that they come out openly to acknowledge their creative activities in law application. He insists that the creative activities of judges introduce a factor of unpredictability into the law. "The judge must choose the facts in the case before him that resemble or differ from the facts in the case, or line of cases, in which prior judicial decisions first announced the rule. The judge no doubt accepts his obligation, made powerful by legal tradition, to 'follow precedent', but he is under no obligation to follow any particular precedent. He completes step one by deciding for himself which of the many precedents are similar to the facts of the case before him and by deciding for himself what they mean."[55]

That law appliers sometimes perform a double function ought not to be in question. What legal theory should do is find out how they discharge this double function and what the real limits are on judicial lawmaking. Such limits will include the limits set by the existing legislative enactments and the general ones set by the natural law of the social formation.

Custom or customary law "Customary law is the primitive form of positive law," wrote N. M. Korkunov.[56] This description fits perfectly with the schema outlined in the present section. Legislation is the most conscious, most articulate mode of laying down the law; judicial usage is only less so; and custom is the least conscious or articulate of them all. It is an instance

53. Allen, *Law in the Making*, p. 290.

54. Benjamin Cardozo, *The Nature of the Judicial Process* (New Haven: Yale University Press, 1921), pp. 103–4.

55. Lief H. Carter, *Reason in Law*, 2d ed. (Boston: Little, Brown, 1984), p. 35. Carter calls this judicial freedom to choose the governing precedent "fact freedom."

56. N. M. Korkunov, *General Theory of Law*, 2d. ed. (New York: Macmillan, 1922), p. 410.

of "practice" nonetheless. "The great majority of customs are non-litigious in origin, and depend for their rise on de facto conduct and repetition."[57] When persons interact in society they give rise to various usages that the direct generators may not even be aware of but that their inheritors come to uphold and augment, with no other sanction than that it was the way their ancestors did things.[58] Antiquity serves as a badge of correctness and legitimacy.

In an order dominated by customs the existence of a custom is its justification. However, with the growing complexity of social formations, the further removed the inheritors are from the source of a custom and the less understanding they have of social forces, the more legitimacy is conferred on the custom. The antiquity of the custom is its justification. Where individuals and groups have acquired some greater understanding of social forces, customs are adapted to the needs of the age; only those customs survive which are relevant to the natural law of the social formation. In such cases, customs serve as positive laws and are so applied. Not all customs are legally relevant. Whether a custom is legally relevant or not will be determined by various tests,[59] the most important of which is the test of legality—by which I mean how well it fits with the natural law of the social formation and with existing legislation. I have illustrated the results of the three modes of positivization of natural law and their relation to the natural law (as described in Chapter 2 above) in a diagram (see "The Law Tree," next page).

Much of what we have been discussing will not be found in many Marxist theories of law. My aim in venturing into territory that Marxists have largely abandoned to non-Marxist jurists is to show that positive law, which is most amenable to class manipulation on the face of it, is itself a very complex phenomenon. As such, it is not enough to talk glibly about the class character of law: the class bias of each specific law may not always be obvious; it has to be established in each case. In the same manner, the class characteristics of entire legal regimes in the same social formation must be identified, and the variations and peculiarities must be extracted from painstaking and meticulous analyses.

---

57. Allen, *Law in the Making*, p. 147.

58. These various usages can be distinguished from the rules in which they are later expressed. When these usages first emerge, they are hardly appealed to in adjudication. They later acquire the form of regularities and are embodied in rules by which social conflicts are adjudicated. The rules represent a subset of usages. In most cases, at this level, they are marked by some measure of reflexivity.

59. See, for details, Allen, *Law in the Making*, pp. 130–46.

THE LAW TREE

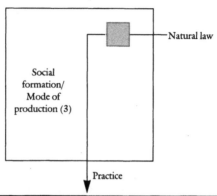

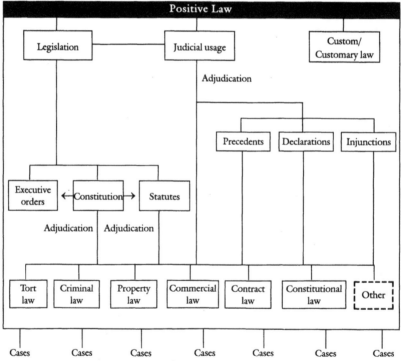

In discussing the various modes of positivization of natural law, I would accomplish another goal: to show how law is profoundly stamped by its class origins while at the same time it can be an object of class struggle. This will be shown by a brief examination of how juridical ideology comes to be and why it is possible for the subordinate classes genuinely to believe that law is on their side—even when, on occasion, they are wrong in their belief. Before doing that, however, it is necessary to integrate the discussion of the processes of positivization into the theory of legal naturalism.

VII

The natural law of an epoch sets the limits of the possible for the positive law of various societies belonging to that epoch. Legislation that profoundly departs from the natural law of the epoch would easily be dubbed "nonlaw" by the savants of the epoch. That is to say, those who are better at deciphering the dictates of the natural law of their social formation will use the natural law to evaluate the legislation concerned. If asked why they think the legal regime is the way it is, their ultimate explanation would be that it is in tune with whatever normative order their social formation embodies.

It is possible, and it sometimes happens, that there are members of the subordinate classes who understand the dictates of the natural law of the social formation. Sometimes, too, they take too seriously the bourgeois freedom of association, for example. Given that part of the "promise" of their social formation is the right to freedom of association, they must feel shortchanged, perhaps even outraged, by legislation that forbids unionization. The occurrence of different understandings of what their social formation presupposes in the area of law is one of the ways that the social formation attains ever-increasing consciousness of its presuppositions. Or, take a situation in which the working class's insistence on its right to freedom of association in unions points to a contradiction with the equally fundamental bourgeois right to freedom of contract. In such circumstances, the savants of the epoch—in the social sciences, judiciary, legislature, etc.—are forced to confront the tension. The resolution of the contradiction, either by harmonizing the two rights or by annihilating one of them, can only expand the understanding the savants possess of the forces at work in the social formation.

The business of discovering the presuppositions of a social formation, apprehending its many possibilities, deciphering the laws of its evolution, and creating appropriate laws in institutional structures is very important, even though it is seldom dealt with in legal theory. Much attention must be paid to the activities of the savants of any epoch, its intellectuals as it were, who in their disputations help their societies to conclude the business just referred to. The more sophisticated the mode of production, the more complex is its division of labor and the more differentiation is to be found in a society in which it is dominant. Judges, in adjudicating, are called upon to harmonize conflicting rights, to hold the tensions wracking a society in some equilibrium, so that the society is not torn asunder. At other times, judges are called upon to help a society find its way, to anticipate new developments, to establish emergent developments—to be sages and prophets, in short. Judges are not the only ones who perform this role. On occasion, judges have to depend on the labors and insights of others within the larger community of savants: sociologists, economists, philosophers, writers, dramatists, and the rest. Thus, a sophisticated society based on the capitalist mode of production can call upon the theoretical exertions of a large community of active thinkers whose sole or main business is to decipher, on behalf of the entire populace, the hieroglyphics of social process (MECW, 5:60). In consequence, such a society might be more adept at deciphering its natural law and acting to positivize it. This is a terrain eminently characterized by contestation among the many classes, groups, or factions that make up a typical society.

It is in this sense that class struggle over the positive law is real, and concessions may not be explained as mere sops that the ruling class throws to the working class. They are also readjustments the rulers must make if their claim to govern in the general interest is to remain credible. Of course, when the divergences in understanding shift from the terrain of positive law to the natural law of the epoch—that is, when what is at issue is the legitimacy and desirability of the social formation itself—those divergences become irreconcilable and the fight is to the death: one side must win out over the other, or both go down to destruction.[60]

When judges invoke policy and principle to justify their particular decisions, when legislators claim that a law is in the public interest, when social scientists warn that some proclamation violates a rule or principle, what they are doing can be interpreted as appeals to the underlying natural law of their social formation *as they understand it*. Sometimes legislators, judges, and others appeal to some transhistorical conception of justice or human rights. Even if there are such human rights, or the like, these are of greater interest to general social theory than to specifically

---

60. Recall the terms of Marx's advocacy discussed at the end of Chapter 2 above.

legal theory. Similar conceptions are appealed to in ethics to justify particular ethical judgments or in politics to justify given political arrangements. Nevertheless, when appeals are made to justify particular laws or legal judgments, those appeals must be analyzed for how much they share with what is conformable to the structure of rights etc. embodied in their social formation. The transhistorical human rights appealed to in these situations are often indelibly marked by the characteristics of the age. We should be less eager to take the words of the legislators on their face value. Whether the appeal is made to an existing way of life or to an emergent one is unimportant.

For example, the "ordinary reasonable man" standard of bourgeois law can be regarded as the juridical equivalent of the "rational economic maximizer" of bourgeois political economy. Oliver Wendell Holmes writes:

> Behind the logical form lies a judgment as to the relative worth and importance of competing legislative grounds, often an inarticulate and unconscious judgment, it is true, and yet the very root and nerve of the whole proceeding. You can give any conclusion a logical form. You always can imply a condition in a contract. But why do you imply it? It is because of some belief as to the practice of the community or of a class, or because of some opinion as to policy, or, in short, because of some attitude of yours upon a matter not capable of exact quantitative measurement, and therefore not capable of founding exact logical conclusions. Such matters really are battlegrounds where the means do not exist for determinations that shall be good for all time, and where the decision can do no more than embody the preference of a given body in a given time and place.[61]

It would seem that Holmes's point buttresses the relativism that is suggested by legal naturalism. Of greater significance is the fact that "the preference of a given body" is anchored on the body's understanding of the natural law of its epoch and what sort of social ordering it commends. An awareness of the relativism of the legal pronouncements of the ruling class might be a catalyst to the process of weaning the subordinate classes from their adherence to the existing legal order. This has implications for class struggle in and over the law.

I have tried in this chapter to tell the story of positive law. The aim has been to show the complexity of positive law, how it comes to be and how

---

61. Oliver W. Holmes, *Collected Legal Papers* (New York: Peter Smith, 1952), p. 181.

it impacts on the class struggle. I have argued that an adequate Marxist theory of law can address in an interesting fashion some of the basic concerns of the philosophy of law. The following chapter will consider the implications for the autonomy of law and juridical ideology of the processes described above.

4

On the Autonomy of Law

In a stable society based on a settled social formation many of whose determinations have become manifest in institutions and social practices, even though the law is made by the ruling class and often bears their imprint, what is remarkable is that law sometimes assumes the character of a common heritage to which rich and poor alike may lay claim. The rich appeal to law and the poor appeal to law and all expect, often unrealistically for the poor, that the law will find for them. "You win some, you lose some" seems to be the dominant orientation of litigants in a stable municipal legal system. Behind these activities lies people's belief in the justice of the legal arrangements and their outcomes—a belief, I suggested in Chapter 3, that is rooted in their acceptance of, or at least acquiescence in, the structure of rights etc. of the social formation and the positive laws founded on them. The farther away we get from the origins of a legal system and of the ruling class that dominates it, the more it seems that the law runs on autopilot. Litigants come before the law with a sense of its majesty, if not totally awed by it. Officials of the law endeavor to take seriously the law's impartiality, generality, and necessity. Judges sometimes are compelled by the law to render decisions that they themselves do not much like or that are not to the liking of the powers that be. Occasionally, the ruling class may appear to be powerless before the determinations of the law. Many people know that the law more often yields outcomes that are more favorable to the rich and the well-placed. Yet everyone keeps insisting that the law be made *autonomous* of private interests and factions. How did it come about that law's autonomy survives the admitted depredations of class and other sectional interests? It is my object here to show how the autonomy of law results from the developments discussed in the preceding chapter.[1] We shall also discuss the impact of this autonomy on the acceptance of the legal system in different societies. Section II deals with the institutionalization of law, a key component in the constitution of the autonomy of law. Sections III and IV, respectively, take up the consequences of institutionalization in the emergence of legal discourse and in the formation of forms of legal consciousness. A final section spells out the implication of law's autonomy for Marxist revolutionary practice.

II

Institutionalization. The practices of promulgation, application and interpretation, and enforcement of law are over time institutionalized in societies. The processes of institutionalization unfold in different ways in different places. But one can discern some general characteristics.

There are three general patterns of institutionalization. The first results from the *creation of formal institutions*. Formal institutions are the products of deliberate action on the part of appropriately authorized individuals or groups and are designated for particular purposes. In the case of law, depending on the complexity of the society concerned and the degree of social differentiation it has attained, the single most important instrument for the creation of formal institutions is a constitution (or any appropriate analogue). Constitutions are the birth certificates of modern legislatures and judiciaries. They specify the formal procedures for the election of legislators, their tenure, and their conditions of service.

Similarly, they contain provisions for the appointment and tenure of judges. In the modern state, the tenure of judges is purposely insulated from the vagaries of politics, and the modern commitment to the rule of law requires that the independence of the judiciary be a supreme ideal. Judiciaries are judged by how impersonal, impartial, and independent of the executive their operations are. The physical spaces exclusively designed for the operations of legislatures and judiciaries are turned into physical extensions of the institutions they house and are thereby endowed with an aura of majesty and importance. Such physical spaces become veritable shrines.

1. The expression "autonomy of law" refers strictly to the autonomy of the positive law; this is the sense in which I use it throughout this chapter.

Their desecration, whether by those who operate in them or by ordinary citizens, is taken very seriously indeed and is visited with the most severe sanctions. Ordinary citizens and officials alike are horrified by the phenomenon of the corrupt judge or other legal official. When judges subvert the law, the act is adjudged to be worse than when nonofficials do so.

Other formal institutions are created by constitutions and various enabling instruments. One example is the law school. Whether in its infancy, when legal education unfolded in the ambit of guilds, or in our day when it takes place in specially designated physical spaces—law schools—there has always been a motley of institutions devoted to the study of law and the training of lawyers. In a country like the United States where there is no centralized system of legal education, the training of lawyers and the institutional loci of this training are not brought into existence by enactment. Matters are much different in Nigeria, where there is a single law school that lawyers have to attend for a year after their university education, and in England, where the Inns of Court and some universities' law faculties are the primary places of training. In the United States, admission to the bar is organized by each state of the Union, while in Nigeria and England there are single, countrywide admission examinations. However the system of legal education is organized, what is of moment is that formal institutions specify the formal requirements for participation in the law as officials.

The legislature, the judiciary, and the system of legal education are complemented by a panoply of other formal institutions in which the law is institutionalized. Bar associations provide a forum where lawyers, an essential component of the legal system, can come together to pursue professional interests, to deliberate on the course of the law and its evolution, and to deal generally with matters ancillary to the operation of the legal system. The Body of Benchers determines the direction of legal education and who should be admitted to the practice of law. Thus is created a community of learned men and women: an intellectual elite that demands and is accorded special treatment by the rest of us. So far, we have been talking of one aspect of the formal institutions in which the law is incorporated. Of equal significance is the operation of these institutions and the rules that guide them.

Many of the activities that take place in the formal institutions are themselves the consequences of following formal rules for the operation of those institutions.[2] For instance, the United States Constitution specifi-

---

2. Formal rules are not the only rules that proliferate in formal institutions; they are a subset. In a moment we will be identifying two other kinds of rules.

cally vested judicial power in the Supreme Court. Thus, every time the Court performs its judicative function it is following the dictates of Article 3 of the Constitution. There are additional formal rules guiding the operations of the legal system. For instance, no court can initiate litigation on its own; it has to adjudicate in causes between parties that bring themselves before the courts. Furthermore, the scope for original jurisdiction in most appellate courts is restricted to fundamental constitutional questions.[3] The judicial hierarchy is rule-bound. There are rules of procedure regarding the placement of causes before the courts, the filing of writs, the use of injunctions and other remedies at bar, and so on.

In the case of legislatures, there are rules of order, elaborate procedures for the promulgation of legislation, and temporal requirements for a bill to become law.[4] Some of these rules have their origins in the instruments that established the institutions. But some postdate those instruments and have been subsequently enacted as rules of the appropriate institution. I discuss them together as aspects of formal institutions because they are the products of deliberate, directed human action.

The second pattern of institutionalization of law and legal practice is to be found in the *formalization of previously unstructured, freely evolving practices.* A good part of what was identified in Chapter 3 above as "judicial usage" comes under this category. Many of the principles that inform judicial decisionmaking, the practice of law at the bar, the procedures for filing papers in court, and so on started out in most jurisdictions as unstructured, freely evolving practices. Immemorial usage and proven expediency have with time led to their formal recognition as rules. The most significant of this species of institutionalization arise from the evolution of *stare decisis* in adjudication. The requirement to decide like cases alike com-

3. We should not overemphasize the importance of this requirement. The Indian Supreme Court has managed to find a way around this limitation. By reinterpreting the rules regarding *locus standi*, the Court has created a new category of "epistolary jurisdiction" under which social activists may act on behalf of the poor who either do not know their constitutional rights or cannot bring suit in their own behalf; these activists can initiate "social action litigation" by addressing a letter to the Court stating the particulars of the violation. The Court was motivated entirely by considerations of the plight of the poor and their inability to actualize rights guaranteed by the Indian Constitution. For discussions of this new type of jurisdiction, see P. N. Bhagwati, "Social Action Litigation: The Indian Experience," in Neelan Tiruchelvan and Radhika Coomaraswamy, eds., *The Role of the Judiciary in Plural Societies* (New York: St. Martin's Press, 1987), chap. 2, and Upendra Baxi, "Taking Suffering Seriously: Social Action Litigation," chap. 3 in the same volume.

4. I have omitted reference to the executive, of which the police/prison system is a part, purely for reasons of limited space. When necessary, I shall draw illustrations from the area of law enforcement.

bines with the need for stability of expectation and for reasonable assurance that the law will not retrospectively criminalize behavior to reinforce the pull of the order of precedent in adjudication. And thanks to *stare decisis*, common law and case law have yielded stable rules of adjudication extracted from centuries of accumulation of cases and from the findings of judges, who always essayed to elicit their *rationes*. Principles of adjudication all fall within this category.

The third and last form of institutionalization is the *consecration of conventions*.[5] Take the doctrine of collective responsibility in the British parliamentary system under which the entire cabinet tenders its resignation when the government loses a vote of confidence in the House of Commons. The practice has no formal enabling instrument; it was a convention that was later consecrated as a rule. How strong a rule it is has never been put to any serious test in Britain: no prime minister has ever failed to heed the demand of this convention. No law requires the prime minister to obey this convention; he or she is merely expected to. Many other conventions have become similarly consecrated. For instance, no law requires that all stand in the courtroom when the judge arrives; nor is it a formal requirement that the marshal of the U.S. Supreme Court shall, every day, gavel the Court to its feet and intone: "Oyez, oyez, oyez! Persons having business before the Honorable, the Supreme Court of the United States are admonished to draw near and give their attention, for the Court is now sitting. God save the United States and this Honorable Court." But this ritual has now become a rule, and it would be hard for those having business before the Court to think of it in session without this ritual announcement, without this consecrated convention. In judicial practice, examples of such conventions will include most common law rules governing the most important writs, especially those of *habeas corpus*, *certiorari*, and *mandamus*.

The manifold processes of institutionalization of law engender diverse consequences. They ensure that, with time, the history of law is not coeval with the biographies of the individuals who momentarily occupy the various institutions. Nor is it a catalog of their interests and predilections. That is to say, the farther we get from the origins of the institutions, the more recalcitrant they are to tinkering by members who momentarily occupy them, and the more their inheritors experience them as near-natural artifacts with

5. See Benjamin Cardozo, *The Nature of the Judicial Process* (New Haven: Yale University Press, 1921), p. 141, for a view of the force of what he called "consecrated principles" on judges.

power to coerce and shape the actions of individuals within them. Few young attorneys will deny the truth of the coercive power of the legal institutions within which they operate. They confront it everywhere they turn: the potential for loss when procedures for filing instruments are not properly followed, the salience of seniority at the bar, and the demand to defer to senior colleagues. Judges themselves are not spared the coercive consequences of the power of institutions: they have to renounce certain previous friendships and associations in order to meet the exigencies of impersonality, impartiality, and necessity. The institutional history of judiciaries and the body of case law that is built over time as a result of the adherence to *stare decisis*, as well as other institutionalizing elements identified above, all act to restrict the room that judges have to maneuver when they decide cases. Judges of lower courts must decide in accord with decisions previously handed down by superior courts. The requirements of comity enjoin judges to take judicial notice of the dicta of judges coordinate with them within the same region or in other regions. When possible, judges must strive to strike compromise among the many contending interests, rights, and entitlements that proliferate in a complex society.

Walter F. Murphy has identified five kinds of checks on judicial power. They are (1) "the restraint of public opinion," (2) "technical checks," (3) "institutional restraints," (4) "political checks," and (5) "judicial self-restraint."[6] Two of the checks—institutional restraints and technical checks—are of especial relevance to our discussion. In addition to the restraint that *stare decisis* provides, we have seen above that judges cannot originate proceedings; they must wait for litigants to bring cases to them. But once a case has been brought before a court, judges are restricted to deciding "only the issues which the litigants themselves raise." There are limits on what kinds of behavior are actionable at law and on who is competent or eligible to sue before the court. The issue at bar must be "justiciable"; that is, it must be "one which is suitable for determination by the judiciary, rather than a 'political' question, for which the Constitution delegates responsibility to one or the other branches of government." Finally, there are "limited kinds of remedies which are available to the Court to settle disputes."[7]

Apart from these technical checks, there are institutional restraints.[8] One such restraint is what is often acknowledged to be the paradox of ju-

6. Walter F. Murphy, *Elements of Judicial Strategy* (Chicago: University of Chicago Press, 1964), chap. 2.

7. Ibid., pp. 21, 22, 23.

8. See ibid., pp. 23–26.

dicial decisionmaking. The judge is called upon *to judge*; that is adjudication's raison d'être. Judging involves primarily the adoption of one outcome rather than another from a set of possible outcomes. Each of the parties to a dispute before the court is called upon to present its case and to support it from the plethora of precedents available in the relevant jurisdiction. Although the judge is called upon to elect for one outcome rather than another, he or she is required simultaneously by the institutional history of the law to suspend his or her own views and preferences and identify the outcome as one dictated by the law. This paradox has been variously described by practicing judges, and it represents one of the most significant consequences of the institutionalization of law. Here is a description of the paradox from Judge Learned Hand:

> The antinomy at the basis of a judge's work has been so often discussed that I can justify no more than a bare restatement of it. His authority and his immunity depend upon the assumption that he speaks with the mouth of others: the momentum of his utterances must be greater than any which his personal reputation and character can command, if it is to do the work assigned to it—if it is to stand against the passionate resentments arising out of the interests he must frustrate. He must pose as a kind of oracle, voicing the dictates of a vague divinity—a communion which reaches beyond the memory of any now living, and has gathered up a prestige beyond that of any single man. Yet the customary law of English-speaking peoples stands, a structure indubitably made by the hands of generations of judges, each professing to be a pupil, yet each in fact a builder who has contributed his few bricks and his little mortar, often indeed under the illusion that he has added nothing. A judge must manage to escape both horns of this dilemma: he must preserve his authority by cloaking himself in the majesty of an overshadowing past; but he must discover some composition with the dominant trends of his time—at all hazards he must maintain that tolerable continuity without which society dissolves, and men must begin again the weary path up from savagery.[9]

The contradictory requirements of the judicial function so eloquently described by Learned Hand are at the core of debates over the role of *discretion* in judicial decisionmaking. A related manifestation of the requirements is to be found in the ancillary debates over judicial activism and judicial restraint. Aside from these debates, judges are venerated or vilified

9. Learned Hand, *The Spirit of Liberty*, 3d ed. (Chicago: University of Chicago Press, 1977), p. 130.

according to how well or ill they are able continually to deal with the two horns of the dilemma apprehended by Hand and other analysts of law.

Certainly these restraints restrict the scope for judicial discretion.[10] Yet they are not absolutely inflexible such that judges may not creatively adapt them to changing specific circumstances.[11] In fact, judicial acumen is sometimes measured by how well a judge is able to use discretion, adapt existing law to changing circumstances, extract new meanings from old phrases, and generally move the law along in new directions while disclaiming any creative activities. In the words of Justice John Marshall Harlan (1833–1911):

> "The courts have rarely, if ever, felt themselves so restrained by technical rules, that they could not find some remedy, consistent with the law, for acts, whether done by government or by individual persons, that violated natural justice or were hostile to the fundamental principles devised for the protection of the essential rights of property." Off the bench, Harlan was even more candid. He once told a class of law students, "I want to say to you young gentlemen that if we don't like an act of Congress, we don't have much trouble to find grounds for declaring it unconstitutional."[12]

To the extent that judges are able to do what Justice Harlan boasted they could and still be able to pass it off as a determination of the law, they indeed manage to deepen the mystique of judicial power and enhance the esteem judges enjoy in public opinion. "The true test of judicial statesmanship throughout the Court's history, however, has been the ability to make this disclaimer convincingly while continuing to play a fundamental and positive role in shaping the development of the American state."[13] So far, I have described the impact of various institutionalizing processes on judicial practice. Analogous considerations can be adduced for legislatures.

Judges are not left without the necessary support infrastructure to ensure that the limits imposed do not hobble them or turn them into minions of the legislature or whatever other powerful forces may exist in society. Thus, in necessary deference to what we identified in Chapter 1 as the reason in law, serious efforts are made to insulate judges from the vagaries of political fortune and changing fashion. Although the ideal is

---

10. See Murphy, *Elements of Judicial Strategy*, p. 31.
11. See Mark Silverstein, *Constitutional Faiths* (Ithaca: Cornell University Press, 1984), p. 19.
12. In Murphy, *Elements of Judicial Strategy*, pp. 30–31, footnotes omitted.
13. Silverstein, *Constitutional Faiths*, pp. 26–27.

often observed in the breach, most modern polities strive to entrench the security of tenure of judges, to isolate and insulate them from social and political pressures. Likewise, generally congenial working conditions are established to enable the judges meet the exigencies of their station as savants of their respective communities. The following is not an atypical statement of the standard courts are held to: "The U.S. Supreme Court is in many ways a monastery of the intellect. To an extent, the framers of the Constitution intended it to be that way. Justices are appointed for life; they are not subject to popular recall or election; they are beholden for their jobs to no one and need not be swayed or intimidated by the passing moods, fears, fancies, or prejudices of a fickle electorate. This isolation enables the Court to protect the rights of the minority from the majority's tyranny with an impunity the system grants to neither Congress nor the president."[14] In the best of circumstances, judges and other officers of the law have access to research conducted by fellow savants in the universities, and they receive qualified support staff and technological resources that will make the discharge of their functions as problem-free as possible. Even in less auspicious circumstances, there is the aspiration to provide optimum working conditions for judges and other officers of the law.

One more consequence of the institutionalization of law deserves comment. The more complex a society is, the more sophisticated its mode of production and division of labor, the more complex its law and legal system are likely to be. It is true that in more primitive times, custom, morality, and solidarity mediate and govern human relationships. At the present stage, though, the area in which law operates is very narrow. With the growing complexity of social formations—manifested in the ever-increasing division of labor, the emergence of classes, and the undermining of kinship and community ties—the law comes to play ever-expanding roles in the mediation and governance of human relationships. As the sphere of law widens, the acts that are regulated by the law increase in number, such that the most advanced capitalist societies with the best understanding of their social formation are also the most litigious. Law has become so complex that it requires the exclusive attention of a professional group—lawyers—for its enactment, application, interpretation, and explication. The growth in the scope and coverage of law has rendered law unsusceptible to tinkering by ordinary folk. Even the most sophisticated and educated in any society can hardly trust their own lights to see them through

14. Michael D. Davis and Hunter R. Clark, *Thurgood Marshall: Warrior at the Bar, Rebel on the Bench* (New York: Birch Lane Press, 1992), p. 140.

the maze of law. As David Luban avers: "It is an obvious fact, however, that all of our legal institutions (except small claims court) are designed to be operated by lawyers and not by laypersons. Laws are written in such a way that they can be interpreted only by lawyers; judicial decisions are crafted so as to be fully intelligible only to the legally trained. Court regulations, court schedules, even courthouse architecture are designed around the needs of the legal profession."[15] The professionalization of advocacy has led some to affirm a unique logic of advocacy. It has also given birth to a debate over the morality of lawyering (Luban's discussion is seminal here). The system of legal education and the hierarchy that dominates the profession both help to reinforce the institutionalization we speak of. And if we are to adopt Oliver Wendell Holmes's view that "the law is made by the Bar, even more than by the Bench," it becomes even more important to pay close attention to the legal profession than is customary among Marxist commentators.[16]

The power of institutionalized law to coerce the choices of those who participate in it, its recalcitrance to change, its inertia, all combine to insulate the autonomy of law, within reasonable limits, from faction, fads and fancies, and expediency. It remains true, of course, that the law is sometimes perverted to the cause of faction or class interest. Law's autonomy persists not because it is free of class perversions or the predations of instrumentalism, but *despite* such perversions and predations. That ruling classes must pay more than lip service to law's autonomy, that they must strive continually to package narrow sectional interests in expensive wrappings, is our best evidence that the autonomy of law is not a sham. Insofar as law's aspiration to autonomy enjoys currency among subaltern or opposition elements in any community, it is unlikely that revolution will be on the agenda of those who sometimes lose out in the operation of law.

In the remainder of the present chapter, we shall consider two consequences of the institutionalization of law: namely, legal discourse and legal consciousness.

III

Legal discourse. The growing complexity of the determinations of the social formation, manifested in part by the institutionalization of law, has led to the constitution of a form of discourse peculiar to law and its insti-

15. David Luban, *Lawyers and Justice* (Princeton: Princeton University Press, 1988), p. 244.
16. Oliver W. Holmes, *Collected Legal Papers* (New York: Peter Smith, 1952), p. 25.

tutions. The language of the law is intricate, often arcane. The silences in the law, its ambiguities and equivocations, require full-time interpreters. Law schools, the Inns of Court, the judiciary, the solicitor's office, the articling year, and innumerable other institutions are dedicated to the socialization of the expounders of the law into legalese. Some observers have, with more than a little merit, compared one instance of the application/explication of law—constitutional interpretation—to the interpretation of sacred texts.[17] The peculiar form of law that we discussed in Chapter 1 is one reason why law has managed to engender a form of discourse all its own. It is impossible for law, any law, to embody all the instances to which it might be applicable. If it did, it would not be adaptable to changing circumstances; nor would it be able to make sense of fresh instances. That law, in its generality, has to be adapted to the particularity of a universe of cases and to the singularity of the specific case requires of the judge some *judgment* about the adequacy of the fit. The terms in which this is done, the many refinements that practice affords over the long haul, yield canons of legal interpretation. Hence the development of a legal hermeneutics that is the standard fare of legal education, judicial practice, and advocacy.

Others have affirmed that law has an immanent mode of reasoning.[18] The uniqueness of legal discourse can be illustrated in other ways. There is a *mode of presentation* of cases that typifies legal discourse. Counsel that refuses to follow this mode risks having the client's case tossed out. So great is the attention sometimes paid to procedural matters and to the technicalities of arguing a case that substantive issues have been known to get lost in the maze. Record keeping becomes central in a jurisdiction in which *stare decisis* is a cornerstone. There are modes of salutation and argumentation, of presenting evidence. On those occasions when practitioners appear to embrace nonlegal—e.g., sociological—evidence, the requirements of legal discourse compel them to render such data in legalese. Thus, when the U. S. Supreme Court appealed profusely to research data from social psychology in the determination of *Brown v. Board of Education*, it had to show that these data had legal-constitutional resonances; the doctrine of "separate but equal" educational facilities for white and black Americans was overthrown not because the doctrine wrought

17. Michael J. Perry, *Morality, Politics, and Law* (New York: Oxford University Press, 1990), pp. 136–45.
18. See Edward H. Levi, *An Introduction to Legal Reasoning* (Chicago: University of Chicago Press, 1949) and Martin P. Golding, *Legal Reasoning* (New York: Alfred A. Knopf, 1984).

havoc with black children, but because such an outcome *violated the equal protection clause* of the Constitution.

The impenetrability of legal discourse to ordinary folk, even if well educated, and its simultaneous indispensability to the cause of justice have led some to argue that there should be a right to the provision of legal services in a complex legal system. Such a case has been made by David Luban:

> Let us make an extravagant supposition. Suppose that a poor person decided to learn the law from scratch so as to be able to represent herself. Suppose that she was able (somehow) to obtain the first year casebooks and other legal texts; suppose that her educational level allowed her to read them; suppose that she had lots of leisure time for study. Suppose that she understood the principle of *stare decisis*, had the knack of "thinking like a lawyer," developed a taste for Byzantine reasoning, logic chopping, and casuistry. Even so, without a civil procedure course under her belt, she would almost certainly be unable to make sense of the most basic features of the cases she had read, namely why they were filed in one court rather than another, why the defendants were chosen as they were, and why the particular cause of action was alleged. These are, after all, questions of tactics as much as of legal doctrine. . . . The inescapable conclusion is that her supposed access to the legal system, based on the bare fact that no regulations forbid her from self-representation, is nothing but a joke.[19]

That representation by competent counsel is a requisite for justice in complex legal systems is one of the strongest indicators of the impact of legal discourse. The indispensability of lawyers and their monopoly on lawyering enhance their prestige and give them a freedom of action as professionals that is seldom matched in other areas of society.

IV

Legal consciousness. The processes of institutionalization and the emergence and consolidation of legal discourse are not without implications for human behavior, the structure of expectations, and the patterns of social interaction. Some of the consequences are discernible in the forms of legal consciousness that pervade societies where legal phenomena are present. The practice of promulgation, application, and enforcement of law induces those whom they affect or who take part in them to develop a view of the world shaped by law. This legally tinted view of the world is what I

19. Luban, *Lawyers and Justice*, p. 245.

mean by "legal consciousness." Forms of legal consciousness are many and diverse. And different individuals and groups exhibit these many forms in endless configurations. Some forms transcend differences of class and social status; others are professionally mediated, while yet others cannot be understood apart from class, ethnicity or sociopolitical affiliations.

Without prejudice to the play of class and other sectional interests in the operation of the legal system, I would like to suggest that there are forms of legal consciousness which are shared by members of society regardless of their class, ethnic, professional, or other affiliation. Law defines many aspects of human activity. Few are the acts that are not potentially acts in law. Under capitalism, everyone is a legal subject either as an autonomous actor or as the victim of someone else's action or as a participant—plaintiff or defendant, suspect, accused—in the legal process. As legal subjects, individuals come to believe that the law is the thing to watch out for, the first consideration before performing an act, legal or not. This continual concern with the legal implications of individual acts is an aspect of legal consciousness. So pervasive is this consciousness that even some people who wish to overthrow their social formation have to be weaned from an attitude that makes them define their struggle legally! Under capitalism, trade unionists, Marxists, and other revolutionaries are not merely mindful of the play of law in their lives and in the lives of their polities. Where it is required, they serve as jurors; they file suits; and often they seize opportunities to embarrass the ruling classes by exploiting the contradictory systemic imperatives of capitalism in order to make incremental progress toward a new social order. But their relationship to the mode of social ordering presupposed by the dominant mode of production is not solely instrumental. Many do "accept," in the way we have specified, the social arrangements based on capitalism, even though some think it is not the best possible system. Hence, oppositional forces file suits and fight court battles. They contest the rules regarding secondary picketing and sympathy strikes; they bring employers before the courts and other bodies established to adjudicate labor disputes. Ordinary people, apprised of the rights, privileges, immunities, and so on that are theirs under capitalism, insist on respect for those rights etc. and demand security in their enjoyment of them. Revolutionaries, too, before the final battle, always try to get the ruling classes to obey their own rules and respect the revolutionaries' enjoyment of those rights etc. Thus, oppositional forces are themselves not without legal consciousness.

The activities of the various institutions of law—law schools, legislatures, judiciaries, bar associations, and so on—are attended by considerable pomp

and ritual, solemnity and sobriety. The imposing architecture of court-
houses, the ornate interiors, the garb of the officers of the law, not to mention the arcane, impenetrable language in which the business of justice is
conducted, all redound to a huge authority-producing potential. By the
"authority-producing potential" of law we mean the tendency of the law to
overawe those whom it binds and to induce in them the appropriate attitudes of obedience to and belief in the law.[20] Consciousness of the authority-producing potential of law is general to all classes and groups in society;
however, its impact on the behavior of individuals and groups is differen-
tially realized. For example, among the lower classes, a feeling of impotence
before the law is much more pronounced than it is among the upper
classes, from whose ranks come the chief operators of the machinery of justice. The language of the law is alienating. The architecture of the law is for-
bidding. The knowledge that the judge is almost superhuman, an oracle of
a divinity, of Law, backed by the power of the modern state, can humble
the stoutest of humans. Except in torts, where the other party is likely to be
just another person like yourself, in most areas of law the ordinary citizen is
ranged against "the state" or the "attorney general," faceless abstractions
embodied in personnel whose effectiveness is determined by how well they
wear the garb of impersonality.[21] The hapless defendant in a criminal case
cannot appeal to the kindness, magnanimity, and so on of the officials of
the legal system, a signal indication of the nonhuman quality of the law.
You cannot plead your own cause no matter how sophisticated you are; before the law, you are incapable of speech. You must get yourself fitted with
a voice, a mouthpiece, what in Yorùbá is aptly called *alágbàwí*, ("one who
accepts to speak for you"): *your lawyer*. For the ruled, the combined effects
of the processes described above show themselves in an attitude that
fetishizes the law, places it on an awe-inspiring pedestal, and makes obedience to as well as acceptance of the law much easier. Moreover, the subordinate classes come to look upon the law as a natural artifact that they are
powerless to change but would do well to take into account in their actions.

The authority-producing potential of law resonates differently for the operators of the legal system. A good proportion of the training that future op-

---

20. See Thomas Mathiesen, *Law, Society and Political Action* (London: Academic Press,
1980), p. 87. Mathiesen's discussion of the authority-producing potential of institutionalized
law is the best I know of from a Marxist point of view, even though the research is based on
Norwegian society.

21. For one American judge's account of the impact of the processes just described on
black, Hispanic, and poor defendants in the courts, see Bruce Wright, *Black Robes, White Justice* (New York: Lyle Stuart, 1990).

erators receive in the law schools and in the offices of senior lawyers consists in the inculcation of a reverential attitude toward the law that sometimes verges on the idolatrous. Authority is everything and everything is authority: the authority of the law exacts respect for its immanent determinations; the authority of precedent acts as a damper on the enthusiasm of an overly activist judge; the authority of tradition and the gerontocratic ordering it enjoins intimidate the young practitioner into deferring to longevity at the bar; the authority of the superior court and the respect it coerces from the operators of the lower courts curbs any proclivity to iconoclasm on the part of the latter; and so on.[22] Little wonder that some have described legal education as "training for hierarchy."[23] This veneration of the law, this bowing down before its authority, can further be seen in the tendency among legal scholars toward the sacralization of law, the petrification of legal practices and, most of all, a strikingly uniform worldview within their ranks. Here is a partial explanation for the convergence of opinions and beliefs that characterize the members of the legal profession, broadly conceived. For those ensnared by this variant of legal consciousness it is hard to imagine a world bereft of the Supreme Court, the chief justice, lawyers, and the rest.

Finally, let us consider another variant of legal consciousness which also has contradictory manifestations for different groups and classes in society: a sense of justice. As I argued in Chapters 2 and 3, the natural law of a social formation provides the criteria of justice for those societies which are instances of it. In Chapter 3, it was argued that the positive law strives to embody this justice and that the functionaries of the legal system seek to dispense justice in specific cases in accordance with their understanding of what the natural legal foundations of their social formation enjoin. We have also seen that acceptance of, or acquiescence in, this natural law in part explains why people—rulers and ruled alike—obey the law; in part, too, it supplies justifying criteria for conforming one's behavior to the dictates of the law and for honoring the outcomes determined by those dictates even when, on occasion, one is hurt by these outcomes. This sense of justice encompasses a sense of the rightness of the social order; a sense of one's own obligation to preserve and enhance this good social order; a sense of the

22. "The longer I remained on the Criminal Court bench, the more I wondered why lawyers would forego the freedom of practice and the unfettered right of free speech to accept employment in a system that monitors conduct so closely. On those occasions when I have been before disciplinary committees, it has always been for speaking my mind, instead of minding my speech." Ibid., p. 77.

23. See Duncan Kennedy, "Legal Education as Training for Hierarchy," in David Kairys, ed., *The Politics of Law* (New York: Pantheon, 1982).

mutual forbearances that successful social living requires in the face of competing interests, scarce resources, and infinite wants; a sense that those who are charged with the onerous task of formulating, explicating, and applying the law have not become partisans of sectional interests; and, lastly, a sustained belief that, though it may fail on occasion, the law in the main works for the benefit of all regardless of individual social circumstances. For the ruling classes who, as part of their ruling function, make the law and try to discover the precepts of the natural law of their social formation, it is easy to see how such a sense of justice might be engendered in them. But this is not so for the subordinate classes. The ruled lack the power to make their will into law, and the dominance of the ruling class means that the law will be fashioned in their own image.

The subaltern classes are not without the form of legal consciousness that I call a "sense of justice." They sometimes believe that the law works for them, and this belief is not groundless. Every society tries to instill in its members a belief in the benefits conferred by their membership and for which they have certain duties imposed upon them. No ruling class can afford to flaunt its partisanship without risking the resentment of the other classes. On the contrary, every ruling class must process its class interests in general corporate terms as the interests of the whole society. It must work sedulously to cultivate the belief by the members of the other classes that its rule is right. Add to that the contradictory systemic imperatives inherent in the capitalist social formation and there is ample ground for the belief of the subordinate classes in the justness of their social order.

Thanks to this belief, suspects and convicts do not routinely question the legitimacy of their trials or the outcomes of those trials. Litigants routinely accept the decisions of the courts. In any stable society, for as long as the ruled remain steadfast in this belief, they are more likely than not to articulate their struggles *within the law*. Such is the tenacity of this belief that for many people, having their "day in court" is as important as prevailing. The willingness to struggle within the law might explain why ordinary folk are genuinely shocked when they think the law has been subverted by the ruling class, or why they accept their losses in litigation and think that if they, too, acquire property, the law will be unstinting in its protection. They are right, to some extent. It is true, as Lief H. Carter points out, that "judicial systems will not remain effective for long if losers regularly accuse the system of crumbling into an unfair power struggle in which the judge simply sides with the winner against the loser."[24]

24. Lief H. Carter, *Reason in Law*, 2d ed. (Boston: Little, Brown, 1984), p. 46.

The ruled sometimes move to force the rulers to live up to the "promise" of the legal system and its natural law foundations. Examples abound in the history of social and political struggles throughout the world. Anticolonial movements forced the colonizers to redeem the promise of *liberté, égalité, fraternité* for their colonial subjects. The struggle for the right to collective bargaining and union representation under capitalism fastened upon one of the contradictory systemic imperatives of capitalism: the right to freedom of association and assembly for its prosecution. The Civil Rights movement in the United States is another instance. In those cases in which Americans of African descent forced the Supreme Court to declare that the proclamations of the U. S. Constitution *do* include them and that constitutional protection must therefore be extended to them, they forced the ruling class to confront some of the implications yielded by the immanent principles of its social formation. These are good examples of how the ruled force the rulers to live up to the promise of their legal system. The following is significant as a description of the man who won the watershed case in the struggle for equal protection of the law in the United States:[25] "Thurgood Marshall was . . . an American patriot. He truly believed in the United States and the Constitution, but that the whole system was tragically flawed by the segregation laws. Wipe away those laws and the whole picture would change. Marshall and his colleagues were no rebels. They felt the social order was fundamentally good. What they wanted was the chance to share in it like men."[26] It is when the struggles of the subordinate classes can no longer be articulated in the terms of the legal system and the natural law of the extant social formation that revolutionary elements make their appearance or become salient players in the society.

v

Law's autonomy results from the interplay of the institutionalization of law, the constitution of legal discourse, and the formation of legal consciousness. Where institutionalization has a long history and legal discourse is highly sophisticated (both of which are a consequence of the stability of the social formation), the law appears to enjoy a lot more autonomy. Legal and other forms of social consciousness are deep-rooted and difficult to do away with in such societies. The repeated practices of

25. *Brown v. Board of Education*, 347 U.S. 483 (1954).
26. Davis and Clark, *Thurgood Marshall*, p. 24.

lawmaking, law-applying, and law-interpreting, of people filing suits, winning some and losing some, of legal officials being punished on occasion for violating the law—in sum, the continual demonstration of law's supremacy—reinforce the appearance of law's independence of class interests and, simultaneously, strengthen the hold of legal consciousness. Marxists and other revolutionaries who work within a positivist framework (whether of the economist, class-instrumentalist, or legal-ideologist variety) are apt to be bewildered by the phenomena we have described in this chapter. Given the tendency to reduce the law to class will, it is no surprise that they are stumped by legal phenomena in which class will is not immediately discernible or in which the force of reason in law has attenuated its impact. Their response is to describe the victories of the subaltern classes as false consciousness or as concessions that the ruling class makes to preserve its position. Contrary to this view, I argue that the subaltern classes' vociferous demands that the ruling classes play by the rules of their social formation are part of the general effort at deciphering the hieroglyphics of social process under capitalism—a process, as we saw in Chapter 3, that is marked by general contestations from the many classes in society. One does not become a dupe of the ruling class or a victim of false consciousness because one insists that the capitalist ruling class should respect the dictates of the natural law of its social formation. The structure of rights, privileges, immunities, etc. inherent in capitalism may not be, and for the Marxist it is not, the best possible. But it is wrong to suggest that it is a sham. Part of the reason that revolutionaries have not been able to wean people off the capitalist system is the failure to take seriously the natural law presuppositions of capitalism and the faith that ordinary people have, in the absence of a revolutionary ferment, in their ability to work to realize conceptions of the good and of the good life under capitalism.

Law, natural and positive, is always class law. It is formulated by the ruling class and its savants, even though other classes may have input in the ways described in Chapter 3. Yet, ruling-class control is limited in the many ways I have highlighted: by the opacity of social processes, inadequate knowledge, sectarianism, the impact of the unintended consequences of even our most deliberate actions, the demands of reason in law, and the pattern of class struggles over and within the law.

One salutary consequence of taking seriously the autonomy of law and the multiplex character of the capitalist social formation is that there may be more room for Marxist legal practice under capitalism than the advocates of economism, class instrumentalism, and legal ideologism anticipate. I take it that this book is proof that a more nuanced analysis of law is possible within Marxism. Marxists who are cognizant of the possibilities within capitalism can make several moves without abandoning their commitment to revolution. Like Karl Marx, they could accept capitalist law as a quantum leap forward in the human condition while still maintaining that humanity is capable and deserving of a better social order. Furthermore, working within the system does not require the assumption of apostasy or instrumentalism. Only those who believe that the Marxism–law relationship is one of mutual exclusion would insist that Marxists cannot work within capitalist law without becoming apostates. The difference between Marxist lawyers and their non-Marxist counterparts is that while the latter may be persuaded that capitalism is the best possible social order, Marxist lawyers have a limited faith in and a qualified acceptance of capitalism. They never abandon the imperative to change the world. The problem of change in law is the subject of the next chapter.

5

Change and Continuity in Law

"Change is a paradoxical idea. It is the notion of alteration combined with the notion of remaining the same. If there were no alteration there would be an unbroken sameness; if there were no remaining the same there would be the recollection of that which had unaccountably gone and the observation of that which had unaccountably appeared. . . . The idea of change is a holding together of two apparently opposed but in fact complementary ideas: that of alteration and that of sameness; that of difference and that of identity."[1] The preceding passage from Michael Oakeshott occurs in the context of a discussion of the concept of historical change. However, it neatly encapsulates the problem posed by the title and theme of the present chapter. We have seen that natural law is a constitutive component of some modes of production or social formations. Positive law strives to embody the precepts determined by the natural law presuppositions. Modes of production are notoriously historical: they come into being, they mature, and they become extinct. If modes of production are historical, and if the natural law of a mode of production is indissolubly bound to it, it follows that natural law is not, and may not be, transhistorical. Given that natural law is historical, the question to ask is: How do changes occur in natural law and from one natural law to another? We also must explain how and why it often happens that the positive laws from

1. Michael Oakeshott, *On History and Other Essays* (Oxford: Basil Blackwell, 1983), p. 98.

one epoch, based on one mode of production, survive and serve in a different epoch based on another mode of production. That is to say, we must explain how the positive laws of an epoch can survive the demise of the natural law of that epoch. In essence, we need to explain how change and continuity cohere in law.

In this chapter, we analyze the dialectics of change and continuity in law. Three principal sets of questions will occupy us. In the first place, we ask: *What is the nature of change in law?* Is it that when law changes, there is an absolute discontinuity between what went before and what came after? Or is it that some modicum of continuity is preserved in the change? Or is change a spurious concept, and is it only continuity that obtains? Secondly: *How does change come about in law?* Does change take place in one fell swoop, as in a revolution, or does it occur only incrementally as in reforms? Does change occur through imposition or through borrowing, coup d'état, legislation, devolution, or chance? Lastly: *Why does law change?* Does law change because of change in society, the emergence of new tasks to be performed, new knowledge of old tasks, desuetude, or other factors?

II

The problem posed by the dialectics of change is that of explaining what is involved when Oakeshott calls change a "paradoxical idea." Perhaps nothing is more obvious in our world than the fact that things change. Yet we see evidence of continuity in spite of change. The problem is well formulated by Oakeshott: "The idea of change is a holding together of two apparently opposed but in fact complementary ideas: that of alteration and that of sameness; that of difference and that of identity."

The theorist is called upon to explain how the dialectic of complementarity is worked out so that we can speak of change even while we can still identify elements of what went before in what has just emerged. Since we are concerned with a given regional discipline, law, our task is to explain at the most general level how the complementarity of change and continuity unfolds in the area of law. We shall begin with a general discussion of change and continuity and then go on to elucidate the applicability of the discussion to law. The following discussion deals with the first set of questions on the nature of change in law. Is change a radical discontinuity or a partial transcendence? As Oakeshott notes, change and continuity are dialectically linked in such a way that if we can explain the nature of change in law, we will have also have explained the nature of continuity in law.

Central to the concept of change is the idea of alteration. When we say that something changes, we mean that it alters from a given state at the beginning of the process to another at the conclusion of the process. However limited this alteration is, for our talk of change to be intelligible the new state of the thing that changes must be in some significant respects different from its state prior to the change. Therefore, difference is a constituent element of change. However, even as a thing changes, there is *some thing* that is the subject of the process. To speak intelligibly about the thing that undergoes change, we must retain some aspect of the thing that will enable us correctly to make the judgment that the thing has changed. That is say, no matter how radically a thing changes, enough of its original character must be left in it at the conclusion of the process to permit us to refer to the same thing as the thing that changed. For if we lost all the original traits of a thing as it changed, the nexus that enabled us to predicate of the same subject that "it" had changed would be lost. When that happens, it is inappropriate to talk of the thing having changed; it is more appropriate to talk of the thing's destruction. A similar situation presents itself when "the thing" refers to an aspect of social life. Let us take an institution like "the University of Ife," for example.

Let us say that "the University of Ife" has changed a great deal in the past twenty-five years. The landscape has changed, the demographic makeup has changed, the methods and content of instruction have changed. When it is predicated of "the University of Ife" that it has changed, we are not saying that each of the things just outlined has changed in the university. At least that much is true. Rather, we are saying that these things which are all components of "the University of Ife" have changed such that the ensemble of which they are the units has itself changed. Throughout, the subject—the University of Ife—remains constant and privileged in all these changes. From one state of being to another "the University of Ife" survives the changes in its component units but is itself changed as a consequence of the changes in its units. "The University of Ife" is thus the subject of the process of change which alters through time, but it retains enough of its original identity to enable us to say that "the University of Ife" has changed. "The University of Ife" is more than a mere phrase, a simple designator. It refers to something, sometimes tangible, often intangible; it is the framework in which all the relevant changes unfold. This something which perdures as the subject of the process supplies the necessary element of continuity that, for Oakeshott, is integral to change.

But "the University of Ife" is an institution made up of people and their relationships. Even though its membership keeps changing, what it is that has the membership is the constant element that enables us to refer to it as the subject of change. It is in virtue of the constant element in the subject that the identity of "the University of Ife" is preserved through the many changes it has undergone. This continuity of identity through change is the continuity that is indispensable to an understanding of change. Put differently, change—when it does not refer to destruction, to a loss of the thing—always contains a moment of continuity, and the preservation of identity in continuity is necessary to a comprehension of change. This is the point of the quotation that opened the present chapter.

It is what I think Oakeshott meant when he affirmed that "[change] is the notion of alteration combined with the notion of remaining the same." Similar considerations will apply, *mutatis mutandis*, to other institutions that undergo change. The preservation of identity through change in the continuity of some basic components that define the subject of change is crucial, not just to the recognition of the institution concerned but also to the preservation of appropriate behavioral attitudes on the part of individuals and groups. If, for example, in the absence of a revolution, an institution were to alter so radically that this basic identity was lost or severely modified, many for whom the institution still had salience could be expected to resist. They would likely deem the new entity illegitimate and, therefore, undeserving of their allegiance. This is one reason why law reform must remain anchored in some basic unchanging or imperceptibly changing principles in order to continue to hold the acceptance of those whom it binds. And it is why constitutional interpretation in a municipal legal regime based on a stable social formation cannot exceed the bounds of its legitimating natural law without provoking the ire of those who remain committed to its natural law foundations. For an illustration, consider the following criterion of exclusion from eligibility for membership on the Supreme Court of the United States: "no Senator should vote to confirm any candidate who believes that the Constitution's guarantees of equality before the law require the complete abolition of private property and contract."[2] In other words, the inviolability of the right to private property and freedom of contract marks the outer limits of possible law reform or constitutional interpretation in a legal regime founded on the capitalist social formation. It needs be pointed out that one direct consequence of the dialectic of complementarity is that, as will be explained below, change in law may not be construed as a radical discontinuity be-

2. Laurence H. Tribe, *God Save This Honorable Court* (New York: Random House, 1985), p. 96.

tween what went before and what comes after a change, even a revolutionary change.[3]

This is where the relevance of the foundations laid in Chapters 2 and 3 above is most obvious. In Chapter 3, it was said that the positive law in any particular society is the total system of more or less consciously adopted rules, regulations, procedures, etc. which exists in a given society and which is generally regarded as binding by the members of that society and widely accepted by them. What gives this legal system its identity is that it is the legal system of a society. So long as this society remains in existence, no matter what changes the constituent elements of the legal system go through, we will still be able to say that the legal system of the relevant society has changed. The element of identity is supplied by the continuity of the society, albeit the fact of change is recognized in our predication of the legal system that it has altered from one state to another. So the society continues and the law changes. But the society serves the same purpose for several other institutions and practices. We therefore must have a more specific analysis that allows us to make sense of law as a regional discipline and autonomous practice but that does not lose sight of the fact that the social existence in which law participates remains crucial.

Moreover, it is not every change in law that represents a significant alteration from one state to another. After all, as Lawrence Friedman aptly puts it, "not every change in a legal system is major change; most change is quite minor. Any alteration, even adding a comma to a statute, is an instance of change in the law."[4] It is necessary to distinguish different kinds of change and the levels at which they occur if we are to make sense of the nature of change and continuity in law. Before that, however, one branch of the analytical structure of legal naturalism remains to be integrated into the discussion.

So far in this section, reference has been made only to the positive legal system in a given society. But ours is a natural law theory. Where does natural law fit into the problem of change and continuity in law? Societies are particular species of social formation. The positive laws of specific societies are founded on the natural law of their social formation. The natural law of the social formation (or mode of production) sets the limits of the possible positive laws in concrete societies. Within these limits, positive legal

3. For this reason, theories of radical discontinuity must be rejected. One such theory is that of Hans Kelsen in his *General Theory of Law and State*, trans. Anders Wedberg (New York: Russell & Russell, 1961).

4. Lawrence M. Friedman, *The Legal System* (New York: Russell Sage Foundation, 1975), p. 269.

systems can be diverse and can unfold to considerable levels of richness and complexity over time.

It follows, then, that in the sphere of law the positive legal system can evolve and change over time and still remain within the limits of its underlying natural law, retaining its identity. In this sphere the identity of a positive legal system is preserved, through change, in the continuity of its natural law foundations while the identity of the natural law is preserved in the continuity of the social formation or mode of production or epoch of which it is a constituent element. We distinguish between changes in specific components of a positive legal system (e.g., writing a new constitution or enacting new legislation affirming human rights)[5] and changes in the positive legal system as a whole consequent upon significant changes in its component units (e.g., devolution of power from a colonial power to a newly independent country, the enactment of legislation creating the welfare state under capitalism, or the emergence of state-regulated monopoly capitalism) and change in the natural law (e.g., the transition from feudal law to capitalist law). For these purposes we identify two major categories of change in law: epochal changes and changes within epochs.

III

Epochal changes correspond to changes from one social formation or epoch to another. In history and sociology this will be used to describe the change from feudalism to capitalism. In law it refers to the transition from the natural law of feudalism to the natural law of capitalism, or from a prelegal world to a legal world. This is the most radical kind of change, and it can aptly be characterized as "foundational change." *Changes within epochs* correspond to changes that do not breach the foundational elements of the epoch but are essentially an evolution of social forms which the epoch allows. In history and sociology such changes include the unfolding of the capitalist mode of production from the era of competitive capitalism to the contemporary period of monopoly capitalism (e.g., in the United States of America) to the state-supported capitalism of countries like Japan, India, and Brazil. In law, changes within epochs embrace the evolution of capitalist law from, say, the period in which contract was almost deified to the contemporary period, in which some even find it apposite to speak of "the death of contract."

5. See my diagram, "The Law Tree," in in Chapter 3 above.

In these two broad categories of change, the element of continuity is located in whatever is the more inclusive form of social life of which the other is a part. In the case of epochal changes, the element of continuity is supplied by the survival of human society (of which the social formations are particular expressions). In the case of changes within epochs, the element of continuity is found in the constancy of the social formation (of which the specific societies undergoing the changes are instances). To make sense of change in law we must be clear at what level we are speaking. Once we are clear about what level of change we are looking at, we can begin to unravel the nature of change and continuity. Legal naturalism is not a theory of absolute discontinuity. It does not seek to obscure the paradoxical nature of the idea of change. On the contrary, it confronts it and establishes the dialectical link between change and continuity. How, then, do we explain change in law?

The starting point should always be a complex whole, a totality. To explain change in the positive law we should look at the whole legal system and try to separate its various parts and their differing strengths. To explain the transformation of one capitalist positive-legal system to another (e.g., in the case of devolution) we should proceed from the social formation, its constitutive natural law if it has one, and the various positive legal regimes it has engendered. If we proceed in this way, we are likely to find that there is never an absolute discontinuity between one state of being of a social artifact and another.

In the evolution of legal systems—natural and positive—the features that come to be dominant in the aftermath of change, especially epochal change, usually start out as embryonic forms in the old configuration. Although the new configuration of the social whole is identified by its dominant form (e.g., capitalism), its erstwhile dominant moment (e.g., feudal forms) does not immediately become extinct; it becomes for a while a subordinate, sublated element in the new dispensation. There is no obliteration; rather, what we have is a *supersession*. Between the time this process commences and the time it is consummated in the emergence of a new social whole, we have a period of *transition*, the high point of which is reached when the two moments—the hitherto dominant and the erstwhile subordinate but emergent dominant—are about equal in strength. At such points it is difficult to identify the social whole. Before these abstract reflections are concretely applied to law, I must first dispose of a possible objection.

If what I have said so far is true, then it may be objected that legal naturalism does not accommodate, because it cannot recognize, revolutionary transformations—that it smacks of gradualism. If so, then its Marxist pedigree is suspect. After all, Marxism prides itself on being the science of revolution par excellence. Additionally, revolutions occur in history and, when they do, they are quite abrupt. Therefore, the objection concludes, while the theory will do for gradual transitions, it is irrelevant to an understanding of revolutionary transformations.

Certainly revolutions are necessary, and it will be a hugely impoverished theory that fails to provide the tools for their analysis and explanation. So this objection appears plausible. But its plausibility is purchased with a dubious currency. The objection works because of an implausible construal of the nature of revolution. It assumes dubiously that revolutions cannot be accounted for by a theory that refuses to admit absolute discontinuity in history. More dubious still, it assumes that revolutions are instances of absolute discontinuity, that between a prerevolutionary and a postrevolutionary regime there is a total break represented in the annihilation of the prerevolutionary order of things.[6] This is the point of view that David Braybrooke has caricatured as the "Extravagances of Total Change."[7] Braybrooke argues that this point of view is unintelligible and incoherent as an articulation of what revolutions accomplish or can accomplish. It is unintelligible precisely for the reasons stated in our discussion of change. Change is a continuum that requires a nexus between the beginning of the process and its end. Unless it can be shown that annihilation is not synonymous with the destruction of the subject of change, it is unintelligible to speak of revolutions as marking absolute and abrupt annihilation of the prerevolutionary order of things.

One may posit continuity in the process of change without eliminating revolutionary change. Periods of foundational change are marked by the maturing of the new forces that are responsible for discrete changes within the social whole. It is true that foundational changes are marked by ruptures, rapidity, and the semblance of absolute discontinuity. Yet we should not be deflected by these momentary phenomena from identifying the moment of continuity in them. For if we are, we will be stumped by the

6. Consider Hans Kelsen. For him, after a revolution a considerable body of norms from the old order cannot survive in the new. Between the old, overthrown constitution and the new constitution, "continuity holds neither from the point of view of the one nor from that of the other. Thus, it is never the constitution merely but always the entire legal order that is changed by a revolution." *General Theory of Law and State*, p. 118.

7. David Braybrooke, "Revolution: Intelligible or Unintelligible," in Robert H. Grimm and Alfred F. MacKay, eds., *Society: Revolution and Reform* (Cleveland: The Press of Case Western Reserve University, 1971), p. 95.

revolution's aftermath, in which there is a lot more continuity than the theorists of absolute discontinuity are willing to accept. Unless this measure of continuity is presupposed, especially on the morrow of the revolution, we will be hard-pressed to understand why so much of the old persists in the new order.

In cases of epochal change in law, the elements of the new epoch have germinated in the body of the old.[8] Let us take an example: feudal law. In its many expressions, feudal law was built on the personal relationship of lord and serf. This relationship guaranteed the privileges of the lord and the obligation of the serf to render personal services to the lord in lieu of usufructuary rights to land under the control of the lord. The lord could requisition services from his serfs, and the serfs did not own the land that they worked. Labor mobility was limited, for the serf's obligation to the lord was lifelong and was passed on to the serf's offspring. However, the bourgeoisie that was later to supplant the manorial lords got its start in the ranks of the artisanal serfs of feudal society. This future ruling class, living on the fringe of feudal society outside the manorial walls, introduced subordinate legal institutions that would later become the dominant legal structures of bourgeois society. I draw historical support from Michael Tigar and Madeleine Levy:

> The great achievement of the bourgeoisie in [the period between A.D. 1000 and 1200] was to wrest from seigneurs in hundreds of separate localities the recognition of an independent status within the feudal hierarchy. The urban movement began in the lower orders of society; many of its members were serfs. It demanded one major concession from the seigneur: a charter, drawn in accordance with the law of the place, setting out that there existed—as there had not existed before—the status of *bourgeois*, *burgher*, or burgess, and establishing that this status implied certain rights and duties.[9]

---

8. This is a very controversial theme in Marxist studies of the transition from feudalism to capitalism. There are those who argue that the main impetus for the emergence of capitalism was provided by factors external to the feudal social formation. Opposite them are those who argue that the roots of the capitalist social formation were already present in the soil of feudalism and that whatever external factors might have been at work only strengthened these roots, they did not create them. As the statement I just made indicates, I agree with the latter point of view. For more on this controversy, see Rodney Hilton, ed., *The Transition from Feudalism to Capitalism* (London: Verso, 1978). See also Maurice Dobb, *Studies in the Development of Capitalism*, rev. ed. (New York: International Publishers, 1963).

9. Michael Tigar and Madeleine Levy, *Law and the Rise of Capitalism* (New York: Monthly Review Press, 1977), p. 111.

This process led to the emergence of chartered cities with different legal systems—existing side by side with seigneurial holdings, administering their own affairs, directly responsible to the princes and kings who, more often than not, were beholden to them for loans to finance their courts. "[B]y the beginning of the eleventh century, the bourgeoisie had carved out areas of autonomy within the feudal system, enclaves within which economic and legal relations were conducted differently than they were on the manors." Thus came "laws that the merchants made for themselves, the legal system they fashioned to serve their own interests. First they set up tribunals to settle disputes among themselves, then wrested or cajoled concessions from spiritual and temporal princes in order to establish zones of free commerce, and finally—over a period of centuries—swept to power over nations."[10] When in the eighteenth century the French bourgeoisie stood at the head of the French people in a final showdown with the forces of the feudal regime, that showdown represented the maturation of forces generated within the feudal epoch; it was not some sudden, inexplicable, discontinuous historical thunderbolt. The transition from feudalism to capitalism was quite long; but even if it had been shorter, our point would still stand. The crucial point about the transition is not its duration but its significance as the crucible in which the struggle between the old and the new is fought out in its final stages and as the crisis which sees the victory of the new over the old.

Such transitional periods are often characterized by what is generally called "dual power" or "dual sovereignty." Whatever its nomenclature in law, it is that phenomenon in which two systems joust for dominance in human society: the old is too weak to predominate, and the new is not strong enough to assert itself. In the transition from feudalism to capitalism this phenomenon was expressed in a dual legal order: the emergent bourgeois order in the cities, which were growing in size and importance, and the waning feudal order in the declining manors. In the twentieth century, an epochal transition in revolutionary Russia yielded another dual order: the new, fast-consolidating government of the Soviets of Workers' and Soldiers' Deputies and the fast-declining bourgeois judiciary. The transition in the Soviet Union was quite short. The Soviets emerged in St. Petersburg in 1905, survived tsarist suppression and, later, became the base of an alternative government to the Aleksandr Kerensky regime in October 1917.[11]

10. Ibid. pp. 91, 5–6.
11. We are now witnessing new periods of transition throughout Eastern Europe, Asia, Africa, and Latin America. In present-day Russia, the transition is toward capitalism and, significantly, the character of the new society is still indistinct; and it is not clear who exactly is in charge. The old Soviet system is moribund, but the new system is visible only in outline.

Clearly, then, we may enlist the support of history for our theory of change in law as it relates to epochal changes in law. The outcome of these transitions was the emergence of a new social formation with its own natural law. These were revolutionary transformations not in virtue of the instantaneity of their emergence or victory but in comparison with the character of the regime that prevailed before them.

Given that these transitions are not illustrative of absolute discontinuities, we can assert that those elements (e.g., rules that regulate interpersonal relationships, the operation of essential services, etc.) which are essential to the survival of human society will contribute significant elements of continuity. These elements are likely to be the best that the overthrown system could offer; they will now be appropriated and absorbed into the new order within the limits of its natural law presuppositions.[12] Survivals can therefore be accommodated. We should not expect to find survivals that are profoundly incongruous with the natural law presuppositions of the new social formation. But if there are some, we can confidently assert that they will not, cannot, be dominant elements in the new social formation. Nor are they likely to be (cannot be) survivals of the defining feature of the old natural law or social formation. For example, the division of labor peculiar to the feudal mode of production could not be sustained in a mode of production in which the mobility of labor and the separation of the laborer from his or her labor power are constitutive.[13] Nevertheless, the farther away we get in time from the origins of the new social formation subsequent to an epochal change, the less likely it is that the survivals will be many or prominent. They are more likely to become bathed in the ether of the new natural law and to become differently validated/legitimated. In some cases they might even become extinct and fossilized; in others, they will fall into desuetude; in yet others, they will survive only by sheer inertia.

12. Speaking of a similar phenomenon in the evolution of law within the same epoch, Benjamin Cardozo wrote: "The work of a judge is in one sense enduring and in another sense ephemeral. What is good in it endures. What is erroneous is pretty sure to perish. The good remains the foundation on which new structures will be built. The bad will be rejected and cast off in the laboratory of the years. Little by little the old doctrine is undermined. Often the encroachments are so gradual that their significance is at first obscured. Finally we discover that the contour of the landscape has been changed, that the old maps must be cast aside, and the ground charted anew." *The Nature of the Judicial Process* (New Haven: Yale University Press, 1921), p. 178.

13. Historical confirmation for some of these postulates can be found in the nonconsummation of the revolutionary transformations of the former European colonies and in the survivals that have contributed to the grotesque distortion of their social and economic identities. Nigeria is a very good example.

What about changes within epochs? Can there be fundamental changes within epochs? Can changes within epochs translate into epochal changes? In this discussion I reserve the expression "fundamental changes" for epochal changes only. It has been contended by some that a series of incremental changes within epochs could translate into an epochal change. For instance, there are socialists (e.g., Fabians) who believe that by means of a series of changes capitalism might evolve into socialism. This is not an incoherent view. There is nothing in the concept of capitalism that forbids such hopes for its transformation. In addition, legal naturalism eschews absolute discontinuity in epochal transformation. In a sense, it builds on a notion somewhat similar to that expressed in the gradualist view: the grounds for revolutionary transformation are prepared by new forces nurtured in the womb of the old society who work on a series of changes within the given epoch.

The critical difference in the two positions is that legal naturalism denies that these changes within epochs would, *in and of themselves*, transform capitalism into socialism. The problem is sociological, not logical. As opponents of an epoch work to engineer changes in it, its partisans too are working to frustrate that effort or, if they fail, to limit the changes to those which will not alter the character of their epoch. I am not aware of any significant example in history in which partisans of a social formation have allowed their opponents to breach the foundations of their epoch without a fight. Here lies the difficulty of the gradualist view. For our purposes, *epochal change requires the sudden irruption of a novel factor on the changes within an epoch*. Only then is it appropriate to speak of a "foundational change."

Changes within epochs can be of different kinds. We should remember that a given epoch is capable of many determinations; so is the natural law of a given epoch. *Changes within epochs are therefore limited to changes in the various positive legal systems that exist within them.* Thus, the birth of independent legal systems in many former European colonies is an example of changes within capitalist natural law. I am speaking only of those colonies in which political independence was not accompanied by a social transformation. For example, when Nigeria gained independence from Britain, the Supreme Court of Nigeria became the court of last resort for all judicial cases in Nigeria, which appointed its own bench and regulated its own legal education. The advent of independence, however, did not constitute a challenge to Nigeria's integration by Britain into the capitalist epoch. Nigeria remains an instance of the capitalist social formation: profitmaking is legal, the legal subject of bourgeois law is the centerpiece of the system, ownership of private property is upheld, and contract plays a large role in legal practice.

Changes within epochs are by no means limited to examples of devolution. Changes may come in the normal unfolding of the determinations inherent in the concept of capitalist law. As I pointed out in the example of the struggle between Roosevelt and Hoover (Chapter 3 above), changes might be in the nature of realizing some of the further possibilities—in that case, the possibility of state-regulated capitalism—inherent in the natural law of the epoch. The diversity of positive legal systems within the capitalist social formation of our present-day world provides solid evidence of how there can be different capitalist regimes united by their participation in the capitalist social formation.

In the discussion so far, I have deliberately refrained from discussing change in law in isolation from other spheres of social existence. The aim has been to show how law is involved in many spheres of social life even when we recognize its autonomy as a regional discipline. Very few changes in law arise from law itself. More often they arise from some perceived inadequacy in law as an instrumental value. I have also intended to show that the concept of a "revolution of law" is a misnomer if what is intended is to describe a process in law that is independent of extralegal considerations. To our first question—What is the nature of change in law?—we answer that change can be of different kinds and can take place at different levels. What it is in each case must be established by analysis. However, even when the change is epochal, it is inapposite to describe it in terms of absolute discontinuity. Nonfoundational change within an epoch can take place bounded by the natural law of the epoch. The modes in which these changes are realized will be elucidated next.

IV

This section seeks to answer the second question we posed at the beginning of the present chapter: How does change come about in law? That is to say, how do epochal changes and changes within epochs occur in law?

There are those who will argue that law is self-sufficient and intelligible in itself. On this view, changes that take place in law are products of the workings of the inner logic of law, of law's own evocation of its immanent determinations. Even though law may be affected by events and processes external to it, the argument goes, the most significant changes in law are those which arise from law's own attempt at self-understanding. While it is arguable that law sometimes changes in accordance with its own nature—especially, as discussed below, by way of adjudication—it can be shown that changes of this sort are quite limited.

There are at least seven ways in which change can come about in law. (Here "change" refers both to epochal changes and to changes within epochs.) Some of them we have already mentioned. The seven ways are adjudication, revolution, reform, devolution, imposition, legislation, and borrowing. There can be considerable overlap among these ways, and particular cases might illustrate more than one.

Adjudication. On one level, law is involved in the more complex forms of the social life of which it is a part. On another level, law is an autonomous regional discipline with its own fully constituted mode of discourse and immanent determinations. In our discussion of Marx's legal rationalism, we identified this aspect of the essence of law as "reason in law." In Chapter 4, we discussed how some attributes of the reason in law become institutionalized, and we considered their subsequent impact on the evolution of legal consciousness. Adjudication brings to the fore and is based on some of these aspects of reason in law. A principal feature of law's reason is its generality. Law is necessarily open-textured because it is impossible for legislators to anticipate every instance of human action that the law is designed to facilitate, regulate, direct, and police. It is not an accident that laws, even those regulating very narrow areas of human activity, are couched in general terms. Being general, laws require, as it were, a middle term—judges, arbitrators, prosecutors, mediators, assessors—to apply the laws to individual cases in the process of adjudication. "The law is universal. The case which has to be settled in accordance with the law is a particular case. To include the particular in the universal involves a judgment. The judgment is problematic. The law requires also a *judge*. If laws applied themselves, courts would be superfluous."[14]

It is this singular feature of law that assigns a lawmaking significance to the law-applying functions of judges. By applying laws to singular cases, law appliers establish usages and arrive at decisions which are used as precedents in future cases that are similar to those in which the original decisions were handed down. The process unfolds through the interpretation of doctrines, the affirmation of principles, the declaration of rights, the granting of restraining injunctions, and so on. One of the ways in which change comes about in law, therefore, is the process of incremental adjustments in legal doctrine through the law's application to specific cases

14. Karl Marx and Frederick Engels, *Collected Works*, published to date: vols. 1–34; 38–47 (New York: International Publishers, 1975–), 1:165–66.

guided by *stare decisis*, formal principles of interpretation (constitutional and statutory), and consecrated convention. The importance of this process of change must not be underestimated, both for common law and for civil code legal cultures. The decriminalization of abortion in the United States, for instance took place by exactly this means.[15]

Change by adjudication, however, is limited to changes within epochs. Reason in law or the form of law is tempered by the content of the structure of rights, entitlements, etc. that it embodies. Adjudication proceeds on the assumption of shared principles, values, and meaning in the society, and it derives its legitimacy therefrom.[16] The breakdown of these values and shared meanings makes adjudication difficult and, in some situations, impossible. These values, I suggest, are largely derived from the presuppositions of specific social formations. The incremental adjustments possible within a given system of positive law, then, are limited by the natural law on which that system is founded. Thus, the judges of the U.S. Supreme Court, except perhaps in a revolutionary situation, cannot be expected to come up with an interpretation of legal doctrine or of the Constitution that will render profitmaking illegal or abolish the freedom of contract, no matter how truncated that freedom has become in contemporary times.

Revolution. Usually revolution is understood in terms of forcible change.[17] In this discussion, though, I will not be concerned with how revolution is brought about or carried through. Instead, the focus is on the scope of change that revolution involves. A revolution is a fundamental transformation of a social whole. A revolution in society refers to the radical transformation of the foundations on which a society is based in such a way that, when the process is consummated, we have to say that a new society has replaced the old one. A revolution in law, on the other hand, will refer to corresponding phenomena altering the character of the law of a given epoch. Since the positive laws in a given epoch derive their

15. See *Roe v. Wade*, 410 U.S. 113 (1973).

16. "Though we read the scales differently in weighing these 'imponderables,' I cannot but feel confident that our scales are the same. In any event our ways do not part and we care no differently for the only things that give dignity to man—the things of the spirit." A note from Felix Frankfurter to Harlan Stone after their failure to agree on a case; quoted in Walter F. Murphy, *Elements of Judicial Strategy* (Chicago: University of Chicago Press, 1964), p. 52. See also David Luban, *Lawyers and Justice* (Princeton: Princeton University Press, 1988), pp. 244, 250–56, and Tribe, *God Save This Honorable Court*, p. 96.

17. Chalmers Johnson, *Revolutionary Change*, 2d ed. (Stanford: Stanford University Press, 1982), p. 12; Crane Brinton, *The Anatomy of Revolution*, rev. and expanded ed. (New York: Vintage, 1965), p. 4.

identities from the natural law of the epoch, only a fundamental change which brings in its wake the overthrow of one epoch and the substitution of a new one, founding (in relevant cases) new legal orders, deserves to be called a revolution. I have argued that changes within epochs cannot, in and of themselves, become epochal changes. Thus, revolution in law refers only to the foundational transformation of the natural law of the epoch.

Consistent with the general theory developed in this work, such a change can only be a part of a revolution in the social formation that encompasses law in its ambit. The change that brought with it capitalist natural law as part of the emergence of the capitalist social formation founded on the ruins of feudalism is an example of revolution in law. But the change that gave Nigeria an independent capitalist legal system after decolonization will not be an example of revolution in law. Revolution in law is tied indissolubly to the occurrence of revolution in society.[18] I have restricted the referential scope of revolution in law because the idea of breaching existing boundaries is essential to the idea of revolution. Any change that does not go that far cannot be a revolution.

Reform. The natural law of any social formation is broad and open-ended enough to permit much diversity in the evolution of positive legal systems in particular societies. Meanwhile, the ruling classes who have to establish concrete legal systems are hampered by an epistemological blind spot. To the extent that they proceed by trial and error in their effort to get at the most proximate embodiment of the natural law of their social formation, there is ample room for experimentation. One way in which the ruling classes tinker with their positive law in order to bring it as close as possible to the natural law of their social formation is by means of law reform. Reform implies a commitment to the foundations—the natural law—while some of the elements of the structure are moved around. Reform is carried out in accordance with the ruling class's understanding of the natural law. Quite often the aim is to protect the natural law foundations from coming under question. Where reforms fail to stem the tide of questioning the foundations of the positive law, a revolutionary upheaval is possibly in the making. For example, it is unthinkable that a program of

18. For a contrary view, see Alan Watson, *The Evolution of Law* (Baltimore: Johns Hopkins University Press, 1985), p. 118, where he says: "A revolution may occur in law or in society. With revolution in law, the legal tradition continues but with appropriate modifications: the basis of law has been changed. With revolution in society the aim must also be to revolutionize law. The legal tradition is then replaced by another legal tradition in whole or in part."

law reform in a capitalist society will ever include the abolishment of private property ownership.

Devolution. Devolution is the process whereby a legal system, in the role of a parent legislature, changes the law in order to grant to another, in the role of an offspring legislature, the power to make law without its having to be validated by the parent legislature. This process usually occurs in colonial situations, between the departing colonizer and the emergent independent territory. An example is the 1960 Act of the Westminster Parliament which divested that parliament of the power to make laws for the then colonial territory of Nigeria and transferred the lawmaking power to the Nigerian Parliament. This normally is a change within an epoch. But if those who received the power in Nigeria had sought to alter the natural law foundations of the legal system they inherited, they would have inaugurated a revolutionary upheaval. Devolution could overlap with law reform.[19]

Imposition. Law changes by way of imposition when a territory becomes the victim of occupation by another which imposes its legal system, along with other cultural forms, on the victim. This is what happens in all colonial situations. As a result of colonization, Britain imposed its common law tradition on the diverse nations and ethnic groups that make up Nigeria. Their law changed insofar as the British common law tradition became the dominant jurisdiction in Nigeria and all the indigenous legal systems were subordinated to it. Thus, even though the transfer of lawmaking powers took place by devolution, the original introduction of the common law tradition to Nigeria was by imposition. Imposition can be part of a social transformation, but it need not be. In the case of Nigeria, it was part of the integration of Nigeria into the world capitalist economy. Imposition may be more or less successful. In the case of Nigeria, many of the indigenous legal systems could not be obliterated. Today, therefore, Nigeria has a multiplex jurisdiction arranged in a hierarchy, atop which sits the common law tradition.

Legislation. Every legal rule established by direct action of the lawmaking organs of a given society is legislation. This mode merits recognition on its own because it is the principal means by which changes are made in most modern legal systems. It overlaps with many of the modes we have so far discussed. For instance, successful coupmakers will likely use legis-

19. Were we to conduct a study of a particular society, adjustments would have to be made to our theory to accommodate the peculiarities of that society. For example, a discussion of the positivization of capitalist natural law in Nigeria must include devolution as one of the mechanics of positivization.

lation as their principal tool for altering whatever they do not like in the instruments of succession and of competence against which they aimed their coup. The act of parliament whereby power devolved on the Nigerian Parliament in 1960 was a piece of legislation. Lastly, proposals for reform when they are accepted are normally executed by means of legislation. In the case of imposition, too, as soon as the period when force is required to subdue the population recedes, legislation is the principal instrument by which the imposition is accomplished.

Borrowing. I owe my awareness of this particular mode of change to Alan Watson.[20] Societies learn from one another. When problems arise in a society for which the society's positive law does not provide any solution, the rulers of the society do not always have to create solutions *de novo*. If the savants of the society in question know that a neighboring society had confronted and solved similar problems before, they sometimes avail themselves of the tried-and-true answers of their neighbors. Borrowing may be on a small or a big scale.[21] It is guided by some principles.

In the first place, for borrowing to take place those who borrow must be aware that another system contains items they could borrow. In many cases, the borrower system holds the donor system in great esteem. Thus, when in 1977 the Nigerian ruling class opted for the presidential system of government over the old Westminster cabinet model, it paid tribute to the U.S. Constitution.[22] Watson identifies three additional factors that affect borrowing. First, "national pride (of the borrowing country) may determine that borrowings should be made, or should be restricted, from some particular system." The Scots, for instance, would rather borrow from French, Greek, Italian, or Dutch sources or even from the Ethiopian Civil Code than from English law. Secondly, where a borrower country turns is partly a result of language and accessibility of the donor system. To

20. Alan Watson, *Society and Legal Change* (Edinburgh: Scottish Academic Press, 1977). As will become obvious in what follows, I owe a huge debt to Watson in this section.

21. Watson has explained the widespread reception of Roman law in Western Europe as an instance of borrowing on a massive scale. See *The Evolution of Law*, chap. 3.

22. I do not agree with Watson that "the factors which determine which system is borrowed from often have nothing to do with the needs of the borrowing society." *Society and Legal Change*, p. 98. This is an exaggeration. Of course, borrowing could sometimes be a product of irrational fascination or aesthetic appreciation. It does not seem to me that ruling classes which decide to borrow from another legal system do not believe that the borrowed practices would help resolve some problems in their own society. It will be more correct to argue that they are often wrong in their assessment of the value of what they borrow, or that they sometimes fail to pay serious attention to the alienness of the practices they borrow which at times results in incongruences between the problem to be solved and the solution proposed.

use Watson's example: "the State of Louisiana and the Province of Quebec both have a Civil Law background and both have a Civil Code based primarily on French Law. No one would deny that Quebec has very much a Civil Law system (though with a Common Law admixture), but the contrary has often been maintained in the case of Louisiana. . . . [P]art of the explanation is that the language of Quebec has remained French, that of Louisiana has become English. French sources have remained open to the former, have become closed to the latter."[23] A similar explanation will suffice for the absence of civil law influences in the Nigerian legal system and the absence of common law influences in that of Senegal. This explanation is closely connected to the third factor identified by Watson: history. In African countries, for example, the character of the legal system depends on which positive law was imposed on them and by whom. In Nigeria the common law tradition predominates because Britain was the colonial power. Legal education and legal practices (down to the wearing of wigs and gowns) follow the British system. Ultimately borrowing must satisfy the presuppositions of the natural law foundations of the legal system in order to be successful. No borrowing will succeed that breaches the natural law of the social formation of which the borrowing society is an instance. We may conclude that only elements of positive law can be borrowed. The natural law is not amenable to our tinkering and is tied in with the epoch of which it is one of the constituent elements.

In this section we have been concerned with elaborating the many modes of change in law. The aim has been to bring together the variegated ways in which change takes place in law even while we admit that ruling classes may emphasize some rather than others and that they sometimes do exploit modes of change for their own ends. However much change in law is mediated by class interests, as a regional and autonomous subject of study the phenomenon of change in law involves considerable complexity and exhibits some elements of uniqueness that force us to consider it on its own. We shall now focus on the causes of change in law.

V

We have so far explained the nature of change in law and modes of change in law. It remains for us to answer the third question posed in the present chapter: Why does law change? Many factors are causally responsible for change in law. They may be divided into two broad groups, depending on

23. Ibid., pp. 102, 105.

what aspect of law we have in mind. What are the factors responsible for change in positive law, and what are the factors responsible for change in natural law? The first group of factors relates to the degree of success with which the positive law performs its functions in the society; the second group relates to the degree of success with which the social formation of which the natural law is a part meets the hopes and aspirations of human beings. Let us take each in turn.

Positive law is an instrument for realizing *in concreto* the structure of rights and entitlements etc. contained in a particular social formation. It performs regulatory, coordinating, and policing functions once this structure is embodied in the relevant institutions. The positive law is a more or less adequate realization of the natural law of the epoch. This is because of what in Chapter 3 above was identified as the abstractness of the natural law of a social formation and the opacity of social processes. A principal cause of change in positive law is a realization on the part of the savants of the epoch of a disjuncture between their positive law and the natural law of the epoch. Change in positive law will then be an attempt to reduce the amount of incongruence between their positive law and the natural law. Some of the modes that we just identified in section IV will be summoned to meet this contingency. Change in positive law may also be a result of social change arising from the further unfolding of the possibilities in a given social formation.

Thus, in the opening years of the twentieth century, the growing concentration of capital in fewer and fewer hands which heralded the advent of monopoly capitalism also gave birth to an entire body of legislation against trusts and interlocking directorships, to the establishment of regulatory commissions to supervise the workings of capital, and so on. Such social change frequently brings in its wake new tasks that require new laws. In these circumstances, change in positive law is the consequence. In some other cases the aim might be to correct perceived flaws in the existing laws. Laws afflicted with desuetude might also call for movement to streamline the law for purposes of rationalization and efficiency. These are all causes of change in positive law because they are not causes arising from the foundations, from the natural law of the social formation.

Change in natural law is radically different in its causative factors. Natural law is a constitutive element of the social formation. The acceptance of a social formation implies the acceptance of its natural law. Insofar as people accept the natural law, their disagreements will be limited to the positive law and how well or badly it approximates the natural law. Additionally, as other members of the society (besides the ruling class) accept that the existing positive law embodies the best their natural law has to offer, they are not likely to question, much less seek to change, the extant social order. Simultaneously, those who believe that there is nothing eternal or permanent about the natural law of the social formation might seek to change the social formation for what they consider to be a better one. Their criticisms will not be aimed at the positive law, but at the natural law. An attack on the natural law is an attack on the social formation of which it is a part.

Given that change in natural law is inseparable from change in the social formation itself, we are right to conclude that change in natural law, or what I have called the "fundamental transformation of natural law," can be understood only as part of a general movement for social transformation or epochal change. The question then is: What must happen before people are willing to struggle to overthrow one social formation and to substitute another? Many writers on revolution are agreed that the old structure must have failed in some significant respects and must have lost its legitimation to continue to exist. Also, its defenders must have largely lost the will to defend the old structure while the partisans of the emergent social formation are growing stronger and increasingly confident about the legitimacy of their goal and the possibility of success. "Law—in all societies—derives its authority from something outside itself, and if a legal system undergoes rapid change, then questions are inevitably raised concerning the legitimacy of the sources of its authority."[24]

Alan Watson identifies two circumstances, among others, in which revolutions in law occur. One is where "the law has, largely through the impact of the legal tradition, become cumbrous and remote from societal realities, and there is profound call for improvement." The other is "where there has been an actual political revolution, and societal conditions have changed."[25] Michael Tigar and Madeleine Levy suggest that "we must make a distinction between opposition to specific parts of the legal ideology of a state, seeking change through the existing, dominant organs of state power, and, on the other hand, rejecting the entire system as illegitimate."[26]

The disagreements that herald a revolutionary upheaval express themselves in many forms. Quite often they are triggered by a fundamental

24. Harold J. Berman, *Law and Revolution* (Cambridge: Harvard University Press, 1983), pp. 16, 20–21.
25. Watson, *The Evolution of Law*, p. 110.
26. Tigar and Levy, *Law and the Rise of Capitalism*, p. 313; also Johnson, *Revolutionary Change*, pp. 93–95, 133–34.

conflict between thought and reality, between the ideological understanding of the epoch and its material reality. On this level, the conflict is usually introduced by the development of the material structures of the social formation, by the irruption of new ideas that articulate the insurmountable limitations of the extant social order. These factors often combine with others—a loss of confidence in their ability to rule on the part of the ruling class, the shifting of allegiance by sufficient numbers of people away from the old ways of doing things, and the articulation by opponents of the old order of the possibility of a new and better world etc.—to generate a social movement which, if successful, inaugurates a new social formation and a new natural law, if the new social formation contains one in its concept. In other words, the eve of the introduction of a new natural law is at the same time the eve of the inauguration of a new social formation. It follows that change in natural law is part of a larger process taking place in the social structure which is reflected in law: a loss of confidence, not in the competence but in the legitimacy of the extant legal practices and institutions; disagreements, not merely over specific outcomes of the legal process but over the foundations of the legal order itself; disputes over the legitimacy of the social order, not just some aspects of it. Sometimes those at the head of the movement might think they are merely modifying the existing order. At other times, they are quite aware of the scope of the changes they are demanding. Overall, the cause of change in natural law is always the perception that the extant means are no longer adequate to their ends and, therefore, that they ought to be replaced.

An attempt has been made in this chapter to identify the nature of change in law, the modes of change, and the causes of change. Where does the dialectic of change and continuity in law lead us? Do we forever have to live with law, no end coming to the dialectic of change and continuity? Does this mean that law is eternal? Since I have argued for the factor of continuity in change, does this mean that law will always be with us? Answers to these questions will form the subject matter of the following chapter.

6

Should Law Wither Away?

I

In this chapter I shall reflect on the future of law. We set out to examine the problem of what will become of law. There are two ways to understand a question about the future of law. The first is to ask: Has law a future? The question can be answered solely by an inquiry that revolves around law: its nature, its evolution, or its structure. Little or nothing need be said about human agency or choices. The discussion can be sustained entirely on the level of the immanent possibilities of law itself, by analyzing whether there is anything in the nature of law that gives us reason to expect it has a future and by prognosticating what kind of future it has on the basis of our understanding of the nature, functions, and limits of law. If we pose the question of the future of law in this way, it is obvious that law has a future unless we are able to discern in law some immanent attribute that exhibits a tendency toward self-destruction. That is to say, if there is nothing in or about law that gives us reason to entertain the belief that law will wither of itself, then there is no basis for asserting that law has no future. We may study law and its structure innocently of its context; but it is law embodied, historical, that interests us. And this is the law of which it is meet to ask whether it has a future. And this brings us to the second way of understanding the question of law's future.

Instead of asking whether law has a future, we may ask: Should law have a future? This way of putting the issue combines the elements of the first way with the elements of human agency and choice. Law is a human artifact; it is a consequence of human interaction. And it is not the only human artifact that has been applied in history to social ordering. Religion was for a long time a universal means of social ordering. At different times torture, war, etc. have also been used for social purposes. But law, except in a few contemporary cases, has become the preferred mode of social ordering. The purpose—harmonious society—that is central to law is the reason that we still embrace it while we have jettisoned other forms or place declining significance on them. We chose law. Doubtless, law has delivered on its promise and has justified its claim as the best means for ensuring peaceable living in society. Over time we have become persuaded that we chose right, in the main anyway. Thus, law is justifiable insofar as it promotes specific human values and ends. The question of the future of law, therefore, raises the issue of whether law will continue to promote, in its regulatory, coordinating, and policing functions, these human values and ends. Even if it is true that law will continue to promote these values and ends, this should not stop us from considering alternative ways of achieving the same aims. Nor should it prevent us from evaluating how well or ill law promotes these values and ends. For, as will become clear in the course of the present chapter, law, *contra* E. P. Thompson, is not an unqualified human good.[1]

Given that alternative modes of attaining the goals of law are always conceivable, an inquiry into the future of law is at the same time an inquiry into good alternatives to law and how they can best be realized. If there are good alternatives to law—that is, modes of social ordering that preserve the best results we have obtained with law, but without the elements that cause us disquiet about law—and if we remain committed to the attainment of the goals for which we have hitherto needed law, then we ought to dispense with law. Here we come to the intersection of the two ways of conceptualizing the issue of the future of law. Whereas it remains true that there is a sense in which the natural law of an epoch is independent of us, it is equally true that law (natural and positive) is a product of human interaction. It is also true that the more we know of the origins of, and tendencies contained in, the natural law of our epoch, the greater the chances that we will be able to affect future outcomes by present choices.

Before we proceed, it is necessary to consider a possible objection to the discussion to follow. It would seem to be implied by legal naturalism that every mode of production comes with its own natural law. If this is

---

1. See E. P. Thompson, *Whigs and Hunters: The Origins of the Black Act* (London: Allen Lane, 1975).

true, then we cannot envisage a future without law, just as we cannot envisage a future without modes of production. This implication is false and unwarranted by our theory. The concept of a "mode of production" is not a monolith. That we cannot envisage a future without modes of production does not mean that we cannot envisage a future without law. For the latter to be the case, it must be that law is a necessary component of any mode of production. But there are several modes of production different enough from one another to be called by different names. Not every mode of production has law in its concept or its history. Law is not always constitutive of modes of production, only of some. Similarly, commodity production is specific to a particular mode of production but not to others. The essential components of every mode of production are raw materials, tools, and labor. Some modes of production are more complex than others, and while some modes of production are complex enough to have law as a constituent element, others are not. If law is eternal, it will not be for the reason that it is constitutive of all modes of production.

It may still be argued that law will forever remain with us because, given the complexity of extant modes of production, we do not have any reason to expect that future modes of production will either be simple or complex without implicating law in their conceptualization. In other words, law is inseparable from complex modes of production. The assumption that law and complexity are inseparable is questionable. It rests on a further assumption that the only alternative to complex modes of production with law is a reversion to simple communities without law. We do not have to accept these assumptions, nor are they implied by the theory developed in this work. What, then, is the prognosis for law?

We have a basis for envisaging a world without law. The extinction of law is conceivable. Whether this occurs or not is very much a factor of what we do or do not do—a factor of how history unfolds. Law is not a prerequisite for civilization or human society; there was human society before there was law. Nor is law, as I will show presently, an unqualified human good. If we could secure the same result for which we revere law while ridding ourselves of some of the unwanted baggage—think of the adversary system—that law brings along with it, then it might be that society will be better without law than with it.

This is not to say that law is an unmitigated evil. Few will deny that "society is, generally speaking, better off under the rule of law [in the contemporary epoch] than under the rule of force or *Diktat*, but can we not also conceive of a form of society existing under a more desirable order than that of the rule of law as we now know it?"[2] My contention in this chapter is that Marxism answers, and must answer, McBride's question in the affirmative. Marxism not only considers alternative social orders possible, it finds some, or at least a particular one—communism—eminently desirable. It sees in law an epitome of the radical insufficiency of the human situation in all present and past social formations. It holds forth the alluring picture of human society organized along lines radically different from any we have thus far known in history: a society without law, the state, division of labor, morality, etc., which are considered forms of mediation that stand between human beings and that are responsible, in part at least, for their alienation from one another, the means of production, the products of their labor, and their own nature.

In this position, which has come to be called the "withering-away thesis," we find an interface (in Marxism) between ethics, social and political theory, and philosophy of law. The issues involved touch upon our ideas about human nature, society, and the structure of authority and human interaction in society. Marx, who devised the Marxist thesis of the withering away of law, here followed a long line of political theorists, mainly Europeans. The thesis will be defended in the present chapter not merely as a description of the fate of law but also, and more significantly, as a prescription of the preconditions for the realization of that brave new world which Marx and Engels and other radical theorists have given the name "communism." We can argue about the cogency of the arguments advanced in support of this thesis, but we may not suggest that it is un-Marxist.

II

Few political theorists claim that law is an unqualified human good and an ultimate value. This is not to say that there are no theorists who believe that law is a prerequisite for civilization or that in the absence of law what we will have is chaos. I am convinced that many people in the present epoch are not very different from Isaac D. Balbus's students, who repeat to him each year: "If we didn't have the law everyone would kill each other."[3] But, even as people trumpet the virtues of law, there is widespread acceptance of the view that law is a second-best option. Law is invested with so

2. William Leon McBride, "An Overview of Future Possibilities: Law Unlimited?" in J. Roland Pennock and John W. Chapman, eds., *The Limits of Law* (New York: Lieber-Atherton, 1974), p. 34.

3. Quoted in Hugh Collins, *Marxism and Law* (New York: Oxford University Press, 1982), p. 97.

much virtue because it is regarded as the best we can hope for in the circumstances of scarce resources and social conflicts of varying degrees of intensity and disruptiveness. The resort to law is a classic case of making the best of a bad situation. For instance, Aristotle asked in *The Politics* "whether it is better to be ruled by the Best Man or by the Best Laws." He answered: "[H]e who asks Law to rule is asking God and Intelligence and no others to rule; while he who asks for the rule of a human being is bringing in a wild beast; for human beings are like a wild beast and strong feelings lead astray rulers and the very best of men. In law you have the intellect without the passions."[4]

It appears that Aristotle is singing the praises of law rather than denigrating it. But when we consider the contrast with human beings, it becomes clear that the merit of law is in direct proportion to the lack of merit of human beings. This lack renders humans unfit to rule. It does not follow that if humans possess as much merit as law does, or more, the rule of humans would not be preferred by Aristotle. It is less the intrinsic merit of law than the lack of merit of human beings that tilts the balance in favor of law. Echoes of the view held by Aristotle can be found in Hobbes's rationale for the institution of the Leviathan. Without the Leviathan human beings will engage in a war of all against all. Once again, it is the inadequacy of the human condition by itself that makes the rule of Leviathan imperative.[5] We find similar sentiments espoused by Rousseau: "[A] country, in which no one either evaded the laws or made a bad use of magisterial power, could require neither laws nor magistrates."[6]

The uneasiness about law is by no means limited to the classics. There is more recent evidence to support this thesis. Jerold Auerbach has ably documented the travails of law in the history of the United States of America.[7] In colonial America there were overarching efforts made by the colonists to order their communities without the aid of law. According to Auerbach, "[d]espite the undiluted praise of its adherents, law raises at least as many questions as it resolves about the nature of the good society."[8] In the words of Grant Gilmore: "The better the society, the less law there will be.

4. Aristotle, *The Politics*, trans. and intro. T. A. Sinclair (Harmondsworth: Penguin, 1962), pp. 139, 143.

5. See Thomas Hobbes, *Leviathan*, ed. and intro. C. B. Macpherson (Harmondsworth: Penguin, 1968), p. 227.

6. Jean-Jacques Rousseau, *The Social Contract and Discourses*, trans. and intro. G. D. H. Cole (London: Dent, 1979), p. 99.

7. Jerold S. Auerbach, *Justice without Law?* (New York: Oxford University Press, 1983).

8. Ibid., p. 13.

In Heaven there will be no law. . . . In Hell there will be nothing but law, and due process will be meticulously observed."[9] The hostility to law of various segments of American society in the period before it became the consummate litigious society is, if Auerbach is correct, near legendary. American colonists rejected law as a matter of conscious choice: "[A]s Christians, utopians, Dutch settlers in New Amsterdam, or merchants, they preferred to live within a communal framework that rendered formal legal institutions superfluous or even dangerous. For them law was a necessary evil or a last resort, not a preferred choice."[10] One colonist, the Reverend John Cotton, regarded litigation as reflecting "a defect of brotherly love."[11] Another called litigation un-Christian because "law was an heart without affection, a mind without passion."[12] Nor was this hostility restricted to churchpeople and the like. Merchants were no less suspicious of law and litigation.[13] And among new immigrants, the hostility was even more pronounced because "not only was litigation expensive, time-consuming and unpredictable, it disrupted harmony" in the immigrant community.[14] The disruptive potential of law and litigation is aptly encapsulated in this Chinese admonition: "Once go to law and there is nothing but trouble."[15]

The uneasiness about law is not limited to political theorists and American immigrants. In different cultures in different parts of the world, uneasiness about law is quite strong. For instance, there is a saying in Yorùbá: *Bíkó bà sí òfin, èsè kò sí* (Without law, there is no crime). One of the most uttered prayers in Yorùbá is that one may not run afoul of the law. The antilaw sentiment is perhaps best articulated in the following saying: *A kìí ti kóòtù bò se òré* (We do not come back from court as friends).[16] I shall shortly

9. Quoted ibid.
10. Ibid., pp. 19–20.
11. Quoted ibid., p. 23.
12. Quoted ibid., p. 22.
13. See ibid., pp. 32–33 and chap. 4.
14. Ibid., p. 74.
15. Quoted ibid.
16. One might explain the antilegal sentiment contained in the Yorùbá sayings just quoted as owing perhaps to the fact that the law talked about is British law which, as I pointed out in Chapter 5, was imposed on the peoples of Nigeria (including the Yorùbá) during the colonial era. It could be that such sentiments articulate the dismay felt by people in the face of an alien system, imposed by force by invaders who spoke a language the Yorùbá did not understand. This is a rational explanation. It will not be adequate, however, for the explanation assumes there was no law in precolonial Yorùbá society. This would mean that the sentiments expressed in the sayings have their roots in the colonial era. But the assumption can be shown to be false. The sayings can be shown to predate British rule. We need only

provide some reasons why law has caused uneasiness in people throughout history.

III

No other part of Marxist theory has drawn more criticism than the supposition that the state, law, and various other forms of social mediation
will, at some future date, wither away. At the same time, one can argue
that no other part of Marxist theory is less understood or so often misun-
derstood. What makes the situation even more interesting is that many
Marxists and Marxist sympathizers have felt the impact of these criticisms
so much that, in recent times, the thesis that law will wither away has been
subjected to significant revision. It is no longer strange to find texts that
claim to expound a Marxist theory of law while arguing with considerable
ardor that although the content of law may and does change, the form of
law will forever remain with us.[17] Recent political and social developments
have combined to undermine the plausibility of the withering-away thesis.
The collapse of Eastern Europe; the resurgence of liberal representative
democracy and its legal twin, the rule of law, in different parts of the
world; the discrediting of erstwhile self-professed socialist regimes—these
have provided grounds for doubting the possibility of future modes of social ordering in which law is absent. There are many for whom the exercise
undertaken in the present chapter is misguided.

   In the justified euphoria brought on by the collapse of East European
communism and its foster children in other parts of the world, what is
often forgotten is that the victory of capitalism over "communism" does
not represent the "end of history." It only clears the decks for social theory
to begin to take seriously—without the ideologically inhibiting influences
of the past half-century—the business of thinking anew about future
modes of social ordering that will preserve the best of what has been

---

refer to the high level of material and intellectual culture among the Yorùbá in the precolonial period to show that the assumption is false. What is required is to show in what respects
the transplantation of the British legal tradition affected indigenous jurisdictions and integrated the two. This would mean that the sentiments against law are not necessarily restricted
to British colonial law but could be against law *simpliciter*. The conclusion might be that even
though very few Yorùbá would deny the value of law as an organizing principle of social interaction, even fewer would deny that it is a mixed blessing.

   17. A good example is the argument of Hugh Collins, in *Marxism and Law*, p. 98, where
he states that Marxists must move in the direction of what he calls the "fetishism of law," understood in one variant as the view that law is a precondition of social order and that civilization without law is inconceivable.

achieved but will minimize, if not eliminate, the less-attractive features. Marxism as social theory is inspired by a commitment to put into place a mode of social ordering that will overcome the diremption of social life which has become the dominant principle of social ordering in the modern era. Admittedly, this is a commitment that Marx and his followers share with the utopian tradition, although Marx founded his commitment on different grounds. The withering-away thesis—concerning law, state, morality, and division of labor—is the theoretical expression of this commitment. Thus it is neither an accidental claim by the original founders of Marxism nor an aberration that they eventually expunged from their theory. On the contrary, there is much truth in Evgeny Pashukanis's contention that "the problem of the withering away of law is the cornerstone by which we measure the degree of proximity of a jurist to Marxism."[18] The withering-away thesis is an essential component of Marxist political and legal theory, and it can be expurgated only at the cost of considerable violence to Marxism, if not its wholesale abandonment.

As far as I know, the phrase "withering away" was Frederick Engels's and it came into existence in his discussion of the prognosis for the state in the revolutionary transformation of the capitalist mode of production. Later Marxists, especially Vladimir Lenin, have built on the foundation provided by Engels. The problem, though, is that neither Engels nor Lenin directly addressed the problem of law and its future on the morrow of the socialist revolution. This is not surprising. From Engels through Lenin to latter-day Marxists, "law" has always been construed strictly as "positive law" and has therefore been seen as deriving from the state as the embodiment of class will, the instrument of the ruling class to keep down the subaltern classes, or the expression of class ideology. This dominant interpretation of Marxist legal theory explains the repeated assimilation of the future of law to the destiny of the state in postrevolutionary society. I have presented arguments in Chapter 3 for why Marxist positivism is inadequate and possibly wrong. Here we need only add that Marx did not give any pride of place to the state; nor, as we have seen in Chapter 2, did he conflate state and law. On the contrary, Marx repeatedly inveighed against *all forms of mediation* that stand between one individual and another and that force them to relate not as persons but as personae in life dramas whose scripts move them away from their humanness. Hence, within the category "forms of social ordering to be transcended in future

---

18. E. B. Pashukanis, *Selected Writings on Marxism and Law*, ed. and intro. Piers Beirne and Robet Sharlet, trans. Peter B. Maggs (London: Academic Press, 1980), p. 268.

society," Marx included not only state and law, but also morality and the division of labor. It is this expansive sense of social transformation and of its possibilities that informs our discussion of the withering-away thesis as it concerns the future of law.

Although the focus of Engels and Lenin on the state makes their discussion too narrow for our purposes, they both make some useful distinctions that help clarify the scope and character of the withering-away thesis. I propose to adopt these distinctions in explicating the thesis. There are two stages in the revolutionary transformation of society from the capitalist mode of production to communism. The first stage is enacted when *"the proletariat seizes state power and to begin with transforms the means of production into state property."*[19] But, however important the state is in the mode of production, it is not the only important constituent of a social formation. As I have argued throughout this book, law is constitutive of some modes of production, and one cannot overemphasize the essentiality of law to the capitalist social formation. It is fair to say that, in addition to the state, the proletariat will also have to take over law and its various institutionalized forms, insofar as these forms of social ordering are necessary to the social formation. As well, the victory of the proletariat means that it will become the new ruling class which will have to operate to preserve the society and keep its inhabitants secure in the enjoyment of their lives and possessions. Of course, given that the transformation is supposed to be an epochal one, we should expect that new forms of entitlement and different principles of distribution derived from the changed mode of production will have to be substituted and enacted as law.

For example, if the overthrow of capitalism is definitive, the preservation of the regime of private property will be incompatible with socialism. Similarly, deliberate efforts will have to be made to undermine commodity production, production primarily for exchange, and the privatized appropriation of surplus production. The new natural-legal presuppositions enjoin new principles and patterns of distribution of burdens and benefits. The emphasis on the meeting of needs rather than on the satisfaction of the profit motive cannot but attract the opposition of the overthrown ruling class and its supporters in the other classes. This is so because, as Marx makes clear in the *Critique of the Gotha Program*, socialist society as it emerges from the womb of capitalism remains, especially in the early stages, a class society characterized by the presence of rights and inequalities which it is called upon to transcend. Hence, the law's policing func-

---

19. Frederick Engels, *Anti-Dühring* (Peking: Foreign Languages Press, 1976), p. 362.

tions will remain germane for life in the newly constituted socialist community. But if all that the proletariat does is preserve the antagonisms for which law is required, not to mention the skewed distribution of burdens and benefits that has characterized all presocialist social formations, socialist society would not represent a qualitative improvement on the capitalist social formation. The superior quality of socialism rests, in part, on its self-conscious historicity which requires its operators to put into place those elements of social ordering in which the reasons for antagonisms, the necessity for class divisions, and the suppression of one class by another are no longer available. That is why Marx and Marxists generally describe socialism as a "transitional phase." The transitional status of socialism has some peculiar resonances for legal naturalism.

It is a fundamental assumption of Marxism as social theory that not only is reality knowable but, within limits, human beings can by their actions alter reality for better or worse. Thanks to this assumption, Marx in his philosophy of history could recommend the capitalist social formation as an improvement over earlier modes of production, in part because it is "a society of knowledge": a mode of production in which humans are less victimized by necessity, more able to understand it, and better prepared to expand the boundaries of freedom. Capitalism never realized the full extent of this potential for freedom because, dominated by the profit motive, it never brought the production process under conscious control. Revolution occurs precisely because of the growing awareness of possible alternative modes of social ordering. This awareness enhances our capacity for conscious control of our life conditions and helps us become less captive to social and natural forces. Those at the head of the socialist revolution are supposed to be imbued with this expansive sense of the possibilities for mediation-free social ordering and keenly aware of its eminent desirability. The requirement to supersede capitalism—putting in place new modes of social ordering which both preserve the best that humanity has achieved and eliminate or mitigate the defects—brings us to the second stage of the transition from capitalism to communism.

If socialism stops at the level of introducing a new ruling class—the proletariat—and entrenching it, that would be a signal failure. The success of socialism will be measured by how quickly it puts into place new social forms from which class cleavages are absent, antagonisms are done away with, the distribution of benefits and burdens is done according to needs and ability, and so on. When these conditions will have been put in place, the necessity for the interposition of forms of mediation like the state, law, or morality would be eradicated. If the necessity for their existence no

longer obtains, then they would become superfluous and fall into desuetude. This latter outcome is what is to be understood by the metaphor of
"withering away."[20]

There are, then, two moments in the socialist transformation: the first is
when the proletariat, "in winning the battle of democracy," seizes state
power and other forms of power in society and installs itself as the new ruling class; the second is when, in realizing the eventual goal of the revolution—communism—the proletariat brings about its own extinction. The
first requires the proletariat to take hold of the institutions of society and
turn them to the purpose of ensuring that there is no reversal; the second
demands that the proletariat dissolve all classes, including itself. This second aspect is what sets Marxist theory apart from the anarchist call for the
"abolition of the state."

Law survives in the first phase of the socialist transformation as a principle of social ordering because the material circumstances that gave law
birth—class cleavages, antagonisms, anarchy in production, and similar
phenomena—continue to exist. Thus, the focus of the proletarian ruling
class is redirected: away from repression and toward the creation of conditions that will eliminate the need for law as an organizing principle of society. When the conditions for the existence of the forms of mediation
become extinct, it is obvious that they will become superfluous. It is very
important to bear in mind this distinction between the "abolition" of the
bourgeois state, law, etc. by the proletarian revolution and the "withering
away" of those forms of mediation after the socialist revolution. For when
applied to law, the abolition of bourgeois law must not be confused with
the withering away of law after the revolution. The withering away of law
is a function of the disappearance of the conditions in which law flourishes.
To the extent that its soil is rendered infertile, law lacks the nourishment it
needs for its sustenance: the logical outcome is its withering.

The abolition of the bourgeois state and law is accomplished by the substitution of the socialist state and law in the proletarian revolution. However, the state and law will wither away after the revolution, according to
Lenin, only when (1) the resistance of the capitalists has been completely
crushed, (2) the capitalists have disappeared, and (3) there are no classes.[21]
When these conditions have been realized and there is complete and unfettered democracy for all, democracy itself, as a political principle, begins
to wither away:

20. See Engels's account of the fate of the state: ibid., p. 363.
21. V. I. Lenin, *State and Revolution* (Peking: Foreign Languages Press, 1976), p. 108.
This is a paraphrase.

(This happens) owing to the simple fact that, freed from capitalist slavery, from the untold horrors, savagery, absurdities and infamies of capitalist exploitation, people will gradually *become accustomed* to observing the elementary rules of community life that have been known for centuries and repeated for thousands of years in all copybook maxims; they will become accustomed to observing them without force, without coercion, without subordination, *without the special apparatus* of coercion which is called the state.

The expression "the state *withers away*" is very well chosen, for it indicates both the gradualness of the process and its spontaneous nature. Only habit can, and undoubtedly will, have such an effect; for we see around us on millions of occasions how readily people become accustomed to observing the rules of community life that are indispensable to them when there is no exploitation, when there is nothing that rouses indignation, [nothing that] evokes protest and revolt and creates the need for *suppression*.[22]

The withering-away thesis is about what we have to do to render the state and law superfluous in the organization of human society and, thus, guarantee their disappearance. We cannot abolish law as an organizing principle of human society until we have eliminated the conditions that necessitated law in the first place. All we can do is abolish particular legal regimes. The thesis has been the target of many criticisms of varying intensity and effectiveness. We shall now consider some of these criticisms.

Hugh Collins has identified the Engelsian-Leninist thesis with what he calls the orthodox Marxist "dogma that a communist society would be able to dispense with law." State and law will wither away because they will be without functions in the future communist society. According to Collins, this thesis is the outcome of a class-instrumentalist analysis of law. He suggests that only class instrumentalism prevented Lenin from recognizing as law the "elementary rules of community life" that would prevail in communist society without any special institutionalized means of enforcement or coercion. In such a society, people would become habituated to observing these elementary rules without any prompting from special institutionalized means of enforcement. Collins asks: "[I]f these elementary rules of social life are not law, what are they?" To his rhetorical question Collins responds that "the whole thesis of the withering away of law

22. Ibid., pp. 108–9; also see p. 124.

rests upon the dubious definitional fiat that rules which serve any other purpose than class oppression cannot be law."[23]

Others have suggested different construals of the withering-away thesis. Maybe what is presupposed by the thesis is not that law per se will wither away in communist society but that some functions of law, especially the coercive function, will die out in communist society. Lenin is quite explicit. Habit, he says, will supplant coercion, and people will observe the elementary rules of community life without being coerced or prompted to do so, without the special apparatus called the state (or law). This interpretation has not been without proponents, and some of William McBride's writings appear to offer this interpretation. McBride has identified the withering-away thesis with the vision of the possibility of a "noncoercive society."[24] A more desirable form of society, one that is neither under the rule of force nor the rule of law, "would be 'a society of individuals so enlightened that, while they would still be confronted with rules of conduct of all sorts, they would constantly be making conscious choices as to whether to accept or to reject any of those rules, and no coercion would be exerted over any member's choice.' "[25] "But in such a state of affairs, the law as we know it today would disappear, just as it would . . . in . . . the totally coercive state."[26]

This does not mean that in such a society there would be no "law" in the sense of rules of social behavior. It is only to say that if coerciveness is taken to be an essential feature of law, and law is identified with an extant set of institutions and procedures, then noncoercive society "could *not* be considered a state of law as we know it."[27] I take it, then, that McBride comes down on the side of the withering away of law as we know it. However, he leaves some room for a position similar to that of Collins to the effect that law is eternal and that it will be present in future communist society. After all, the social rules of behavior that will be observed in communist society will be some form of law once we elimi-

23. Collins, *Marxism and Law*, p. 103, 106. See also William Leon McBride, "Non-Coercive Society: Some Doubts, Leninist and Contemporary," in J. Roland Pennock and John W. Chapman, eds., *Coercion* (Chicago: Aldine-Atherton, 1972), p. 191.

24. See McBride, "Non-Coercive Society"; also Rudolf Schlesinger, *Soviet Legal Theory* (London: Kegan Paul, 1944), p. 24.

25. McBride, "An Overview of Future of Possibilities," p. 34. The inside quote is from an earlier paper by the author: "The Abolition of Law as a Standard in Legal Decision-Making," in *Legal Reasoning (Proceedings of the World Congress for Legal and Social Philosophy)*, ed. H. Hubien (Brussells: Establissements Emile Bruylant, 1971), p. 317.

26. Ibid., p. 35.

27. Ibid.

nate coercion as one of the defining features of law. There may be rules of social behavior in the future communist society. But what makes such rules law? Is it the case that all social rules of behavior are law? Obviously not. If they are, then the concept of law will be too vague to aid theoretical reflection. If not all social rules are law, and if it is not the case that law is social rules plus coercion, then an argument for the occurrence of law in communist society cannot have for its premise the presence of social rules of behavior.

McBride criticizes Lenin's elucidation of the withering-away thesis on another score. Lenin has argued that when the state has died out, habituation would replace coercion as the principal means by which the elementary rules of community life are observed. McBride argues that Lenin ignored the coercive aspect of the mechanisms of habit formation and the fact that "internalized coercion" is coercion nonetheless. If indeed Lenin identified habituation with the internalization of coercion, then McBride would be right to conclude that "such a society can hardly be regarded as one in which coercion has been eliminated, and there is no hint that Lenin envisages a dramatic reversal with respect to the employment of this subtle but total, internalized coercion in the highest phase of communist society."[28]

Did Lenin mean the internalization of coercion when he spoke of habituation? I am not sure that he did. In fact, contrary to McBride's argument, I think Lenin *could* assent to McBride's advocacy of the acceptance of a legal system by those it binds being based not on fear of coercion or force of habit, but on a recognition by those concerned that the system's rules are the best for achieving certain desirable goals.[29] Lenin could rejoin as follows: given that practical action is central to human existence, learning by doing as it were, we have reason to believe that human beings would become so accustomed to observing these rules that their initial rationale recedes farther and farther from their collective memory, and the only reason for observing them would come to be that it is the thing to do. In other words, habit formation is not essentially coercive. It should be conceded that much habit formation (e.g., in child-rearing) is an internalization of coercion. Nevertheless, the view that regards habituation as internalization of coercion stands in need of more arguments than McBride has provided.

28. McBride, "Non-Coercive Society," p. 183.
29. Ibid., p. 192.

IV

In section II, I pointed out that even in the best of its manifestations law has always caused considerable uneasiness in theorists and ordinary people alike. Sometimes this uneasiness metamorphoses into outright hostility. Why is this so? Let us recall our definition of law: a structure of rights, entitlements, duties, privileges, immunities, and so on which regulates and directs the relations in society between one individual or group and another, and among individuals and groups with reference to the material, instrument, and product of labor. The implications of this characterization of law need to be spelled out at this point. The first is that *law is irreducibly social*. It makes as little sense to talk of language without people living together and talking to one another as it does to talk of law without people living together and honoring and infringing one another's rights, duties, etc. Some may see some Hohfeldian debts here.

Although I think Wesley Hohfeld exaggerates when he at least seems to imply that all strictly fundamental legal relations can be exhibited "in a scheme of 'opposites' and 'correlatives,' "[30] his principal insights are invaluable. The sociality of law is best exemplified in the fact that the fundamental legal conceptions unearthed by Hohfeld always draw at least two parties into relations with each other. For example: "[I]f X has a right against Y that Y shall stay off X's land, the correlative (and equivalent) is that Y is under a duty toward X to stay off the place."[31] The same relation can be expressed in terms of jural opposites: X's "right" to enter his or her land is Y's "no right" that X shall not enter. Law, therefore, is a structure of mutual expectations and forbearances.[32]

We have so far talked in the abstract. How law is realized *in concreto* in given social formations will be determined by the requirements and presuppositions of each social formation. Hence the historicity of natural law, understood as that law which is natural to a given social formation. But not all social formations have embodied natural law in their concept. History tells of times when societies had existed without law. How, then, does law emerge in some social formations and not in others?

---

30. Wesley N. Hohfeld, *Fundamental Legal Conceptions*, ed. W. W. Cook (New Haven: Yale University Press, 1920), p. 36.

31. Ibid.

32. This dialectic of recognition, as we saw in Chapter 2 above, is one feature missing from Gerald Cohen's attempt to purify law of rights, to describe law primarily in terms of power.

Accounts of the origins of law vary from theorist to theorist. Still, recurrent themes in many of these accounts permit us to make some generalizations. First, those social formations have some natural law as constituent elements which exhibit *a considerable level of complexity in the way they reproduce the material conditions of their existence*. Let us analyze what is involved in this notion of "complexity." The population will be big enough so that the preponderant exchanges within the society are more and more between "strangers" rather than among kith and kin. I use "strangers" here not in the sense that those who are involved in the exchanges do not know each other, although that may well be the case. More significant, "stranger" here suggests that the exchange is not direct but, rather, is mediated in such a way that if the mediating factor were absent the parties would not necessarily deal with each other.

For instance, the exchange between a father and his son in which the son works for his father to save for the cost of his wedding is a mediated exchange, and it is between strangers even though the parties know each other. In some cultures it is part of the duties of a father to furnish his son with the wherewithal to enable the son to pay the necessary costs of getting married. In some situations, like that depicted in our example, father and son are cast in the roles of employer and employee, and the requirement of remuneration is mediated by the roles assumed by the two parties and by the rules and regulations governing those roles. It is a secondary relationship in which each of the principal parties could have been different—each assumes a different persona that is external to the primary father–son relationship. This is a different relationship from that in which the son works for the father as part of the family network of expectations. In the latter situation, payment is not required because the father–son relationship is direct: there is no mediating factor like that supplied in the former situation by the assumption of roles outside those of the family. In a complex society, the bulk of the transactions between individuals and groups in it will be marked by secondary, role-defined relationships between "strangers." There are two more factors without which the kind of complexity we are looking for will not be present.[33]

The population would likely be spread over a large territory. But the staking out of a large territory is impossible where the division of labor, and therefore the development of the forces of production, is rudimentary and backward. Lastly, the division of labor must be sufficiently advanced so that individual subsistence can no longer be assured by the puny production of

33. Cf. Roberto Unger, *Law in Modern Society* (New York: Free Press, 1976), pp. 137–38.

the individual. Rather, the individual or group has to exchange the surplus that is produced but not needed for that which is not produced but is needed. My point is the commonplace in legal anthropology and sociology of law that the emergence of law is indissolubly linked to the evolution of human society from the undifferentiated unity of the earliest primitive societies to the dawn of the division of labor, and on to the excessively litigious era of capitalism and socialism. It is this emergence of complexity that Rousseau laments so much in his *Discourse on the Origin of Inequality*. In a study of law and economic organization in preindustrial societies, Katherine Newman, too, has pointed out that the classical theorists of the evolution of law (Maine, Durkheim, Marx, Engels, and Weber) differ on what underlying forces moved legal evolution along the path it has taken historically. Nevertheless, she avers, "this much they hold in common: The prime mover of legal evolution is the increase in socioeconomic differentiation and stratification that can be observed throughout history."[34]

The above brief sketch of the evolution of law is relevant to the withering away of law in two ways: (1) Insofar as there was a time in the past when human society did manage without law, there is nothing utopian about entertaining the idea of a future human society in which law is absent. We can disagree only about its desirability and probability; its possibility cannot be questioned. It is not logically foreclosed. (2) The circumstances of the historical emergence of law have a lot to tell us about the nature of law, information that might enhance the desirability of a future order without law.

Talk of law in a situation where there is no societal conflict over the production and consumption of surplus products will be foolhardy. It will be more so where the conflict can be resolved by a shared understanding of mutual expectations and forbearances among the parties.[35] The pervasive-

---

34. Katherine S. Newman, *Law and Economic Organization* (Cambridge: Cambridge University Press, 1983), p. 32.

35. In a recent book self-consciously titled *Order without Law: How Neighbors Settle Disputes* (Cambridge: Harvard University Press, 1991), Robert C. Ellickson has shown how residents of rural Shasta County, in California, create order without law. The work is significant because it shows in a convincing way how people who are members of what is admittedly the most litigious society in the world consciously attempt to steer their interpersonal relations — business and otherwise — away from and without law. As the author puts it in his introduction, "The Shasta County findings add to a growing library of evidence that large segments of social life are located and shaped beyond the reach of law. Despite this mounting evidence, the limits of law remain too little appreciated. In everyday speech, for example, one commonly hears the phrase 'law and order,' which implies that governments monopolize the control of misconduct. This notion is false — so utterly false that it warrants the implicit attack it receives in the title of this book" (p. 4).

ness of law and its widespread appeal in the contemporary period tend to occlude the underside of law. It is arguable that at no other time in human history has law enjoyed so much acceptance or attracted so much enthusiasm as it does now in all parts of the world. Even those who do not play by the laid-down rules know the importance of keeping up the appearance of operating according to law. Such is the seductiveness of law in the contemporary situation. Despite this mass appeal, those of us who are not entranced by the sweet sound of legalism cannot but stress that in its glorious present, law is a mixed blessing, a classic instance of making the best of a bad situation.[36]

Think of what the law does not require us to do in the scheme of everyday living. Law does not require us to love our neighbors; it does not ask us to befriend lonely hearts; it generally does not require us to rescue people in distress; rather, it quibbles over whether we should be Good or Bad Samaritans; it does not ask us to be exemplary husbands, wives or parents, or siblings; it does not ask us not to cheat on our spouses; it does not ask us to strike friendships; nor does it facilitate the operation of friendships once they are struck; it does not ask us to be good employees or employers. The list goes on. Little wonder that Aristotle called law "intellect without the passions."

Now, consider the occasions for law's intervention. Law intervenes when amity breaks down between friends; when consensus is lost among associates—the law has no role where a handshake will do; when spouses have become each other's scourge; when families are no longer united in love; when employer and employee are no longer talking to or with each other; when neighbors are snarling at each other. Law is inseverably linked to the breakdown of concord. When law is brought in to restore concord, the quality of the resolution leaves much to be desired. Mediation is about the least friction-ridden mode of dispute resolution under the law. It is also the least frequently used—so infrequently that it has become a special case in most places, requiring extraordinary steps to draw people's attention to it. Still, so long as mediation is brokered by law, it cannot produce

---

36. "What is legalism? It is the ethical attitude that holds moral conduct to be a matter of rule following, and moral relationships to consist of duties and rights determined by rules. . . . Its most nearly complete expression is in the great legal systems of the European world. It [is] the political ideology of those who cherish these systems of law and, above all, those who are directly involved in their maintenance—the legal profession, both bench and bar. The court of law and the trial according to law are the social paradigms, the perfection, the very epitome, of legalistic morality." Judith Shklar, *Legalism* (Cambridge: Harvard University Press, 1964, 1986), pp. 1–2.

a resolution that does not leave the parties to the dispute less reconciled than they might have been had they resolved it outside the law. Other resolutions mediated by law are often concerned to establish winners and losers, blameworthiness, fault, responsibility, or negligence, thereby leaving loser resentment in their wake. Such outcomes are definitely not conducive to good-neighborliness.

So long as we act *humanly*, law has no interest in our affairs and we do not work with it. To seek to bring law into the comity of friends is to display bad faith or a complete lack of faith which is corrosive of friendship. For spouses to read to each other the Marriage Act is to fail to have a marriage or, at least, to have a defective marriage. When neighborly relations fall victim to mutual resort to property law and tort, it is a sign that the parties involved have become neighbors in name only. Moreover, in most life situations, we remain unmindful of law. How often do people *routinely* read car rental contracts or laundry/dry-cleaning contracts? Certainly ignorance of what the contract contains might be a mitigating factor but, ordinarily, ignorance does not exculpate one in the event of a breakdown in understanding. Yet, in most situations, we proceed on good faith, on the assumption that the other party will not seek any undue advantage so long as we do not.[37] Only when there is a failure or noncompliance do we invoke law.

I conclude that in all those activities which define what we value most in our humanity—social harmony, good-neighborliness, loving and being loved—the law is completely excluded or, at best, plays a negative role. The argument that without law we would be at one another's throats as-

---

37. The force of this point was brought home to me in a real life situation when I sued a car rental company to recover towing charges it had billed to my account after an accident. I had thought that the insurance I purchased at the time of rental covered all eventualities should I have an accident. It turned out that, in the fine print on the back of the rental contract, towing charges were excluded from my insurance coverage. I argued in court that this was not pointed out to me by the sales agent, who had directed my attention to other parts of the agreement that he deemed important. The judge agreed with me in part and split the cost of the towing between the company and me. I cite this experience here only because of what happened after judgment had been rendered. The judge instructed the court reporter that the remarks he was about to make should be off the record. Then he proceeded to say essentially the following: "Even I, a judge, do not ordinarily read the fine print at the car rental or the dry cleaners. So I might have been in your situation. Perhaps this case will make this company and possibly others put the most important points in bold print and at the front of the contract in the future." We routinely sign such everyday agreements: think of the airline ticket with its myriad limitations on the liability of the carrier. Only in crisis situations are we confronted with the ugly realization that many rights we assume we have do not exist or do not carry the implications we think they do or should.

sumes that without law we cannot trust ourselves to be human, that law is essential to our humanity. But if what I have been saying is true, then this assumption and the argument founded on it are implausible. For even in its best manifestation, in its most positive form, we try to hide the play of law, we strive to banish it from our most treasured relationships. Law is an acknowledgment of failure; it is what we resort to when we are unable otherwise to achieve our ends. *Law is always a second-best option.*

It might be objected that I have painted an overly negative picture of law, that I have completely ignored the many positive ways law intervenes in our lives. After all, it would be pointed out, law facilitates social inter- action, empowers us to bring about new social relations and generally to arrange our affairs for the preservation of concord and harmony in society. We incorporate clubs; we set up judiciaries and joint-stock companies; we make wills; we have adoption laws that enable us to create families where there would have been none; we make people secure in the enjoyment of their estates. Admittedly, law does all the foregoing and more; and this is good. But it is not clear to me that these facilitative dimensions of law are enough to obviate the force of my argument.

The question that needs to be posed is this: If law is such a harbinger of good, why do we work so hard to keep it from our most cherished rela- tionships? Why do we not use law to structure such relationships? Fur- thermore, the areas that are touted as shining manifestations of law's goodness are precisely those areas in which the predominant interactions are between "strangers" working beyond the pale of shared understand- ing, values, and principles. Law is crucial to operations in these spheres largely because in them the lure of gain from bad faith is very great and the danger of loss of face, an important marker of social standing in close-knit communities, is minimal.[38] The importance of law, then, is predicated on the insufficiency of trust, on the assumption that people will not do what they are supposed to do in the absence of law, and that they cannot be held to the performance of their duties unless they are interpellated as legal sub- jects. If we could do all the things for which law is a facilitator without law, we would prefer it. Additionally, we may still establish rules for the execu-

---

38. "Indeed, one reason people are frequently willing to ignore law is that they often pos- sess more expeditious means for achieving order. For example, neighbors in rural Shasta County are sufficiently close-knit to generate and enforce informal norms to govern minor irritations such as cattle-trespass and boundary-fence disputes. This close-knittedness enables victims of social transgressions to discipline deviants by means of simple self-help measures such as negative gossip and mild physical reprisals. Under these circumstances, informal so- cial controls are likely to supplant law." Ellickson, *Order without Law*, p. 282.

tion of the tasks for which law is a facilitator; but these rules do not have
to be *legal*, they may be purely *technical*.[39]

I conclude that law, in a sense, is an admission of the irreconcilability of
contradictions in society, and a recognition of the inevitability of conflict—
some individual's "right" is someone else's "no right"; somebody's privilege
is another's duty; one person's (legal) power is the other's disability; and so
forth.[40] This conflict-ridden evolution reaches its apogee in capitalist society where the enjoyment of rights etc. becomes a matter of mutual indifference between monadic individuals. This is a society in which the

> dominant conception of right imagines the right as a zone of discretion
> of the rightholder, a zone whose boundaries are more or less rigidly fixed
> at the time of the initial definition of the right. The right is a loaded gun
> that the rightholder may shoot at will in his corner of town. Outside that
> corner the other licensed gunmen [and women] may shoot him [or her]
> down. But the give-and-take of communal life and its characteristic con-
> cern for the actual effect of any decision upon the other person are in-
> compatible with this view of right and therefore, if this is the only
> possible view, with any regime of rights.[41]

Although it may be argued that the conception of "right" just quoted is
a peculiarity of the capitalist social formation, I should insist that if talk
about law is about rights, entitlements, immunities, and privileges, on and
against individuals and groups, law is not and cannot be a facilitator of
communal life of the sort that we value most. Law is indelibly marked by
the imprint of the circumstances of its emergence, and the recovery of a
more satisfactory form of community must be premised on its supersession.
It should be obvious that if we could constrict the spheres in which

39. E. B. Pashukanis makes a distinction between legal and technical rules: "Finally, even
in bourgeois society there are things like the organisation of the postal and rail services, of the
military, and so on, which cannot be related in their entirety to the sphere of *legal* regulation
unless one views them very superficially and allows oneself to be confused by the outward
form of laws, statutes and decrees. Train timetables regulate rail traffic in quite a different
sense than, let us say, the law concerning the liability of the railways regulates its relations
with consigners of freight. The first type of regulation is predominantly technical, the second
primarily legal." *Law and Marxism: A General Theory,* ed. and intro. Chris Arthur (London:
Ink Links, 1978; London: reprint, Pluto Press, 1983), p. 79.

40. For details see Hohfeld, *Fundamental Legal Conceptions,* p. 36.

41. Roberto Unger, "The Critical Legal Studies Movement," *Harvard Law Review* 96
(1983): 597. Unger, of course, does not believe that this is the only possible view; in fact, he
goes on to set out a regime of rights that accommodates, among other things, community
(see pp. 599–600).

we need law, and expand the spheres from which we ardently banish law, then law, lacking relevance, is sure to wither away on account of its superfluity. I have presented arguments that such an outcome is possible; it remains to provide grounds for its desirability.

V

At almost every level of their political and intellectual development, Marx and Engels arguably considered law as a kind of cancerous growth on human society. It is this normative appraisal of law that led to their insistence on the withering-away thesis. They differed from utopian critics because their thesis was firmly anchored in their account of the historical emergence of law and in the tendencies they were able to discern in the evolution of capitalist social formation. It is failure to attend to the *prescriptive* significance of the thesis that accounts for the persistent criticism that history gives us no reason to expect law will become extinct. A concomitant failure to appreciate the historical roots of the thesis leads to the charge that it is utopian. Both lines of criticisms lose sight of the fact that understanding the world is only a preliminary step to changing it. Marx's future communist individual, as Shlomo Avineri has rightly remarked, "is both a criterion for measuring existing political institutions and a paradigm of future society."[42]

Law grows in the ashes of community.[43] The lamentation of the loss of community is a recurrent theme in political theory. Marx followed this trend

42. Shlomo Avineri, *The Social and Political Thought of Karl Marx* (Cambridge: Cambridge University Press, 1968), p. 33.

43. I have deliberately left unexplicated the notion of "community." This is quite consistent with the speculative thrust of the present chapter. I am aware of the contemporary debates about liberalism and communitarianism. But these debates do not even begin to broach the radical thesis that I insist is Marx and Engels's true legacy: the requirement that we rethink human community and modes of social ordering in ways that have not hitherto been contemplated. In this, I follow their pattern of refusing to prognosticate the future character of communism or what it will be like to live under it. I hope, however, that my argument casts sufficient doubt on the claim of law to being the preeminent principle of social ordering in that changed world. A cautionary note, though: one formidable obstacle to the appeal of community is that it sometimes evokes justifiable fears of excessive conformity, herd instinct, and the obliteration of individuality. If, in attempting to reinvent community in extremely novel ways, we cannot do better than the simple, undifferentiated, tribal community of antiquity, we must accept failure. What we may not do is pretend that the ills we speak of are inevitable features of community, however configured. To show that these ills are not peculiar to community, one need only look at the remarkable sameness of life under late capitalism in the United States of America, despite the plurality of cultural institutions and the spurious claims of the captains of consciousness to genuine diversity in social life.

and made it a starting point. We take as our starting point the condition of modern society, of capitalist society, which is typified by the dominance of motley binary divisions: civil society and political society, individual and community, and so on. The key diremption of modern life, though, is that between the individual and the community: it is the ground of all the other divisions in the society.[44] The most essential embodiment of this phenomenon is the preservation of a zone of individual expression from which community or communal demands are excluded. Notwithstanding the relational nature of rights, the predominant relationship in civil society is one of mutual indifference among the atomistic individuals—sovereigns whose individual zones are sacrosanct and for whom community is inessential—that make it up. The complement to this sphere of unrestricted egoism is one in which these individuals have to recognize the need for community—recognize the interests of others, negotiate with other individuals to work out the conduct of everyday living and ensure that infringements of one another's spaces are kept to a minimum—the sphere in which sociality is recovered through law's mediation. The consequence is the illusion that community is external to and inessential for the individual, that community is a hostile or burdensome presence on the path to individual self-expression. Legal theorists take this doctrine of separate spheres as their starting point. Consequently, the unity that is essential to social life becomes an accidental requirement to be constructed with the aid of law and other forms of mediation.

Marx's argument is that the rigid separation in modern society between the individual and the community, and the attempt to effect their unity through law and other forms of mediation, rest on a misconstrual both of human nature and of the form of life most conducive to what is best in human nature. In capitalist society the principle of division is the organizing principle of human relationships. Rights are understood in individualist terms. Those who wish to affirm the rights of groups have a hard time establishing the legitimacy of their quest. Law consecrates individual rights and establishes them as the basic building blocks of social relations. But, for reasons outlined above concerning the impact of law on our most treasured relationships and our general unease about law, I submit that rights are corrosive of community.[45]

---

44. For a discussion of the diremption of life under modernity and its various manifestations, see Jürgen Habermas, *The Philosophical Discourse of Modernity*, trans. Frederick G. Lawrence (Cambridge: MIT Press, 1990), esp. lectures 1 and 2.

45. It is not accidental that in many of the controversies raging across American college campuses at the present time—concerning multiculturalism, affirmative action, racial discrimination, sexual harassment, etc.—the arguments of both sides are articulated in the language of

Contrary to the presuppositions of modern capitalist society, it is so-cial existence, or communal living, that defines the human essence. To live in community, to live in association with others, to cooperate with others in securing the conditions of life, these are the essential modes of life for human beings; and that mode of social ordering is best which en-hances this essential sociality. Does the mode of social ordering that has law for its organizing principle enhance such sociality? In section III above, it was argued that we exclude law from all those spheres in which our sociality is best manifested. In the areas where law predominates, the community that is facilitated is a community of convenience, marked by instrumentalism and typified by transience. We eagerly desire to be rid of it in order to return to the safe haven of family and friends. The law is one of the means by which human beings are drawn into a semblance of communal life counterposed to what is said to be a monadic existence in their private spheres. In law-inspired communal relations, individuals re-late as legal subjects, as infinitely variable personae simultaneously en-abled and hobbled by law: enabled because law defines the relationship, makes it possible; hobbled because they are restricted to the legally rele-vant personae they assume, rather than the persons that they are. This is the exact opposite of what real community is: we do not summon the law in forming friendships, nor do we interpose law in our relationships with friends. The community facilitated by law is an "illusory commu-nity"[46] which is built on the assumption that conflict is inevitable in the relation between the individual and the community or among individu-als left to their own designs.

Marx argued that bourgeois society has ensured the greatest efflores-cence of freedom in human history. The modern age is also justly cele-brated by Hegel and other philosophers as that age in which the principle of subjectivity, the sovereignty of the individual, has become the principle of social ordering. But the victory of individuality has been achieved at a very great price: the loss of genuine community. One need only look at some of the cleavages that typify bourgeois society for evidence of the lim-its of law as a facilitator of genuine communal living.

---

individual rights. This, I suggest, may be one reason why these controversies seem intractable. The right to free speech comes into conflict with respect for persons; the remedy for past and present discrimination conflicts with the right to equal protection of the law; and sometimes the instrument used for solving one problem helps create another. It should be clear that rights discourse does not contain within itself the solutions to the many problems it generates.

46. Karl Marx and Frederick Engels, *Collected Works*, published to date: vols. 1–34; 38–47 (New York: International Publishers, 1975–), 3:154. Hereafter cited as MECW.

Consider the problems of racial and sexual discrimination that are the subjects of such acrimonious debate in contemporary American society. Although there have been attempts by some radical-liberal theorists to affirm collective rights,[47] the dominant form of rights discourse is still in terms of individuals. Libertarian critics of radical liberalism insist that any effort to redress the wrongs of racial and sexual discrimination by appealing to the enjoyment of rights as a consequence of group membership, rather than individual identity, is wrongheaded. We may dismiss, as many tend to do, the protestations of libertarians as ideological special pleading. It seems to me, though, that rights discourse and its inherent contradictions pose insurmountable obstacles to community and the amicable resolution of conflicts. Somebody utters a racial insult to another; another person is a dealer in hard-core pornography. The utterer of the insult claims a right to freedom of expression; the offended party would invoke a right to respect and, ultimately, to equal protection of the law. As for the purveyor of pornography, he will invoke his right to free speech. Meanwhile, quite a few feminists now insist that pornography is not speech, that it is a harmful act which injures women qua women. In these cases, we confront the force of the underlying presuppositions of capitalist law.

These presuppositions determine on whom falls the burden of proof in particular cases. In criminal cases, such is the strength of the principle of individualism that the onus is always on the prosecutor to prove guilt, not on the accused to prove innocence. Little or no reference is allowed to what the consequences might be for society should the prosecutor fail to discharge the burden: what matters is upholding the rights of the individual. In free-speech cases, the opponent of offensive speech assumes the burden because *"free speech is the rule, not the exception. The restraint to be constitutional must be based on more than fear, on more than passionate opposition against the speech, on more than a revolted dislike for its contents. There must be some immediate injury to society that is likely if speech is allowed."*[48] The underscored statement has serious disabling consequences for the prospective anti-free-speech litigant. Because free speech is the rule, the onus is on the party who feels insulted to show that there will be injury to society. I suggest that it is an acknowledgment of the near impossibility of discharging this burden that has caused some

47. See, for example, Will Kymlicka, *Liberalism, Community, and Culture* (Oxford: Clarendon Press, 1991).

48. Justice William O. Douglas, dissenting, in *Dennis v. U.S.*, 341 U.S. 494. Quoted in Alan Barth, *Prophets with Honor: Great Dissents and Great Dissenters in the Supreme Court* (New York: Vintage, 1974), p. 238. My emphasis.

feminists[49] to try to process speech as an *act* which will then open a new line of attack that has a solid pedigree in capitalist law: if it harms another, it may not be done. But I am interested in a different kind of consequence: the impact on community.

Imagine for a moment that instead of proceeding from a presupposition of the sovereignty of the individual, we proceed from one concerning the value of social solidarity. But maybe we do not even need to imagine this different scenario. Recall what was said above about the areas of social living from which we strive strenuously to exclude law. An appreciation of the value of friendship suffices to disincline us to make snide remarks about our friends to their faces. And when we do so behind their backs, so long as we judge the friendship worth salvaging or preserving, we vigorously deny such remarks when confronted by our friends. We do not appeal to our right to free speech in such situations. In addition, considerations of social harmony and amicable coexistence lead us to refrain from insulting our neighbors, colleagues, students, etc., even when such relationships are defined by law. In these diverse situations law plays no role in dissuading us from saying hurtful things or behaving obnoxiously: the sole consideration is the preservation of community. The greater the likelihood that these associations will endure, the greater the lengths we go to to exclude the corrosive influence of law.

Now, consider what the consequence will be in a social formation where the principle of social solidarity is the basic presupposition of the law. We should expect that the burden of proof would fall on the utterer of hateful speech to show that the speech does not cause harm or that it is promotive of community, rather than on the person or group that alleges the speech causes harm. If the commitment to community were to become the principle of social ordering, it is obvious that just as law is superfluous in those areas of social life where community, other-regarding considerations, and concord command a premium at the present time, it will be superfluous in this future society. That such an outcome is desirable is evidenced in our qualified enthusiasm for law, on balance. That law thrives on the diremption of individual and social life is the principal reason why it cannot be the preferred principle of social ordering in a better social formation than the capitalist one.

A social ordering that separates these two moments of human life and opposes one to the other cannot be the best or most adequate for human flourishing. Of course, this statement implies that there is a truly human existence

49. Notably Catharine MacKinnon, *Feminism Unmodified* (Cambridge: Harvard University Press, 1987).

that corresponds to the way humans are. Marx did try to show how our social nature cannot be realized save in a social ordering that has transcended the
spurious community that law facilitates. Although this is a "new principle," it
is developed from an analysis of the "existing principles of the capitalist
world." The solution lies in the abolition of state, law, and other forms of mediation which stand between humans and the realization of their essence.

Law, as a structure of rights etc., presupposes that society has become
riven with contradictions and conflicts that are no longer amenable to settlement and resolution within the bounds of mutually shared understandings and expectations. As a mediating institution, law is external to people;
it stands between them and their fellows. That is why a qualitatively superior social formation must include the supersession of law. How shall we
bring about this new state of affairs? According to the outlines of the withering-away thesis, there are two fundamental prerequisites for the transition to that mode of life which Marx called "communism":

(1) The proletariat must use the power—legal, political, economic—it
wins in the socialist revolution to remove all the fetters that inhibited material production in the capitalist mode of production. The means to this
is the transformation of private property in the means of production to
public ownership and the elimination of the anarchy that characterized
capitalist production. The rational organization of production is crucial.
One of the essential differences between socialism and capitalism is that
the former does, and the latter does not, in the main, subject production
to conscious social regulation.[50]

(2) The proletariat must use the same power to deepen democracy and
socialize the means of production. The deepening of democracy must
mean (it can mean nothing else) the broadening of control over the levers
of social life to cover the widest spectrum of society imaginable. In production, it must mean (a) that the means of production are employed in
the interests of society and (b) that society has effective disposition over
the means of production it owns and the products of the process of production. "The basic criterion of socialization of the means of production
therefore, in our understanding, is the criterion of democratism."[51] If the

50. See Marx's letter to Ludwig Kugelmann in Karl Marx and Frederick Engels, *Selected
Works* (Moscow: Progress Publishers, 1969), 2:419.
51. W. Brus, *Socialist Ownership and Political Systems* (London: Routledge & Kegan Paul,
1975), p. 30. Brus points out that "the term 'democratism' instead of simply 'democracy' is to
emphasize that this is not only a matter of constitutional principles but also of the extent to
which they are implemented in practice, of real 'democraticness'. Of course, we do not attach
any fundamental importance to the distinction between these shades of meaning" (p. 96).

conditions adumbrated are met, the demise of law follows as a matter of course in postcapitalist society. It is important to stress that (1) and (2) are the *minimum* conditions for the construction of the future society. By themselves, they do not exhaust what has to be done to realize the mode of social ordering that we are to understand by Marxian communism. When these conditions are met, we will have laid the foundations for a radically different future. The withering away of law is the outcome of the conditions to be created by the socialist transition.

Now that we have explained the goal and adumbrated the conditions, the question arises: "What premises do we have to admit in order to believe that a social organization free from any mediating and coercive power and from any political bodies is practicable? What conditions would make conceivable a society which can 'administer things' without 'governing people'?"[52] I take it that there is not much I, or anyone else, can say to somebody (e.g., a fascist) who does not allow the desirability of the kind of future society envisaged by Marx. But there surely is room for disagreement on its practicability.

There are people who argue that the communist vision cannot be attained. The impracticality of the vision is a common criticism of the withering-away thesis. Here I consider the criticisms of Leszek Kolakowski and Timothy O'Hagan. Kolakowski, reflecting on what he calls "the myth of human self-identity" in socialist thought, set as the aim of his enterprise "to point out a soteriological myth hidden in the traditional Marxist anticipation of socialism as based on the identity of civil and political society. I will try to reveal a continuity (though not identity) between this soteriology and contemporary totalitarian variants of socialism and to say why the Marxian ideal of unity is in my opinion impracticable."[53] Similarly, O'Hagan insists:

The search for the withering-away of the *Rechtstaat*, I argue, leads to the alternatives of authoritarianism, on the one hand, or to an unattainable reversion to a simplified form of life, incompatible with advanced technology, on the other. If socialism is to be a reality, it must allow both popular access to the levers of power within a complex productive system and also the flourishing of Millian pluralism. To do this, it must have at its disposal a correspondingly complex constitutional system to guarantee the

52. Leszek Kolakowski, "The Myth of Human Self-Identity: Unity of Civil and Political Society in Socialist Thought," in Leszek Kolakowski and Stuart Hampshire, eds., *The Socialist Idea* (London: Weidenfeld & Nicolson, 1974), p. 22.
53. Ibid., p. 18.

twin aspirations of democracy and pluralism and to mediate between them.[54]

Let me quickly dismiss the second part of O'Hagan's argument. Of course, socialism—a transitional stage—would very much remain, especially in its earlier phase, a sphere needing mediation.[55] But the progress of the transition will be measured by how quickly it is creating the conditions to make superfluous the necessity for coercion and mediation. To the extent that this is not the case (as it obviously is not in the picture painted by O'Hagan) his criticism is misaimed: a society that still stands in need of a mediating instrument is *not* a postpolitical, postlegal society. We now turn to the arguments adduced to show that postpolitical society is unattainable.

Kolakowski gives two reasons for his pessimism. First, he finds it very difficult to imagine what reasons there could be for the belief that the abolition of classes (in the Marxian sense) would lead to elimination of the conflict of private interests. The class struggle in bourgeois society is historically specific. It is a particular instance of the "struggle for the distribution of surplus product." According to Kolakowski, there is no reason to presume that the struggle will not be replayed in a different historical form in socialist society, be it democratic or authoritarian. Socialist society with its public ownership must, he insists, "inevitably beget social layers endowed with privileges in controlling the means of production, the labour force and the instruments of coercion."[56] If the last statement is true, and Kolakowski thinks it is, there are no reasons to deny that the occupiers of these privileged layers will employ every means to safeguard their position and increase their privileges.[57] There are two problems with Kolakowski's first argument:

(1) The argument that the emergence of a new ruling class is inevitable in socialist society and beyond rests on a questionable conception of human nature. Kolakowski affirms this questionable conception of human nature when he concludes that Marx "entirely overlooked the possibility that some sources of conflict and aggression may be inherent in the permanent characteristics of the species and are unlikely to be eradicated by institutional changes."[58] That this is the way our biological nature *is* is not

54. Timothy O'Hagan, *The End of Law?* (Oxford: Basil Blackwell, 1984), p. 3.

55. See Marx and Engels, *Selected Works*, 2:19.

56. Kolakowski, 'The Myth of Human Self-Identity," pp. 31–32.

57. "Unless, of course, we predict a sudden restoration of the angelic nature in the human race." Ibid., p. 32.

58. Ibid.

proven as far as I know. Kolakowski's claim, then, is not obviously correct, but let us suppose that it is. What follows from such a supposition? Perhaps some sources of conflict and aggression are inherent in the species. But it does not follow that conflicts arising from them are not amenable to institutional mitigation, if not eradication. Our many natural instincts are profoundly affected by the institutional media through which they are expressed. As Marx would say, hunger is a natural instinct in us. But hunger satisfied by raw meat is a different hunger from that which is sated by steak eaten with fork and knife. Thus, even if Kolakowski is correct, he still has to defeat the argument that our instincts of aggression and conflict are typically expressed in institutional arrangements and cannot remain unaffected by these media. Furthermore, it may be that these sources of aggression and conflict are ineradicable. But there is little doubt that they can be reduced and, sometimes, channeled into productive outlets.

Nor is Kolakowski's pessimism about human nature the only possible view. Without doubt, the history of the twentieth century and its misbegotten "socialist" revolutions must make us pause and qualify our enthusiasm for the possibility of epochal change. It is also true that Marx's faith in technology and progress coupled with the amoralism of many putatively Marxist regimes have created some unspeakable horrors in recent history. But to think that all these horrors are traceable to human nature is to offer only one possible interpretation. There is ample evidence from these horrors for the opposite assumption that human beings could just as well be altruistic, benevolent, and kind. While some human beings were busy constructing the horror chambers, a lot more were dedicated to dismantling them and to bringing those responsible to book. Humanity has survived the many grotesque horrors in its evolution precisely because it has not been completely overtaken by the human proclivity for self-destruction. If the evidence from history and anthropology is any indicator, there is more reason to be optimistic about the possibility of eradicating particular kinds of conflict that disintegrate society than there is to be pessimistic. Part of the underlying assumption of Marxist philosophy of history is that we shall continue to increase our knowledge of our own nature and of the nature of social processes. This is the basis of the Marxist optimism concerning the human condition. That Kolakowski comes down on the side of pessimism and Marxists on the side of optimism is a matter of choice with respect to the possibilities for improvement in the human situation. How this could be held by anyone to vitiate the withering-away thesis remains unclear and unconvincing to me. If Kolakowski's point is the limited one that the zeal with which some Marxists have tried to create the millennium has tended to overlook some sources of conflict and aggression in human nature, and that this has led in practice to totalitarianism, there is no reason for us to demur. A cautionary note of this sort need not lead to an acceptance of a conservative pessimism about the possibilities for improvement in the human situation.

(2) Kolakowski simply read Marx wrong if he took Marx to assert that postpolitical, postlegal society will be without "conflicts of private interest." A similar criticism can be made of Christine Sypnowich's more recent attempt to cast doubt on the plausibility and feasibility of the withering-away thesis. She argues that the "orthodox Marxist's rejection of the possibility of socialist law rests on two assumptions: first, that there would be material abundance under socialism, so legal rules regulating scarce resources would be superfluous; and second, that socialism accordingly would be devoid of interpersonal conflict, so there would be no need for the mediating role performed by legal institutions." These assumptions, she says, are problematic. To begin with, the promise of material abundance under socialism remains to be realized. In the second place, the elimination of scarcity does not mean that conflict would disappear. There are other possible sources of conflict, besides scarcity, in any society. One possible source of conflict might be disagreement "about the best way to mobilize and distribute resources." If conflict "would outlive capitalism, law could continue to be necessary to mediate socially useful conflicts between individuals and groups."[59] For Marx, contrary to the interpretations offered by Kolakowski and Sypnowich, communist society does not herald the annihilation of human individuality. The unity of the individual and the community does not mean the dissolution of either of them or the complete absorption of one by the other. Individuals will populate postpolitical society. As individuals, they will necessarily be different and will, we should expect, have differing interests that may conflict from time to time. The claim that Marxism assumes a conflict-free society is unwarranted.

59. Christine Sypnowich, *The Concept of Socialist Law* (Oxford: Clarendon Press, 1990), p. 7. Sypnowich does not take seriously the distinction between "socialism" and "communism" which is pivotal to the withering-away thesis. Marx and Engels did not deny that law would be necessary in that earlier phase of postcapitalist society to which they gave the name "socialism." But they insisted that this is merely a transitional phase in which the conditions are put in place for the emergence of that higher and qualitatively superior mode of social ordering that they called "communism." Thus, I see no reason why most Marxists would have any problem conceding the relevance of different forms of mediation under the socialist phase. The real revolutionary force of Marxist social theory is contained in its insistence on creating a mode of social ordering that has no antecedent in human history: one that does not need law, state, morality, religion or, yes, the division of labor. See MECW, 3:297, 5:81.

Here we directly encounter the interface between philosophy of law, ethics, and social and political theory. The reason law cannot be the facilitator of genuine community is that it embodies a structure of rights, entitlements, etc. Rights are claims assertable by one individual or group against another or among individuals in particular groups. The presence of law in a society is a recognition that the society is riven with irreconcilable contradictions. Law essentially presupposes division between one individual and another, the individual and the group, or one subgroup and another in a bigger social whole. At the same time, law is brought in to pull these divided elements back into harmony; to restore, ultimately, community (MECW, 3:297, 5:78–80, 86).

The same problem expresses itself in ethics in the dichotomy between self-interest and the common good; in politics, between the person and the citizen. In other words, the general problem in social theory of eliminating the tension between individuality and collectivity is exactly the one to which, at this level, according to Marx and Engels, communism is the resolution. Communism is the stage at which the individual no longer experiences community as a burden, as a hostile presence. The community, in turn, no longer seeks to curb individuality in order to preserve itself.[60] The restoration of community, therefore, is not a simple elimination of individuality or a condition of perfect unanimity where there is no difference and, hence, no conflict. So it is false to assert that the withering-away thesis presupposes the elimination of conflict from human society. To this extent, Kolakowski and Sypnowich are simply wrong. What will be different in postlegal society will be the *nature of social conflict* and the *modes of dispute resolution*.

We should make a distinction between two broad kinds of conflict: *social conflicts* and *personal conflicts*.[61] Social conflicts are those which concern the crucial aspects of social existence: production, distribution, consump-

---

60. "Only within the community has each individual the means of cultivating his gifts in all directions; hence personal freedom becomes possible only within the community. In the previous substitutes for the community, in the state, etc., personal freedom has existed only for the individuals who developed under the conditions of the ruling class, and only insofar as they were individuals of this class. The illusory community in which individuals have up till now combined always took on an independent existence in relation to them, and since it was the combination of one class over against another, it was at the same time for the oppressed class not only a completely illusory community, but a new fetter as well. In the real community the individuals obtain their freedom in and through their association." MECW, 5:78.

61. These do not exhaust the kinds of conflict there are in human society. Moreover, there is an infinite variety of manifestations within these broad categories.

tion, and exchange. The objects of conflict under this heading range from power (political, economic), to prestige, family form, and modes of socialization. They do not have to be class conflicts, but class struggles are included in this category. They are social because, if unchecked, their occurrence must over time lead to the degeneration of society itself. Personal conflicts, on the other hand, have typically limited consequences and have those consequences only for the persons who are party to them. Personal conflicts may have social ramifications and, when they do, they pass over into social conflict. For example, a fight between two individuals, in which one person ends up killing the other, may degenerate into a social conflict: a feud.[62] The distinction between social and personal conflicts is not a new distinction. We already make similar distinctions in daily life, as I have tried to show in previous sections. There are many conflicts that we consider to be beyond the reach of law.[63] The challenge is whether we can expand the sphere of nonlegally mediated conflicts and constrict that of legally mediated ones in the future. For Marxism, this challenge is not only worth being met; it is considered feasible.

The more postlegal society approximates its concept, the fewer social conflicts we should expect to see. The personal conflicts that arise from individual differences would no longer require a force standing outside society, like law and the state, to resolve them. On the contrary, we should witness an efflorescence of what are now regarded as alternative (to legal) modes of dispute settlement (e.g., arbitration) and/or mediation (by other members of the community). We have already argued that the nuclei of those future modes of dispute resolution are present in even the most litigious society. It is not uncommon to have judges encourage litigants to work out settlements between themselves in noncriminal cases, especially those involving filial and other emotional ties. The effort to exclude law from the most treasured human relationships is yet another indication of the possibility of alternative modes of social order.[64] "[T]he success of nonlegal dispute settlement has always depended upon a coherent community vision. How to resolve conflict, inversely stated, is how (or

62. See Jacob Black-Michaud, *Feudal Societies* (Oxford: Blackwell, 1980).

63. For an account of contemporary attempts at dispute resolution and social interaction without law, see Ellickson, *Order without Law*, chap. 14, esp. the many sociological studies cited there.

64. Courts do not rush to adjudicate divorce cases until it is obvious that the marriage has irretrievably broken down. Even then, judges never cease to encourage the parties to explore any possibility of reconciliation. We feel betrayed when a friend drags us to law before exploring an amicable settlement.

whether) to preserve community."[65] Auerbach further points out: "The enduring Edenic vision of a harmonious community may invariably be undercut—but even in the American experience, where law reigns supreme,
the vision is never entirely stifled."[66] That Auerbach is correct is the best
hope we have for the realizability of postlegal society against the acerbic
pessimism of people such as Kolakowski, O'Hagan, and Sypnowich. For
where the unity of civil and political society that galls Kolakowski so much
is achieved, the meaning of justice would be clear to its members: "Precisely that clarity [in earlier communities] rendered courts and lawyers not
only superfluous, but even subversive. Only when there is congruence between individuals and their community, with shared commitment to common values, is there a possibility for justice without law."[67]

The argument of the preceding paragraph has a double function. At a
descriptive level, it is a prediction of what will be in a situation where the
preconditions we identified earlier have been fulfilled. The corroboration
of this aspect of the argument will have to await historical development.
The argument also has a normative dimension. It paints a picture of a state
of affairs that is desirable by Marxist criteria. It is a part of the Marxist
project. It has to be judged not by how appealing a picture it paints of the
future, but by how good the grounds are for its acceptance. The normative
claims rest on the premise discussed above that political theorists and ordinary people alike view law as a second-best option. That is to say, a
world in which we can do without law will be a better world than one in
which we cannot. The problem is that even a world without law will not
be a world without conflict. The question, then, is whether the presence of
conflicts per se entails the presence of law. This is not the case.

A possible objection is that law and conflicts of any kind are inseparable;
that is, where there is conflict, there is law. Our reply is that, even under
present conditions, there are many conflicts (e.g., family quarrels, misun-
derstandings between friends, disputes among allies or business associates)
that are not brought within the purview of law. At the least, efforts are
made to keep the law out of some spheres of life. Part of the task enjoined
by the withering-away thesis is that of widening those spheres where law
plays no role and narrowing those where law is relevant or necessary.

Is the program just suggested practicable? The conflicts that will likely
occur in postlegal society can unfold in many ways that we cannot antici-

65. Auerbach, *Justice without Law?* p. 4.
66. Ibid., p. 7.
67. Ibid., p. 16.

pate. What gives us grounds to think that these ways will not include some which require some kind of law? It must be conceded that there is no basis for such an expectation. People might still kill one another, there might still be occurrences of drunk driving, and so forth. How will our nonlegal society cope with these problems? Some of these questions touch on larger issues of democracy, popular control over decisionmaking, decentralization of authority, understanding of human nature, and others that cannot be satisfactorily addressed here. It is probable, though, that if the conditions for a genuinely communist society were fulfilled, there would be so few incidences of some of these infractions that it would not require law to deal with them. This is so because such infractions would no longer be couched in terms of violations and affirmations of rights, duties, entitlements, etc. It might even be that the best we can hope for is a minimal presence, not an absence, of law. Whatever the future outcome is, it remains plausible to argue that the pursuit of a nonpolitical, nonlegal society is worthwhile and desirable.

The second argument that Kolakowski deploys against the attainability of postpolitical society is closely related to the first. This argument states that even if there was a time when the unity of civil and political society was achieved, in "stagnant primitive communities," there is no reason to expect that a restoration is possible. Were a restoration possible, there is no reason to believe that "it could be secured by institutional means." This is so because the hope of restoration "would presuppose an unprecedented moral revolution running against the whole course of the past history of culture" by which people who were once coerced to do something out of fear would later do the same thing willingly and cheerfully.[68] Kolakowski is led to this conclusion by his pessimistic view of human nature which I have already criticized.

What Kolakowski refuses to concede is the educability of human beings.[69] He has also chosen to ignore the material preconditions for communism. It is an integral part of the Marxist project that the society of the future cannot be built until humanity possesses the means to create the material wherewithal to satisfy everybody's basic needs fully (MECW, 3:306, 5:64, 75, 76, 81, 87). The presence of abundance is required to minimize temptation and, ultimately, enhance the educability of human beings. A variant of Kolakowski's second argument is advanced by O'Hagan in the passage already cited. According to this ver-

---

68. Kolakowski, "The Myth of Human Self-Identity," pp. 32–33.
69. See also the last two paragraphs of McBride, "Non-Coercive Society," pp. 196–97.

sion, the vision of postpolitical society can be realized only under an authoritarian regime or in an unattainable reversion to a simplified form of life incompatible with advanced technology. I am *amazed* that O'Hagan thinks that Marx's withering-away thesis even remotely resembles a call for a return to the undifferentiated substantiality of the infancy of the human race. Not even Rousseau could be charged successfully with this error.[70] O'Hagan's reading of the thesis turns Marx, a dialectical theorist of history into a cyclical theorist: the future will and must always be in the past. This is nonsensical. O'Hagan's own thesis of the eternality of law appears more plausible than it is only when placed beside this distortion and bastardization of Marx's position.

The withering-away thesis does not presuppose a reversion to a simplified form of life. On the contrary, it is today's complex modern technology, which creates the abundance of wealth we have witnessed in our time (MECW, 5:64, 75, 80), that permits us to envisage a future when complexity will no longer dominate humans but, rather, will be put at the service of the new individual of postpolitical, postlegal society. I cite the description by Marx and Engels of what this new mode of social ordering will look like:

3) In all previous revolutions the mode of activity always remained unchanged and it was only a question of a different distribution of this activity, a new distribution of labour to other persons, whilst the communist revolution is directed against the hitherto existing *mode* of activity, does away with *labour*, and abolishes the rule of all classes with the classes themselves, because it is carried through by the class which no longer counts as a class in society, which is not recognised as a class, and is in itself the expression of the dissolution of all classes, nationalities, etc., within present society; and 4) Both for the production on a mass scale of this communist consciousness, and for the success of the cause itself, the alteration of men on a mass scale is necessary, an alteration which can only take place in a

---

70. In the concluding paragraph of the appendix to *A Discourse on the Origin of Inequality*, Rousseau wrote: "What, then, is to be done? Must societies be totally abolished? Must *meum tuum* be annihilated, and must we return again to the forests to live among bears? This is a deduction in the manner of my adversaries, which I would as soon anticipate as let them have the shame of drawing. . . . As for men like me, whose passions have destroyed their original simplicity, who can no longer subsist on plants or acorns, or live without laws and magistrates . . . [t]hey will respect the sacred bonds of their communities; . . . [b]ut they will not therefore have less contempt for a constitution that cannot support itself without the aid of so many splendid characters, much oftener wished for than found." *The Social Contract and Discourses*, pp. 112–13.

practical movement, a *revolution*; the revolution is necessary, therefore, not only because the *ruling* class cannot be overthrown in any other way, but also because the class *overthrowing* it can only in a revolution succeed in ridding itself of all the muck of ages and become fitted to found society anew. (5:52–53; also see 5:47,81)

There is contained in the above passage, and others like it, the kernel of Marx and Engels's commitment to the most profound and radical restructuring of human society in history. The idea of a return to some pristine earlier state represents a grotesque misconstrual of the communist revolution. That this optimism about human nature and its possibilities is the ground of the withering-away thesis should no longer be doubted. That we are still a long way from the communist society of the future is an assertion that no Marxist worth the name would deny. Covering the distance in the shortest time possible is the challenge of the future. Bringing more and more people to the realization of the possibility of a postpolitical, postlegal society is an urgent task the present forces on us.

VI

I should not end this work without pointing out some of the problems that are bound to arise in the construction of postlegal, postpolitical society. This is not the first time that the problem of the future of law has been articulated in Marxism. For example, one cannot help but be impressed by the optimism exuded by those who anticipated the withering away of law on the morrow of the October Revolution in the former Soviet Union.[71] However, the experiences of the past seventy-five years which have witnessed, first, the strengthening of laws in the former "socialist" countries and, lately, their collapse, as well as the current enthusiasm for law and its appurtenances, must induce some questioning in even the most optimistic of Marxists. The ebullient optimism of that era has long since yielded to a widespread pessimism that makes some Marxist interpreters concede that the whole withering-away thesis is an aberration. Hence, they readily opt for bourgeois liberal solutions.[72] Among those who hold forth the banner of the postlegal, postpolitical society and its possibility, there is a more pronounced mood of resignation that this new society is not going to happen "in our lifetime." Consequently we see renewed interest among Marx-

71. See in general the collection *Soviet Political Thought: An Anthology*, ed. and trans. Michael Jaworsky (Baltimore: Johns Hopkins University Press, 1967), esp. pt. 1.
72. E.g., O'Hagan, *The End of Law?*

ists in discussions of the rule of law or socialist legality. Among non-Marxists, there is renewed confidence in the necessity of law to civilization.

I am not inclined to discount the enormous sociological problems that have to be overcome on the path to realization of the future communist society. But postpolitical, postlegal society presents such an alluring picture to us because it promises a social order in which humans will relate to one another without legal mediation. In such a society, we are supposed to dispense with the innumerable personae or masks that we have assumed hitherto in history in order to relate to one another in complex social formations. I have argued that doubts about the attainability, rather than the desirability, of communist society motivate our opposition to the form of social ordering it enjoins. These doubts are not without grounds.

It seems to me that such a social formation will require either small, relatively homogeneous communities, in which "everybody knows everybody else," or forms of social ordering as yet unknown to us for administering large population concentrations and economic units. Outside of self-consciously utopian speculations, insufficient work has been done on this.[73] Many helpful hints are scattered throughout Marx's own writings. A more adequate and, I should say, more convincing account of the withering-away thesis requires that Marxists pay more attention to the problem of the sociological prerequisites for the realization of postlegal, postpolitical society. I surmise that these sociological prerequisites would include units of administration that are small enough to enable every person who wishes to to participate in the running of such units.

The twentieth century, however, is the century of the emergence of megalopolises, of octopus-like transnational conglomerates and vast corporate industrial and commercial concerns, of stupendous advances in technology which, for the first time in human history, turns the idea of the society of abundance from fiction into fact, from utopia into reality, and gives content to the idea of *world history*. Whatever odious consequences are associated with this tremendous growth in the development of the productive forces in our time, few will deny that the economies of scale and the productivity this development generates are the best bets we have for ushering in the future society of abundance that we said is the material prerequisite for the withering away of law. They were also the basis of Marx's optimism about the future and of his embrace of the capitalist

73. Exceptions include Robert A. Dahl, *After the Revolution? Authority in a Good Society* (New Haven: Yale University Press, 1970) and John Friedmann, *The Good Society* (Cambridge: MIT Press, 1979).

mode of production as a necessary staging area for entry into the communist society of the future.[74]

The snag is that there is an almost necessary connection between the development of the productive forces, the large economies of scale they afford, and the emergence of the alienation-ridden megalopolises in which there are more personae than persons. Given that it seems the postlegal, postpolitical, post-division-of-labor society must be founded on a high degree of decentralization and on the proliferation of small units of administration, the question that arises is the following: Can we retain sufficient efficiency in the utilization of the highly developed forces of production that we have and, at the same time, operate them within the context of small-enough units of administration in which the face-to-face society of the future might be realized?

I confess that I do not have answers to this question. In addition, an adequate answer must be multifaceted, since we are talking about remaking society in ways for which we lack antecedents. This task requires a competence in politics, economics, sociology, urban and regional planning, and other disciplines that I do not pretend to possess. Perhaps this is the ultimate challenge of this book: that it calls upon all those for whom law-mediated social ordering is a second-best option to restore utopian reflections on human possibilities to the center of the social-scientific agenda. As for me, I will conclude on an optimistic note. A refusal to abandon what Jerold Auerbach has called the Edenic vision of a harmonious community might be the only reason for plodding on, for pursuing the path to that society in which the poet Thiago de Mello's "The Statutes of Man (A Permanent Act of Law)" will have become the guiding principles of everyday life:

> FINAL ARTICLE: The use of the word freedom is hereby
> prohibited,
> and will be struck from every dictionary
> and from the deceptive mires of the
> mouth.
> Henceforth

74. Consider the following passages from Marx: "Only with large-scale industry does the abolition of private property become possible." MECW, 5:64. "Competition separates individuals from one another, not only the bourgeois but still more the workers, in spite of the fact that it brings them together. Hence it is a long time before these individuals can unite, apart from the fact that for the purpose of this union—if it is not to be merely local—*the necessary means, the big industrial cities and cheap and quick communications, have first to be produced by large-scale industry.*" MECW, 5:75. My emphasis.

freedom will be something living and
transparent
like a fire or a river,
like a grain of wheat,
and its home will always be
within the heart of man.[75]

75. In *Latin American Revolutionary Poetry: A Bilingual Anthology*, ed. and intro. Robert Marquez (New York: Monthly Review Press, 1974), pp. 95–97. Copyright © 1974 by R. Marquez. Reprinted by permission of Monthly Review Foundation.

Selected Bibliography

Aarnio, Aulis. *Philosophical Perspectives in Jurisprudence*. Helsinki: Societas Philosophica Fennica, 1983.

Acton, H. B. *The Illusion of the Epoch*. London: 1955.

Agresto, John. *The Supreme Court and Constitutional Democracy*. Ithaca: Cornell University Press, 1984.

Allen, C. K. *Law in the Making*. 7th ed. Oxford: Clarendon Press, 1964.

Althusser, Louis. *For Marx*. Trans. Ben Brewster. London: Verso, 1979.

——. *Montesquieu, Rousseau, and Marx*. Trans. Ben Brewster. London: Verso, 1982.

Aquinas, Thomas. *Treatise on Law*. Dominican translation. Chicago: Regnery Gateway, n.d.

Ash, William. *Marxism and Moral Concepts*. New York: Monthly Review Press, 1964.

Auerbach, Jerold S. *Justice without Law?* New York: Oxford University Press, 1983.

Avineri, Shlomo. *Hegel's Theory of the Modern State*. Cambridge: Cambridge University Press, 1972.

——. *The Social and Political Thought of Karl Marx*. Cambridge: Cambridge University Press, 1968.

Ball, Terence, and James Farr, eds. *After Marx*. Cambridge: Cambridge University Press, 1984.

Barth, Alan. *Prophets with Honor: Great Dissents and Great Dissenters in the Supreme Court*. New York: Vintage, 1974.

Bartholomew, Paul C., and Joseph F. Menez. *Summaries of Leading Cases on the Constitution*. 12th ed. Totowa, N.J.: Rowman & Allanheld, 1983.

Bass, Jack. *Unlikely Heroes*. New York: Touchstone, 1982.

Battaglia, Anthony. *Toward a Reformulation of Natural Law*. New York: Seabury Press, 1981.

Beirne, P., and R. Quinney, eds. *Marxism and Law*. Toronto: Wiley, 1982.

Berman, Harold J. *Justice in the U.S.S.R.* Rev. ed., enlarged. Cambridge: Harvard University Press, 1963.

——. *Law and Revolution*. Cambridge: Harvard University Press, 1983.

Blackshield, A. R., ed. *Legal Change: Essays in Honour of Julius Stone*. Sydney: Butterworths, 1983.

Bobbio, Norberto. *Thomas Hobbes and the Natural Law Tradition*. Trans. Daniela Gobetti. Chicago: University of Chicago Press, 1993.

Bober, M. M. *Karl Marx's Interpretation of History*. 2d rev. ed. Cambridge: Harvard University Press, 1962.

Burman, Sandra B., and Barbara E. Harrell-Bond, eds. *The Imposition of Law*. New York: Academic Press, 1979.

Cain, Maureen, and Alan Hunt. *Marx and Engels on Law*. London: Academic Press, 1979.

Cardozo, Benjamin. *The Nature of the Judicial Process*. New Haven: Yale University Press, 1921.

Carter, Lief H. *Reason in Law*. 2d ed. Boston: Little, Brown, 1984.

Chkhikvadze, V. *The State, Democracy, and Legality in the USSR*. Moscow: Progress Publishers, 1972.

Cohen, G. A. *Karl Marx's Theory of History: A Defence*. Princeton: Princeton University Press, 1978.

Colletti, Lucio. *Marxism and Hegel*. Trans. Lawrence Garner. London: Verso, 1979.

Collins, Hugh. *Marxism and Law*. New York: Oxford University Press, 1982.

Cotta, Sergio. "Positive Law and Natural Law." *Review of Metaphysics* 37 (1983): 265–85.

Cover, Robert M. *Justice Accused: Antislavery and the Judicial Process*. New Haven: Yale University Press, 1975.

Dahl, Robert A. *After the Revolution? Authority in a Good Society*. New Haven: Yale University Press, 1970.

D'Entrèves, A. P. *Natural Law*. 2d rev. ed. London: Hutchinson, 1970.

Dobb, Maurice. *Studies in the Development of Capitalism*. Rev. ed. New York: International Publishers, 1963.

Dworkin, Ronald. *Taking Rights Seriously*. Cambridge: Harvard University Press, 1977.

Edelman, Bernard. *Ownership of the Image*. London: Routledge & Kegan Paul, 1979.

Elias, T. O. *The Nature of African Customary Law*. Manchester: Manchester University Press, 1956.

Ellickson, Robert C. *Order without Law: How Neighbors Settle Disputes*. Cambridge: Harvard University Press, 1991.

Engels, Frederick. *Anti-Dühring*. Peking: Foreign Languages Press, 1976.

——. *The Origin of the Family, Private Property, and the State*. New York: International Publishers, 1972.

Fine, Bob. *Democracy and the Rule of Law*. London: Pluto Press, 1984.

Finnis, J. M. *Natural Law and Natural Rights*. Oxford: Clarendon Press, 1980.

Friedman, Lawrence M. *The Legal System*. New York: Russell Sage Foundation, 1975.

Friedmann, John. *The Good Society*. Cambridge: MIT Press, 1979.

Fuller, Lon L. *Legal Fictions*. Stanford: Stanford University Press, 1967.

——. *The Morality of Law*. Rev. ed. New Haven: Yale University Press, 1969.

Gerety, Tom. "Iron Law: Why Good Lawyers Make Bad Marxists." J. Roland Pennock and John W. Chapman, eds. *Marxism: Nomos XXVI*. New York: New York University Press, 1983.

Golding, Martin P. *Legal Reasoning*. New York: Alfred A. Knopf, 1984.

Grene, David, and Richmond Lattimore, eds. *The Complete Greek Tragedies: Sophocles I*. Chicago: University of Chicago Press, 1954.

Habermas, Jürgen. *Legitimation Crisis*. Trans. Thomas McCarthy. Boston: Beacon Press, 1975.

——. *Theory and Practice*. Trans. John Viertel. Boston: Beacon Press, 1973.

Hand, Learned. *The Spirit of Liberty*. 3d ed., enlarged. Chicago: University of Chicago Press, 1977.

Harris, Errol. "Natural Law and Naturalism." *International Philosophical Quarterly* 23 (1983): 115–23.

Hart, H. L. A. *The Concept of Law*. Oxford: Clarendon Press, 1961.

——. *Essays in Jurisprudence and Philosophy*. Oxford: Clarendon Press, 1983.

Hegel, G. W. F. *Natural Law*. Trans. T. M. Knox. Intro. H. B. Acton. Philadelphia: University of Pennsylvania Press, 1975.

——. *The Philosophy of History*. Intro. C. J. Friedrich. New York: Dover, 1956.

——. *Philosophy of Right*. Trans. T. M. Knox. Oxford: Clarendon Press, 1952.

Hilton, Rodney, ed. *The Transition from Feudalism to Capitalism*. London: Verso, 1978.

Hirst, Paul. *On Law and Ideology*. Atlantic Highlands, N.J.: Humanities Press, 1979.

Hofstadter, Richard, and Beatrice K. Hofstadter, eds. *Great Issues in American History*. Rev. ed. New York: Vintage, 1982.

Hohfeld, Wesley N. *Fundamental Legal Conceptions*. Ed. W. W. Cook. New Haven: Yale University Press, 1920.

Holmes, Oliver W. *Collected Legal Papers*. New York: Peter Smith, 1952.

Hook, Sidney. *From Hegel to Marx*. Ann Arbor: University of Michigan Press, 1962.

Hyppolite, Jean. *Studies on Marx and Hegel*. Ed. and trans. John O'Neill. New York: Harper & Row, 1973.

Jawitsch, Leon S. *The General Theory of Law*. Moscow: Progress Publishers, 1981.

Jaworsky, Michael, ed. *Soviet Political Thought: An Anthology*. Trans. Michael Jaworsky. Baltimore: Johns Hopkins University Press, 1967.

Johnson, Chalmers. *Revolutionary Change*. 2d ed. Stanford: Stanford University Press, 1982.

Kain, Philip J. *Marx and Ethics*. Oxford: Clarendon Press, 1991.

Kairys, David, ed. *The Politics of Law*. New York: Pantheon, 1982.

Kantorowicz, Hermann. *The Definition of Law*. Cambridge: Cambridge University Press, 1958.

Kelsen, Hans. *The General Theory of Law and State*. Trans. Anders Wedberg. New York: Russell & Russell, 1961.

Kolakowski, Leszek, and Stuart Hampshire, eds. *The Socialist Idea*. London: Weidenfeld & Nicolson, 1974.

Korkunov, N. M. *General Theory of Law*, 2d. ed. New York: Macmillan, 1922.

Kosik, Karel. *Dialectics of the Concrete*. Dordrecht: D. Reidel, 1976.

Kymlicka, Will. *Liberalism, Community, and Culture*. Oxford: Clarendon Press, 1991.

Lefcourt, Robert, ed. *Law against the People*. New York: Vintage, 1971.

Lenin, V. I. *State and Revolution*. Peking: Foreign Languages Press, 1976.

Levi, Edward H. *An Introduction to Legal Reasoning*. Chicago: University of Chicago Press, 1949.

Lewis, John U. "The Basis of Positive Law: An Essay toward the Advancement of 'Integrative Jurisprudence.' " *The Monist* 49 (1965): 434–57.

Luban, David. *Lawyers and Justice*. Princeton: Princeton University Press, 1988.

Luhmann, Niklas. *The Differentiation of Society*. Trans. Stephen Holmes and Charles Larmore. New York: Columbia University Press, 1982.

MacGregor, David. *The Communist Ideal in Hegel and Marx*. Toronto: University of Toronto Press, 1984.

MacKinnon, Catharine. *Feminism Unmodified*. Cambridge: Harvard University Press, 1987.

Marcuse, Herbert. *Reason and Revolution*. Boston: Beacon Press, 1954.

Marx, Karl. *Capital*. 3 vols. Moscow: Progress Publishers, 1954–59.

——. *A Contribution to the Critique of Political Economy*. Ed. and intro. Maurice Dobb. New York: International Publishers, 1970.

——. *Grundrisse*. Trans. M. Nicolaus. New York: Vintage, 1973.

Marx, Karl, and Frederick Engels. *Collected Works*. Published to date: vols. 1–34; 38–47. New York: International Publishers. 1975–.

——. *Selected Works*. 3 vols. Moscow: Progress Publishers, 1969–70.

Mathiesen, Thomas. Law, *Society and Political Action*. London: Academic Press, 1980.

McBride, William Leon. "The Acceptance of a Legal System." *The Monist* 49 (1965): 377–96.

——. *Fundamental Change in Law and Society*. The Hague: Mouton, 1970.

——. "Marxism and Natural Law." *American Journal of Jurisprudence* 15 (1970): 127–53.

McCloskey, Robert G. *The American Supreme Court*. Chicago: University of Chicago Press, 1960.

McMurtry, John. *The Structure of Marx's World-View*. Princeton: Princeton University Press, 1978.

Meikle, Scott. *Essentialism in the Thought of Karl Marx*. La Salle, Ill.: Open Court, 1985.

Mepham, John, and D.-H. Ruben. *Issues in Marxist Philosophy*. 4 vols. Atlantic Highlands, N.J.: Humanities Press, 1979–81.

Mitias, Michael. *Moral Foundations of the State in Hegel's Philosophy of Right: Anatomy of an Argument*. Amsterdam: Editions Rodopi, 1984.

Moore, Barrington, Jr. *Injustice: The Social Bases of Obedience and Revolt*. White Plains, N.Y.: M. E. Sharpe, 1978.

Murphy, Walter F. *Elements of Judicial Strategy*. Chicago: University of Chicago Press, 1964.

National Deviancy Conference / Conference of Socialist Economists. *Capitalism and the Rule of Law*. London: Hutchinson, 1979.

Newman, Katherine S. *Law and Economic Organization*. Cambridge: Cambride University Press, 1983.

Nicolaievsky, Boris, and Otto Maenchen-Helfen. *Karl Marx: Man and Fighter*. Harmondsworth: Penguin, 1976.

Oakeshott, Michael. *On History and Other Essays*. Oxford: Basil Blackwell, 1983.

O'Hagan, Timothy. *The End of Law?* Oxford: Basil Blackwell, 1984.

O'Malley, J. "Editor's Introduction." *Karl Marx's Critique of Hegel's Philosophy of Right*. Cambridge: Cambridge University Press, 1982.

Pashukanis, E. B. *Law and Marxism: A General Theory*. Ed. and intro. Chris Arthur. London: Ink Links, 1978. London: Reprint, Pluto Press, 1983.
——. *Selected Writings on Marxism and Law*. Ed. and intro. Piers Beirne and Robert Sharlet. Trans. Peter B. Maggs. London: Academic Press, 1980.
Pelczynski, Z. A., "Introduction." *Hegel's Political Writings*. Trans. T. M. Knox. Oxford: Clarendon Press, 1964.
——. ed. *Hegel's Political Philosophy*. Cambridge: Cambridge University Press, 1975.
——, ed. *The State and Civil Society*. Cambridge: Cambridge University Press, 1984.
Pennock, J. Roland, and John W. Chapman, eds. *Coercion*. Chicago: Aldine-Atherton, 1972.
——, eds. *The Limits of Law*. New York: Lieber-Atherton, 1974.
——, eds. *Marxism: Nomos XXVI*. New York: New York University Press, 1983.
Perry, Michael J. *Morality, Politics, and Law*. New York: Oxford University Press, 1990.
Phillips, Paul. *Marx and Engels on Law and Laws*. Totowa, N.J.: Barnes & Noble, 1980.
Rader, Melvin. *Marx's Interpretation of History*. New York: Oxford University Press, 1979.
Raz, Joseph. *The Authority of Law*. Oxford: Oxford University Press, 1979.
——. *The Concept of a Legal System*. Oxford: Clarendon Press, 1970.
——. *Practical Reason and Norms*. London: Hutchinson, 1975.
Reasons, C. E., and R. M. Rich, eds., *The Sociology of Law*. Toronto: Butterworths, 1978.
Renner, Karl. *The Institutions of Private Law and Their Social Functions*. London: Routledge & Kegan Paul, 1949.
Rommen, H. A. *The Natural Law*. Trans. Thomas R. Hanley. St. Louis: B. Herder, 1948.
Rousseau, Jean-Jacques. *The Social Contract and Discourses*. Trans. and intro. G. D. H. Cole. London: Dent, 1979.
Schlesinger, Rudolf. *Soviet Legal Theory*. London: Kegan Paul, 1944.
Schmidt, Alfred. *History and Structure*. Trans. Jeffrey Herf. Cambridge: MIT Press, 1983.
Shaw, William H. *Marx's Theory of History*. Stanford: Stanford University Press, 1978.
Shklar, Judith. *Legalism*. Cambridge: Harvard University Press, 1964, 1986.
Silverstein, Mark. *Constitutional Faiths*. Ithaca: Cornell University Press, 1984.
Simpson, A. W. B., ed. *Oxford Essays in Jurisprudence*. Oxford: Clarendon Press, 1973.
Skillen, A. *Ruling Illusions*. Hassocks, Sussex: Harvester Press, 1977.
"Social Sciences Today" Editorial Board. *The Marxist Conception of Law*. Moscow: Progress Publishers, 1980.
Soper, Philip. *A Theory of Law*. Cambridge: Harvard University Press, 1984.
Sorokin, Pitirim. *The Sociology of Revolution*. New York: Howard Fertig, 1967.
Stein, P. *Legal Evolution*. Cambridge: Cambridge University Press, 1980.
Stepelevich, Lawrence. *The Young Hegelians: An Anthology*. Cambridge: Cambridge University Press, 1983.
Sumner, Colin. *Reading Ideologies*. London: Academic Press, 1979.
Symposium: "The Duty to Obey the Law." *Georgia Law Review* 18 (1984).
Symposium on Jurisprudence. *Virginia Law Review* 67 (1981).
Sypnowich, Christine. *The Concept of Socialist Law*. Oxford: Clarendon Press, 1990.
Thompson, E. P. *Whigs and Hunters: The Origins of the Black Act*. London: Allen Lane, 1975.

Tigar, Michael, and Madeleine Levy. *Law and the Rise of Capitalism*. New York: Monthly Review Press, 1977.

Tiruchelvan, Neelan, and Radhika Coomaraswamy, eds. *The Role of the Judiciary in Plural Societies*. New York: St. Martin's Press, 1987.

Tribe, Laurence H. *God Save This Honorable Court*. New York: Random House, 1985.

Tumanov, V. I. *Contemporary Bourgeois Legal Thought*. Moscow: Progress Publishers, 1974.

Tyler, Tom R. *Why People Obey the Law*. New Haven: Yale University Press, 1990.

Unger, Roberto. *Law in Modern Society*. New York: Free Press, 1976.

Watson, Alan. *The Evolution of Law*. Baltimore: Johns Hopkins University Press, 1985.

——. *Society and Legal Change*. Edinburgh: Scottish Academic Press, 1977.

——. *Sources of Law, Legal Change, and Ambiguity*. Philadelphia: University of Pennsylvania Press, 1984.

Weber, Max. *Economy and Society*. Ed. Guenther Roth and Claus Wittich. Berkeley: University of California Press, 1978.

Weinreb, Lloyd L. *Natural Law and Justice*. Cambridge: Harvard University Press, 1987.

Wolff, Robert Paul, ed. *The Rule of Law*. New York: Simon & Schuster, 1971.

Wood, Allen. *Karl Marx*. London: Routledge & Kegan Paul, 1984.

Xueming, Chen. "An Inquiry into Marx's Early Views on Philosophy of Law and His Early Legal Thinking." *Social Sciences in China* 4 (1983): 23–62.

Index

absolute discontinuity, 148–54. *See also* radical discontinuity

acceptance, 101, 106; of a legal system, 123–24, 135–37; and sense of right, 53; of a social formation, 161

Acton, H. B., 46–47

adjudication, 155–56

Allen, C. K., 95, 117n; on judicial usage, 115

anticolonial movements, 139

Aquinas, Thomas, 43–44

apartheid, 65

Aristotle, 168

atomism, 11

Auerbach, Jerold S., 168–69, 197n, 202

authority-producing potential of law, 136–37

Avineri, Shlomo, 185

Balbus, Isaac D., 82, 167

base/superstructure, 45, 84; and problem of legality, 46–54

Battaglia, Anthony, 37, 43, 45, 73n

Baxi, Upendra, 126n

Bhagwati, P. N., 126n

Bober, M. M., 45

borrowing, 155, 159–60

bourgeoisie, 150, 151

bourgeois law, 153

Braybrooke, David, 149

Brazil, 147

Brinton, Crane, 156n

Britain, 127, 153, 158, 160

Brown v. Board of Education, 133

Bush, George, 91n

Cain, Maureen, 8, 29

canon law, 64, 84

capitalism, 51–52, 59, 91–92, 94, 96–97, 135, 139–41, 147, 153, 170, 173; as best mode of production, 74; nature of, 59, 71; ruling classes under, 3; South African, 65; and structure of rights, etc., 54. *See also* mode(s) of production

capitalist: commodity production, 67, 82; law, 154; mode of production, 65–66, 82, 96, 147, 157; social formation, 91, 96, 105, 154, 157, 172

Cardozo, Benjamin, 116, 127n, 152n

Carter, Lief H., 116, 138

certiorari, 127

change, 142–47; in natural law, 161, 163; in positive law, 148, 161. *See also* changes within epochs; epochal changes; foundational changes

changes within epochs, 147, 153–57

civil disobedience, 104

civil rights movement, 139

class instrumentalism, 82, 85–88, 90, 111, 132, 140, 175

Marxist legal positivism, 80–90, 95
Marxist theories of law: class
  instrumentalism, 80–81, 85–88;
  criticism of, 83–85; economism, 80–83;
  legal ideologism, 80, 88–90
materialism, 30–31
materialist hue, 31
material mode of production, 55, 60
McBride, William Leon, 35, 73n, 101,
  167; on withering-away-of-law thesis,
  175–77, 198n
McCloskey, Robert G., 93n
McMurtry, John, 45, 84n
Meikle, Scott, 10–12
mode of cooperation, 55, 58
mode(s) of production, 1–2, 32, 52,
  55–58, 65, 67, 78, 81, 120, 131, 135,
  142–47, 166, 172–73; as capitalism,
  51–52; Cohen on, 55–56; essential
  components, 166; locus of natural law,
  67; the natural law of, 58, 66; nature of,
  32, 59. *See also* division of labour;
  mode of social ordering; social
  formation
mode of social ordering, 4–5, 135,
  169–71, 187
Murphy, Walter F., 128–29, 156n

natural law, 1, 4, 10, 20–21, 34–35, 37,
  40–41, 43, 62, 67, 77, 79, 97, 104–5,
  108–9; axiological system, 67;
  capitalist, 4, 68, 106, 137–39, 142–48,
  152, 157–62, 178–79; conservative
  essence of, 69; distinguished from law
  of nature, 40–41; distinguished from
  positive law, 22; duality of legal
  systems, 61, 78; feudal, 147;
  foundations of, 69, 74; framework law,
  skeleton law, 45; of God, 40; historicity
  of, 73; of human reason, 9, 19, 24, 30;
  of the mode of production, 54, 64, 65,
  104–5, 108, 116–17; order of practical
  reason, 44; practical character of, 41;
  regulative role of, 68; tradition, 1–2,
  20–21, 34–40, 70
nature, 24; of capitalism, 59; of mode of
  production, 59
Newman, Katherine S., 180
Nigeria, 125, 152–53, 157–60

Oberdiek, Hans, 63
objective law, 17–18; as essence of positive
  law, 17
Offe, Claus, 94n
O'Hagan, Timothy, 191–92, 197–99
ownership, 48, 50; matching power and
  owernship right, 48; of private property,
  66

Pashukanis, Evgeny B., 7n, 34–35, 81–82,
  171, 184n; commodity exchange theory
  of law, 82; commodity form, 83
Pelczynski, Z. A., 9–10, 77n
Phillips, Paul, 21–22
Plamenatz, John, 46–47
political rationalism, 9
Popper, Karl, 87
positive law, 1, 4, 9–10, 17–20, 23, 30,
  37, 38, 40, 45, 56–70, 74, 77, 79, 83,
  89, 91–94, 96–97, 100, 108, 117,
  120–21, 137, 142, 146, 156–62;
  acceptance of, 80; diversity of, 96;
  explication of, 103; gaps in, 94–95; as
  legislation, 56; regime, 69, 71
positivization of law, 4, 79, 108;
  mechanics of, 112–19; nature and
  processes of, 79
precedent, 114–15, 129, 137, 155
production relations, 47–48, 51–52,
  55–56; of capitalism, 53; as legal
  relations, 54, 56
proletariat, 172–74
property, 50; forms of, 61–62; ownership
  of, 154, 158; private, 62; relations,
  46–48; right to, 145; tribal, 61

Quebec, 160

Rader, Melvin, 45, 60
radical discontinuity, 145. *See also*
  absolute discontinuity
rational law, 19–20, 24, 30
Raz, Joseph, 80
Reason, 8, 24; locus of law, 67
reason, in law, 23–24, 27, 38, 77, 113,
  130, 140, 155–56. *See also* law: form of
rechtsfrei: descriptions, 51, 53–54;
  powers, 51; production relations, 48
reform, 155, 157–58